A SHAVIAN GUIDE TO THE
INTELLIGENT WOMAN

BARBARA BELLOW WATSON is Associate Professor of English at The City College of New York. She holds the Ph.D. from Columbia University and has published both poetry and criticism. She lives in New York City.

A Shavian Guide to
The Intelligent Woman

By

Barbara Bellow Watson

With a new Introduction

The Norton Library

W · W · NORTON & COMPANY · INC ·

NEW YORK

To
David · Jonathan · Robert

Books That Live
The Norton imprint on a book means that in the publisher's
estimation it is a book not for a single season but for the years.
W. W. Norton & Company, Inc.

SBN 393 00640 9

PRINTED IN THE UNITED STATES OF AMERICA

1 2 3 4 5 6 7 8 9 0

Introduction
to the Norton Library Edition

BOOKS on women through the decades (in this field there is
no need to speak of centuries) show an amusing consistency
in their openings. Each author admits that far too much has
been written on the subject already, that the matter has now
been settled and the last word—the last word but one—has
been said. I seem to have followed that convention when I
wrote this book some eight years ago, but only for one paragraph. After that I returned to my conviction that Shaw's
vision was very much needed and, being inclusive and complex as the subject demands, was not likely to be understood
by a reader who took Shaw's work piecemeal or out of the
context of his ideas on politics, economics, evolution, drama-
turgy, diet, and all the rest of his omniferous thought.

In the normal paradoxical process of social change, the
need for Shaw's insight and advice seems greater now than
eight years ago, before books and articles on women began
to crowd the presses. As more argument appears in print,
more information, more revelation, there is less and less
ground for thinking that the last word has been said or will
soon be said. Apparently the vein that seemed so narrow near
the surface needed only to be worked a little deeper to show
impressive yields. And the same process that has made Shaw's
work more necessary has also made a guide to his work more
necessary. As the argument about women goes on without the
needed clarification, it comes closer and closer to intellectual
stalemate. And as a new consciousness of the subject has
spread in widening circles, the value of genuine thought,
thought that clarifies the essential issues, has become even
more apparent, and the Olympian qualities of Shaw's mind
a more necessary corrective.

Nor is it possible to say, "Read Shaw," and bow out. The
Risks in Reading Shaw that I mention in my first chapter
have not changed at all. If anything, as the movement towards
emancipation goes on, the hazards have increased. Publicity
and passion are mad masters. Shaw's mode—comic, ironic,

3

subtle—seems like fragile equipment for the battlefield, yet
it is exactly what is needed. Like his own chocolate soldier,
Shaw knew that the prancing romantics of the battlefield
should be court-martialed. If war is to be superseded, it will
have to be by the exercise of intellect and not merely by
what Yeats called "ignorant good will."

The very words of controversy hold us back. Feminism, a
term Virginia Woolf dropped into the wastebasket in 1938
as "a vicious and corrupt word," has been replaced by
women's liberation, another catchword of virulent potential.
In fact, the real issues will remain unmanageable as long as
they are talked about in abstractions. Here Shaw the dramatist
is a real help. As Shaw himself pointed out in asserting the
sacredness of the theater, every moral conflict on stage must
be embodied in situations and characters teaching the one
moral lesson we can believe in, the consequences of a given
course of action. Dramatization, then, resists abstraction. If
it is tiring to be asked whether you are for or against women's
liberation, that is because it is an abstract, or wooden horse,
question. The real business is concealed inside. In this case
the real business, what is sometimes called "the hidden
agenda," is a question Shaw recognized as coming close to
the heart of the controversy: that is, Can I count on you to
play the game by the present rules and pick up the scheduled
rewards, or are you going to cause trouble, insist on having
your own selfish way, forfeit credits earned to date, and show
base ingratitude for past favors? Shaw's advice on this real
question was unequivocal: "Be as selfish as you can." As I
explain in Chapter Two, Shaw stood for the woman's right, as
a normal, human matter, to exercise her intellect and her
will, without any fuss about gender, to have self-respect, self-
love, self-direction, as far as her spirit will carry her.

As for other abstractions, nouns like Freedom and Equality
will have to be deflated to their original status as honest
adjectives modifying nouns we can understand. "Equal pay
for equal work" is so simple even a president can understand
it. Free day-care centers can at least be discussed. The right
to have children without being married to their fathers, the
right to have sexual experience without either husbands or
children, the right to abstain from sexual experience, the

right to be as intelligent as one can, and all such specific rights can be usefully discussed. In that kind of discussion, Shaw's clarity about the basic issues, the humanity of his insights, and the brilliance of his formulations, have much to contribute. The dramatist's pen, like the poet's, takes vaporous ideas ". . . and gives to airy nothing/ A local habitation and a name." For example, Shaw knew that there is no such thing as adultery, except in cheap fiction and sentimental drama where it is stocked in bulk, but only an endless variety of connections between people of a certain legal status, and that any set attitude toward "adultery" is therefore absurd. For the same reason, arguments about equality in the abstract are also absurd, and Shaw was aware, as I show in "Beyond Feminism," that the concept of equality, if it remains vague and airy, can be used in punitive ways against women. In its place he offers the far more workable goal of equal consideration.

In a sense Shaw believed in the equivalence of the sexes, but in a sense he believed in what might be called the slight superiority of women. Beyond all that, he entirely believed in our common humanity, in the woman's soul as a comprehensible human soul, free of mysterious additives, in the woman's mind as exactly like the man's, only reacting to different treatment. Some of the ordinary man's hostility to Shaw derives, I suspect, from a dim resentment of this unduly sensible belief. One corollary that seems more useful now than ever is that Shaw values equal consideration primarily because it benefits the whole society. Justice to the individual female remains a necessary part of any social reform, but it is dangerous to forget that such justice is never essentially in conflict with other values, but actually an integral part of any forward step. That truth is perfectly obvious, but it gets lost in the adversary mood of the moment.

Higher civilizations seem always to have involved greater equality for women. Claims for a high culture in societies that oppress women are likely to be claims for an elaborated and accomplished savagery. But, as Tocqueville pointed out long ago, rebellion becomes more likely, not less, when the burden of oppression grows lighter. At some later stage, the oppressed group stops asking for favors and begins to demand its rights.

Women seem to have reached that stage. In the past decade, gratitude, humility, tact, and even reasonableness have been conquered, as they must be before any movement can escape from the circle of guilt and accusation. At this point the way begins to be clear for a new understanding that is not based on dependence or dominance.

One response to the new female aggressiveness has been a male backlash of alarming timidity. Has the door been standing open all this time, as in Kafka's parable of the doorkeeper in *The Trial,* while we wasted our lives outside, waiting for permission to enter? Or is this timidity merely a way of retreating from the contest, leaving the real issues, the issues that go beyond politics and polemics, uncomfortably unsettled?

In the midst of all this, it is finally not enough to speak of Shaw's ideas. His value to our time may be most of all in the spirit that pervades his work, a spirit that lifts us out of the realm of glum contest. The air is very clear here, and the light is excellent. We may even be able to glimpse, in the phrase of Ellie Dunn in *Heartbreak House,* that prototype of all the aspiring young women of our time, the vision, however distant, of "life with a blessing."

Barbara Bellow Watson

January 1972

Contents

Acknowledgments   *page* 9

CHAPTER

1 *Shavianism and Feminism*   11
    The Eternal Woman Question   11
    Portrait of the Shavian Woman   14
    Beyond Feminism   27
    Risks in Reading Shaw   30

WOMEN AND THE IDEAL

2 *Pedestals and Petticoats, Paragons and Parrots*   37
    The Double Woman   37
    My Dear Dorothea   40
    The Quintessence of Ibsenism   45

WOMEN AND MEN

3 *The Comedy of Courtship*   59
    Ana, Huntress Chaste and Fair   59
    The Tyranny of Women   64
    The Saving Woman   68
    The Duel of Sex   74
    The Devil's Granddaughters   78

4 *Mothers Married and Unmarried*   83

5 *Marriage: The Mystery of the Unhappy Ending*   100

6 *The Real Thing*   124

WOMEN AND THE WORLD

7 *Bread and Circuses: The Career Woman*   149
    The Economic Woman   149
    Cardinals on Stage: A Portrait of the Actress   153
    Career Women in Love   160
    Is Woman Houyhnhnm?   164

8 *Emancipation and its Discontents*   *page* 177

9 *Second Sex First*   204

Notes   215

Bibliography   235

Index   244

Acknowledgments

It is a pleasure to record here my large debts of gratitude to Jacques Barzun and to Lionel Trilling.

I am indebted also to Dan H. Laurence, editor of the *Collected Letters of Bernard Shaw*, who has kindly allowed me to examine and quote from a number of heretofore unpublished letters in his possession. These letters may not be further quoted or in any way used without the permission of Mr Laurence and of the Shaw Estate, which holds copyright.

A Note on the Notes

The sources of all quotations, as well as other necessary references, are listed by page number in the notes, which begin on page 215.

CHAPTER 1

Shavianism and Feminism

1 THE ETERNAL WOMAN QUESTION

THE subject of Woman has inspired in recent years a flood of words and a drought of fresh ideas. Obsession takes the place of interest. Yet the dullest of subjects can fascinate if we dig deep enough, and Woman, far from being the dullest of subjects, is one of immediate and enduring interest to people of all kinds. There must be some reason for the torturing ennui that threatens us whenever, after a hundred years of controversy, yet another article on this 'problem' appears. Men and women squabble in print over unconnected trivia, each assuming that his preferences constitute a universal law, his grievances a final argument. Even when critics try to generalize they are trapped in the lines of assumptions which automatically close certain avenues.

One trouble with our present ideas about the status of women is that, as an intellectual community, we are bemused by superficial changes. In the last hundred years the outward woman has changed more than she had in the thousand years before. Men have noticed that they are losing certain immunities – their immunity from domestic work and their immunity from female competition, among others. Women try to stay their unhappiness by comparing themselves with the women of a century ago, thus persuading themselves that life must be better than it seems to be. Moreover, women are led to overvalue certain gains like the suffrage, because they are full of uncertainties, having all the ignoble greediness of half-fed creatures. For both men and women the mistake lies in assuming that the emancipation of women is a quantitative matter about which we need only ask: How far?

As Camus says of mankind in general, 'Actual freedom has not increased in proportion to man's awareness of it.' Our society wastes its breath congratulating itself on having covered a great distance, but without taking bearings at either end. And yet the children of the Second World War are so avid of folly that they consider the Victorians smug, whose great writers fulminated against the crimes of their own society like the

Hebrew prophets and were yet recognized as great writers in their own time.

On the subject of women we are particularly prone to deceive ourselves. I do not for a moment deny that the life of an intelligent woman is far better in my own time than in my grandmother's. Also I am bound to agree with Shaw's statement that '. . . no change that has taken place in this century has been more obviously a change for the better than the change in the relations between men and women'. Observe, however, that the century Shaw refers to is the nineteenth, and the generation his New Woman belongs to is my grandmother's, not my own. Even in 1895 when Shaw made that statement, the New Woman, with her disruptive independence, assertiveness and attraction, was being blamed for all the ills of mankind, anything from unemployment to impotence. Two questions now arise. The first is the question of time-lag: What does it mean that the New Woman continues after seventy-five years to seem eternally new, that the ruin of society by her private and public misbehavior seems to be always impending? The second question is: Does our literary treatment of women's status stem from a way of thinking which closes doors on the answers to this Woman Question, instead of opening them? If so, the time-lag is really a full stop. I believe that, in a certain sense, our ideas on the subject (not denying our practical progress) are at a standstill; also that Shaw's views on the subject open doors instead of closing them. Yet in all the furore over more feminity or less, more matrimony or less, more sexuality or less, more childbearing or less, more political power or less, more professionalism or less, there seems to be no recognition that Shaw long ago made a synthesis of all these oppositions, a delightful synthesis full of love and realism but ignored by some because they find Shaw too true to be good, by others because they think love too good to be true.

Shaw's reputation, a decade after his death, suffers in two ways from his very success. One of these is the oblivion which follows genuine success. Dr Johnson said, 'A writer who obtains his full purpose loses himself in his own luster. Of an opinion which is no longer doubted, the evidence ceases to be examined.' Many of Shaw's opinions, particularly those about women and the relations between the sexes, are no longer doubted, even though sixty years ago they seemed monstrous paradoxes. This is precisely what Shaw predicted at the turn of the century:

> But the whirligig of time will soon bring my audiences to my own point of view. . . . By that time my twentieth century characteristics will pass unnoticed as a matter of course, whilst the eighteenth century artificiality that marks the work of every literary Irishman of my generation will seem antiquated and silly. . . . Reputations are cheap nowadays. Even were they dear, it would still be impossible for any public-spirited citizen of the world to hope that his reputation might endure: for this would be to hope that the flood of general enlightenment may never rise above his miserable high-watermark.

That prediction has come true, in some respects, within a surprisingly short time. The daily bread of twentieth-century assumptions (not our blood-thirsty behavior) is in large measure Shaw. He has created just the sort of thing he parodied in *You Never Can Tell* in listing Mrs Clandon's Twentieth Century Treatises: Twentieth Century Cooking, Twentieth Century Creeds, Twentieth Century Clothing, Twentieth Century Conduct, Twentieth Century Children, Twentieth Century Parents. We have forgotten how much Shaw taught us as naturally as a child forgets learning to read.

On the other hand, most of Shaw's teachings are also suffering the kind of oblivion that comes to an author when his public, weary of his stings and discouraged by the loftiness of his aspirations, decides to call him a classic and put him on the shelf. That was Ibsen's fate as Shaw observed in 1913: 'Now that Ibsen is no longer frantically abused, and is safe in the Pantheon, his message is in worse danger of being forgotten or ignored than when he was in the pillory.' This observation applies with even more force to Shaw, whose genial comedy allows its victims to smile even as they are being transfixed by its arrows.

Shaw's ideas about women have suffered both kinds of eclipse. Although much of what he began to say about women eighty years ago is commonplace today, much more that he has tried to tell us remains closed among the classics, ignored in favor of easier and more congenial teachings.

Yet one has only to read Shaw's plays (or to see them on the rare occasions when an actress gives as much humanity as the author requires) to know that character comes first and ideas after.

2 PORTRAIT OF THE SHAVIAN WOMAN

The relation between male writers and the female characters they create has almost always been a strange one, marred by a lack of personal sympathy. I am not ignoring that horde of authors in love with their heroines, but theirs is a sexual sympathy which engenders its own kind of error. In the adored heroine, as in the other female characters, the lack of character development, even allowing for the lack of character development in the female humanity the author has observed around him, is as striking as the lack of variety. There are types, of course, but these remain theatrical: the mooning ingénue, the vivacious soubrette, the whore with a heart of gold, the dreadful dowager, the malicious witch, the angel child – all pre-fabs as monotonous as the houses in a company town; and with good reason, as all have been set up by The Management to serve its own purposes. A writer who creates male characters in this way can expect severe treatment from his reviewers; but the paper-doll woman is accepted because the ordinary critic has never known anything else, because she is no more unreal than all the others. If a writer will glue a different sort of wig to the empty head, try an unexpected color scheme, or hinge some of the wooden joints, he may reasonably hope to be praised for his insight into feminine character.

In this connection one might reverse the comment G. K. Chesterton made on the Brontës when he said that they '. . . treated the male as an almost anarchic thing coming in from outside nature; much as people on this planet regard a comet'. Chesterton, himself a great explorer of the obverse, goes on to say: 'The reply may be made that the women in men's novels are equally fallacious. The reply is probably just.' He says also that the Brontës were '. . . perpetually making the masculine creature much more masculine than he wants to be'. If we change the gender of that statement, we see at once the error against which Shaw, like Ibsen, stood out so strongly: that men in their writing were perpetually making the feminine creature more feminine than she wants to be.

An especially thoughtful writer may observe his own bias, as Keats did.

I am certain I have not a right feeling towards Women – at this moment I am striving to be just to them but I cannot – is it because they fall so far beneath my Boyish imagination? When I was a school-boy I though[t] of fair Woman as a pure Goddess . . . I have no right to expect more than their reality. I thought them etherial [sic] above Men – I find them perhaps equal – great by comparison is very small.

For a very young man to question himself this way in 1818 requires a superb fairness of mind that makes the disappoint-ment of the writer, his '. . . evil thoughts, malice spleen . . . obstinate prejudice . . . complication of feelings . . .' all the more significant. Shaw would have agreed that it was the im-possibly high ideals of boyish romanticism that made all real women seem, in that bewitching light, 'equally smokeable'.

Of Dickens, in whose work he was steeped, Shaw said, 'In my youth it was commonly said that Dickens could not draw women.' Shaw agrees that the heroines were 'ridiculous ideal-izations' but points out that the shrews, featherheads, warped spinsters, were masterpieces – and all unamiable. He even suggests that Dickens's women were prototypes of Strindberg's.

The inability to create women characters is only one sign of something wrong in the literary treatment of women. Writers seem also to suppose that women cease to exist when men leave the scene. The physical presence of men may not always be required, but in normal fictional procedure, women are given scant attention unless they are talking about men or thinking about men or doing something that is to impinge on men. Stories without women are fairly common, although not as common as stories in which one woman exists to give men something to fight over. How many stories without men are offered to the reading public? Of course, there are reasons for this imbalance, which is partly a reflection of the dull lives most women have led. Still, it is only reasonable to assume that women do something between love duets.

Shaw points out a similar state of affairs in sociology and economics: '. . . all these books are addressed to men. You might read a score of them without ever discovering that such a creature as a woman had ever existed. In fairness let me add that you might read a good many of them without discovering that such a thing as a man ever existed.'

The rise of the woman novelist has somewhat obscured this

hiatus in literature, for our memories are peopled also by the characters created by Jane Austen, George Eliot and the Brontës, in whose novels women have a genuine existence and in some of which (e.g. *Emma* and *Shirley*) they are granted a right to consciousness and initiative that is positively feminist. Otherwise, the difference between the real women and the fictional women of the same era and circumstances can only be accounted for by a preference of the writer, a preference described by Charlotte Brontë's analysis of one male character exposed to her unwomanly heroine, Shirley:

> At heart, he could not abide sense in women: he liked to see them as silly, as light-headed, as vain, as open to ridicule as possible; because they were then in reality what he held them to be, – inferior: toys to play with, to amuse a vacant hour and to be thrown away.

The chief reason for the scarcity of interesting women in literature must surely be a lack of sympathy. Lack of familiarity is not enough. Different as the lives of men and women have always been, the male writer has been more familiar with lives of women in his household than with those of many of the male characters into whose moods and adventures he has imagined himself. But in writing about the male stranger the writer's sympathy, his ability to imagine how such a man might feel, can bridge the gap of circumstances. In writing about women, that imagination has had to be artificially fired, either by sexual interest, or by the doubly artificial device that has produced the paragons, from Griselda on, who have sprung, without the participation of any mother, straight from the heads of male authors.

It remained for Shaw to voice the equal and opposite reaction, when he caused Mrs George in *Getting Married* to say: 'The Women are all different. It is the men who are all alike.'

By Shaw's time, a change in the literary perception of women had begun to take place, partly because of a shift in emphasis which turned many novels from outward adventures to inner consciousness. Meredith portrayed a spirited woman in *Diana of the Crossways*. Henry James, with his concentration on the inner aspect of events, on the interplay of relationships, dealt with the part of life in which a woman's participation is as real and as eventful as a man's. But these are only indications that the temper of the time was showing its ripeness for change. Shaw was the change for which his time was ripe.

Gathering up all that was implicit in the time, notably in the work of Ibsen, Shaw made explicit in his theories and vivid in his fiction, the 'new' assertion about women: that they exist as individuals, quite apart from their sexual role. Even this, however, fails to do justice to Shaw's assertion unless we add that his women can be characters and also heroines, that in their eccentricity and egotism they are neither ridiculous nor horrible, but charming and triumphant. Further, they have a genuine importance as protagonists.

Even the titles of the major plays give some indication of the importance of women in Shaw's work: *Candida, Mrs Warren's Profession, Major Barbara, Saint Joan, The Millionairess*. And it is the woman who manages *Captain Brassbound's Conversion*, forges the link between *Man and Superman*, and speaks for the universe in *Getting Married*. The only men who are a match for the women in Shavian plays are those who, like Dick Dudgeon, Caesar, Androcles, King Magnus and King Charles, are independent of romantic love and act on principles of worldliness (or other-worldliness) that are scarcely different from disillusionment. These men have apparently learned the lesson of Ibsen as interpreted by Shaw: 'Men are waking up to the perception that in killing women's souls they have killed their own.' In other words, the only men who are a match for the Shavian woman are those who have given up the old illusions about the relations between the sexes.

Shaw's boast to Mrs Patrick Campbell (to induce her to play Eliza in *Pygmalion*) was, '. . . I am a first class ladies tailor. . . .' Of course the business of a tailor is not to create a woman but to clothe her suitably. If he either idealizes her anatomy (as the woman-worshippers do their heroines' souls) or emphasizes its worst points (as the woman-haters do with *their* heroines' souls), he cannot give satisfaction. Shaw's portrayal of women shows a great attention to their real characteristics, even to the non-sexual details of their outward appearance. Shaw's stage directions, especially those for his earlier plays, bear out Archibald Henderson's observation that 'In feminine details – name, dress, hat, gown, ribands, costume illustrative of character – Shaw was more meticulous, and sensitive to nuances than many women.'

Shaw's portraits of women have been deprecated from two points of view, the lady's and the sensualist's. The lady's point of view is well represented by Constance Barnicoate's article in the *Fortnightly Review* of March 1906. The early date of this article makes it all the more significant, as Shaw's later heroines, with a few exceptions, merely intensified the traits this writer objected to: and later this kind of objection was to be expressed less forthrightly. Shaw's women, she says, are '. . . unlovable, unpleasing . . . if not more or less disagreeable . . . they are either hard as nails, like Vivie . . . [*Mrs Warren's Profession*] or merely bleating old sheep like Mrs Whitefield. . . .' [*Man and Superman*]. She supports my claim for Shaw's uniqueness by saying '. . . no one else has drawn such utterly, hopelessly, weakly, contemptible types of women. . . .' She feels shame that any man could so depict a woman and wonders how Mr Shaw conceived so low an ideal of woman, but claims that '. . . we are not so bad as Mr Shaw makes out'. But for her the heart of the matter is that Shaw never draws a genuine lady. And here an avowal that more accomplished critics mask in jargon is quite openly made. 'The term "lady" may be weak and question-begging, but what other is there?'

Shaw had his own ideas, quite aristocratic ones, about what was ladylike and what was not. He defended the laundress in one of Brieux's plays for spitting on her iron and saying things like, 'Stir your stumps', which Shaw claims is just what an ideal duchess would say. Shaw's women shock a bourgeois audience just as the aristocratic ladies shocked Mrs Tarleton in *Misalliance* by talking about drains and, most certainly, other unmentionable realities as well.

Oddly enough, Shaw's women, scorned by the ladylike critics. are thoroughly irritating also to the sensualist critics. Frank Harris, editor, biographer and self-advertised seducer who told somewhat more than all in his memoirs, quite loses patience with Shaw over his 'sexless dolls'. The women in the early plays he calls '. . . distinctly unpleasant, practically unsexed women. Their bodies are as dry and hard as their minds and even where they run after their men . . . the pursuit has about as much sex appeal as a timetable.' Harris obviously was so muddled that he confused sex appeal with solicitation. What is this '. . . vital defect in Shaw's women', this '. . . lack of mystery, grace, divinity, allure and charm . . .' which, according to Harris, everybody has noticed?

This 'defect' is simply Shaw's departure from the conventional treatment of women in fiction, a departure which makes women both less feminine and more.

The outward behavior of Shaw's women characters is in part an act of rebellion against the ladylike and thoroughly impossible standards of polite pretense flourishing about 1880. When the glorious Gloria, queen of fatal fascination in *You Never Can Tell*, shows the rudeness reserved for those we love in a bewildering way, she reveals at once true passion, which lets down the barriers of ordinary politeness before it lets down any others; but her mother, an authority on modern woman, offers an explanation which applies to much of the aggressively unladylike behavior in the works of Bernard Shaw:

> Mr Valentine, you must excuse us all. Women have to unlearn the false good manners of their slavery before they acquire the genuine good manners of their freedom. Don't think Gloria vulgar: she is not really so.

In one sense this is perfectly true, although it is not the real explanation of Gloria's behavior when she falls in love and finds herself enslaved in quite another way. It is true that women have had to discard some part (without any guidance about how much or which part) of what had been normal good manners, in order to behave as free human beings. Every emancipated woman has had to make up her manners *vis-à-vis* men as she goes along, which means that, as in all such improvised societies, offense is taken where none is intended. Much of the ill-temper engendered by the emancipation process is caused by this need to improvise one's manners, which has faced both women and Negroes in the twentieth century. The instinctive defense against subservience is arrogance; yet arrogance in a newly liberated chattel is not an endearing or reassuring trait. Only persons who have a rare combination of natural tact with a highly informed social sense can avoid a failure that, although less perilous for women than for Negroes, is far more personal. The novels of clever women like Doris Lessing, Iris Murdoch and Mary McCarthy, writing about love or something that has something to do with love, are full of the disasters that result from our uncertainties. Shaw's women, even when endowed with the glamor an infatuated author can bestow and gifted with all his verbal grace, sometimes fall into the kind of arrogance that is clearly the assertion of a newly-won freedom.

Besides this need for Shaw's women to reject the good manners of slavery as conspicuously as possible, a difficulty that might not have existed fifty years later, there is a more essential reason for those qualities that repelled both the ladylike and the sensualist critics. This quality is the existence in Shaw's women of two terribly unwomanly characteristics: wit and will. Neither of these is unprecedented in literature. Clever women and willful women have been observed by authors since the beginning of literary time, but with rare exceptions they have been mocked or dreaded, not admired. Where is there a virtuous Lady Macbeth or a strong-minded Desdemona? In Shakespeare's comedies there are 'modern' women, but Shaw says, 'Nothing will persuade me that Shakespear ever carries a modern woman with him right through. . . .' Except for Millamant in *The Way of the World* (of whom I have more to say in the next chapter), we come up to Shaw's time without meeting in the drama a woman of wit and will whose author thoroughly likes her. It has been pointed out, of two contemporaneous plays about fallen women, that Pinero in *The Second Mrs Tanqueray* punishes his heroine, but Shaw does not punish Mrs Warren in *Mrs Warren's Profession*. Mrs Warren is punished by life, no doubt, in its quiet, ironic style, when the daughter whom she has given a gentlewoman's education on the earnings of a prostitute, turns against her in horror, but Shaw does not grind his heroine down according to the flamboyant terms of what Kenneth Tynan calls 'the dramatists' convention'.

Shaw will not punish his women for domineering any more than for sexual misbehavior. Mrs Warren's daughter, Vivie, goes to work in a flare of relief after sending her mother and her suitors packing. She sheds no tears; she bites no pillows. And all through the plays that follow, the domineering Shavian woman goes consistently unpunished. The only exception is Joan of Arc, over the broad outlines of whose story Shaw had no control. Only in Strindberg, as Augustin Hamon points out, are there such overpowering women; but in Shaw their triumph is a good thing, whereas in Strindberg it is bad. It is Hamon who gives us the supremely suitable word for the Shavian woman: 'la triomphatrice'. Lacking the feminine ending in English, we might substitute the ambiguity of the phrase, 'a winning woman'. Hamon concludes, 'Le théâtre de Shaw est . . . un théâtre féministe'.

Shaw's own answer to the critics who dislike his women characters is first of all a literary one:

> I declare that the real secret of the cynicism and inhumanity of which shallower critics accuse me is the unexpectedness with which my characters behave like human beings, instead of conforming to the romantic logic of the stage.

Still, it will never do to rest any playwright's reputation on a claim to verisimilitude. Until the philosophers find a more helpful way to talk about reality, and until the critics come to some sort of understanding about the many sorts of realism possible (and impossible) in the theatre, that claim is always open to dispute. Shaw's women do not speak like real people, being infinitely more articulate, more expressive, and more elegant. They do not live like real people, their lives having the logic of fulfilled principles which we are denied. But they do give expression to states of mind which we recognize as our own and our opponents'. This realism about states of mind is accounted for by Shaw's pseudo-mystical talk about '. . . Woman, projecting herself dramatically by my hands (a process over which I assure you I have no more control than I have over my wife). . . .' This might, I suppose, be dismissed as mere banter, but I think it is actually one of Shaw's assertions of the androgynous nature of personality, and refers to the same process as the following:

> I am a dramatic author, and people wonder what is the secret of my extraordinary knowledge of women which enchants the whole world. Women come to me and ask: 'Where did you get this amazing knowledge of women?' Very often I am suspected of having in the course of my life been a most abandoned character, and that is how I acquired this knowledge. But I never acquired it at all. I always assumed that a woman was a person exactly like myself, and that is how the trick is done.

One odd consequence of this androgynous point of view is that the women who result are so much more feminine than most real or imaginary emancipated women. This seems less paradoxical if we realize that the male consciousness through which this female character is being sifted, does not feel itself 'unsexed' by the mere fact of having ideas and independence and a career. Logically the feminine character need feel no more 'unsexed' than her counterpart. If women are rendered more masculine by entering 'a man's world', is the real reason not simply the terms on which they are allowed to enter?

In a state of genuine equality, a woman can be clever, active and bossy without being what J. B. Priestley calls 'a Yang girl'. Priestley, urging the incorporation in our lives of more of the feminine principle, points out that '. . . many women, including the most aggressive feminists are devotees of Logos, Yang girls', whereas the feminine principle is Eros, the Yin portion of the human sphere. Shaw would not entirely have disagreed with this. The only aggressive feminists he portrays, those in 'Press Clippings', are obviously deficient in the feminine principle, Eros, although they are '*triomphatrices*' enough to beat the Yang boys at their own game. Apart from this exception, all the women in Shaw's plays who set the standard for feminine character have 'the feminine principle' in a high degree and an equally high degree of the qualities most often called 'unwomanly'.

Shaw's views on women's dress show that his belief in the androgynous nature of personality is by no means a plea for the masculine woman. His objection to the Victorian costume for women is that it '. . . dressed them up in an extraordinary manner which entirely concealed the fact that they were human beings . . . .' When crinolines went out of style, the woman became '. . . like the parlor table, which had a round top on one central leg'. On the other hand he says in the same piece, 'Woman Since 1860':

Masculine affectations were always a mistake . . . the followers of John Stuart Mill and Henry Fawcett cut their hair short; put on men's stiff collars and cravats; wore waistcoats and shirtfronts and watch-chains; and made themselves mannish above the waist whilst remaining quakerish below it. There was no sense in this, as women were much more sensibly and pleasantly dressed than men in these parts. . . .

On this matter Shaw passed the ultimate test of sincerity: he applied his principles to his own wife.

I remember when we went to the first Fabian Summer School she was dressed in a very masculine costume, tailor-made, with a stiff white collar; and I said, not to her but to the assembled gathering, how much I disliked the way women had of dressing like men: it detracted from their charm and made them look ridiculous. That evening she appeared in a lovely dress with a low-cut chiffon bodice, through which her skin showed very attractively, and she never reverted to the masculine garb again.

Mrs Shaw ought to have heeded her husband's description of Mrs Clandon, the advanced woman in *You Never Can Tell*:

She has never made herself ugly or ridiculous by affecting masculine waistcoats, collars, and watch-chains, like some of her old comrades who had more aggressiveness than taste. . . . She therefore dresses in as businesslike a way as she can without making a guy of herself, ruling out all attempts at sex attraction and imposing respect on frivolous mankind and fashionable womankind.

Shaw's criticism of the Victorian costume is simply intended to remind us that we must not disguise our common humanity. He concludes: 'I do not regard women as animals of another species. . . . The sexes wear different boots and bonnets, not different souls: that is why I have left the souls out, and concentrated on the boots and bonnets.' But the most important sentence in 'Woman Since 1860' is: 'It was clear to me that what women had to do was not to repudiate their femininity, but to assert its social value; not to ape masculinity, but to demonstrate its insufficiency.'

What is the value of this new creation of Shaw's, this good-humored yet clever and selfish lady? Is it to shock the bourgeoisie? If so, she is as dead an issue as the paragon who preceded her, for the bourgeoisie have, with diabolical ingenuity, inured themselves to shock on the anti-toxin principle, building up their resistance by submitting to more and more massive doses in which, however, the ideas have been killed. Is she, on the other hand, merely a comic figure, one of the mistaken? If so, the actress must traduce the author's lines, playing between them so as to suggest that the woman who speaks thus can succeed only by behaving otherwise, behaving, in brief, just like the conventional stage notion of Woman. Or is she, as some might suppose, a monster, an ideal conceived by a man whose humanity was defective, even though defective in an exalted way? No, it is not Shaw's weakness that has invented this kind of woman, but his strength.

Shaw's comments on his boss-women make it quite clear that they are intended to destroy a cliché which is more than boring: it is dangerous; for it maintains that only by being submissive and reasonably stupid can a woman hope to be loved by mortal man. Hollywood, guardian of the cliché, issues a reminder on the subject frequently. In these instructive films, the female executive or teacher learns to remove her glasses, curl her hair and stop thinking. Any intellectual work a woman does is, we learn, only an inferior substitute for sex and domesticity. It is with relief and a violin accompaniment that the heroine puts down her book, her chisel, or her dictaphone, and (reversing the fate of Henry James' spinster heroine in *Washington Square*) settles down in the clinch – 'for life, as it were'.

This silly picture may not seem dangerous, but it is presented with such assurance and consistency that life tries to follow art. Men are made uneasy about having clever or eminent wives. An even more common result is that women, drilled in the belief that cleverness and activity mean sexual unattractiveness, often hide or pervert their talents. Furthermore, if we follow Shaw's reasoning, it will be the most vital – that is, the best – women who refuse to give up motherhood, and therefore retire from the frontiers of intellectual life, robbing society of part of its most precious asset, intellectual vitality.

Of course, the influence of fiction on real lives is unmeasured and probably unmeasurable, since the evidence is so complex. There remain, however, questions of intent and meaning. Even if we question the influence of the prig-heroine of yesteryear or the whore-heroine of yesterday (since the established is necessarily passé) on the real women who see her admired, we cannot reasonably question the influence a new kind of heroine might have, one who presents a possibility previously unimagined. Such is this heroine of Shaw's, who knows her own mind, speaks and acts her own mind, and in all the exuberance of her selfish vitality is irresistibly attractive to men.

The strangest fact about this Shavian woman is that she has had no successors. The main stream, at least, of English and American fiction neglects her, probably more out of perplexity and a failure of imagination than dislike. Edmund Fuller says, in *The Image of Man in Modern Fiction*, 'Rich, complex portraits of women are not common in recent fiction or, indeed, in the fiction of any period.' His explanation of the vogue for what he calls 'female zombies' in recent fiction is that 'They are vessels for male use. It is assumed that man is a person and woman a receptacle.' The same state of mind is given another interpretation in Leslie Fiedler's *Love and Death in the American Novel*. Behind the broad outlines of his theory lies the still broader and more shadowy assumption that woman is an adjunct to man's personality and is to be judged by her effect on him. As Simone de Beauvoir puts it, 'Thus humanity is male and man defines woman not in herself but as relative to him. . . .' This conviction of the 'otherness' of women is still largely unchanged. Modern portrayals of woman, showing her dramatically emancipated from the restrictions of a hundred years ago, are blind to the fundamental restriction which remains – that of being treated, not as an end in herself, but as a means to an end.

. . . it is not surprising that our society, being directly dominated by men, comes to regard Woman, not as an end in herself like Man, but solely as a means of ministering to his appetite. . . . Now to treat a person as a means instead of an end is to deny that person's right to live. And to be treated as a means to such an end as sexual intercourse with those who deny one's right to live is insufferable to any human being. Woman, if she dares face the fact that she is being so treated, must either loathe herself or rebel. As a rule, when circumstances enable her to rebel successfully . . . she does rebel; but circumstances seldom do. Does she then loathe herself? By no means: she deceives herself. . . .

This is one important part of Shaw's doctrine that has been set aside in the process of removing him from the pillory to the Pantheon. Another, which contains a message for men as well as for women, specifically denies that civilization has mitigated the danger of sexual tyranny.

Is the cultured, gifted man less hardened, less selfish towards the woman, than the paleolithic man? Is the woman less sacrificed, less

25

enslaved, less dead spiritually in the one case than in the other? . . .
Ibsen's reply is that the sacrifice of the woman of the stone age to
fruitful passions which she herself shares is as nothing compared to
the wasting of the modern woman's soul to gratify the imagination
and stimulate the genius of the modern artist, poet, and philosopher.
He shews us that no degradation ever devized or permitted is as
disastrous as this degradation: that through it women die into
luxuries for men, and yet can kill them; that men and women are
becoming conscious of this; and that what remains to be seen as
perhaps the most interesting of all imminent social developments is
what will happen 'when we dead awaken'.

This vision makes clear so much that is obscure about the
struggle over emancipation that there must have been some
compelling reason for ignoring it. One reason is the impervious-
ness of society to ideas which will mean giving up some of its
cherished weaknesses. If the world were to adopt Shaw's view
of women, it would have to give up a large part of what Shaw
called its silliness and vulgarity, and some of the comforts of
home, most notably its illusions. It has never been forgiven
Shaw that he had some of the feelings of the future. As John
Stuart Mill put it:

To see the futurity of the species has always been the privilege of
the intellectual élite or of those who have learnt from them; to have
the feelings of that futurity has been the distinction, and usually the
martyrdom, of a still rarer élite.

Shaw's advance beyond the 'otherness' concept of women
requires 'the feelings of futurity' more than it requires any kind
of knowledge or idea.

Furthermore, modern writers have consumed much creative
energy in rebelling against a tradition which has tended therefore to shape them in its own image, even though in reverse.
Only a few minds of exceptional clarity and assurance have
escaped this compulsion. In that tradition a civilizing self-
control was closely bound up with the evils that were poisoning
the relations between men and women. Therefore it is not surprising that a whole trend, of which D. H. Lawrence is only the
most vivid example, should have begun to move in an opposite
direction. The possibility which such writers have apparently
failed to consider is that the need they feel so powerfully is a
need for more civilization, not less.

Or, to be exact, it is not *more* civilization that is wanted, but enough intellectual pride in the critic to assert that civilization is not, as his enemies have insisted, a matter of mills, mines and banks, but a matter of the quality of human life. By accepting the first definition of civilization, the opponents of hard facts and hard times have placed themselves in a bitter dilemma.

Shaw's strategy was not to retreat from the nineteenth century, but to supersede it; not to reject civilization, but to reject the obvious forgery that had been set in its place. Thomas Carlyle in *Past and Present* fulminated against this fraud and demanded a return to the enlightened practices of the eleventh century. Shaw, although unbemused by the illusion of progress, as his preface to *Saint Joan* demonstrates, knows that historical time cannot turn back, that the dilemmas of the present are an inextricable part of the present. Some may say: 'Precisely. And Carlyle is that which Shaw knows.' Yes, Carlyle, like all the social critics of the nineteenth century, is part of what Shaw knows, but something more interesting than chronology is at work here: that is, character.

Concerning women and the relations between men and women, that difference of character speaks clearly. Lawrence yearns to return to an archaic idyll, perhaps not quite primitive, but certainly far removed into an imaginary Arcadian past. Even if such an era could have existed, and even if it could have satisfied men as Lawrence dreams of its doing, we know quite well what archaic sexual systems mean for women. Shaw, in contrast, yearns for a move forward, beyond the period of artificial commercial monogamy, beyond the pleasure principle, but not (in the foreseeable future) beyond pleasure itself, into a period in which men and women can meet happily in a hut in the woods, but also in drawing-rooms and kitchens and banks and factories, sometimes to make love, but at other times to work and talk and carry on all the other pleasures of social existence.

3 BEYOND FEMINISM

Shaw's sympathy with the woman's point of view is not enough to explain his feminism. The men who like women most are often most afraid of anything that will change or distract them. The vital difference between Shaw and susceptible mankind at large is his ability to see the value for man of the emancipated woman, and above all her value for the large concerns of society in which differences of sex make no difference at all. As a result, his claims for the political, economic and professional rights of women go beyond feminism, into a realm so new that it does not yet exist.

Feminism is related to that unpleasant pleasantry of the twentieth century, the war between the sexes. As I show in Chapter III, the war between the sexes is not represented in Shaw's work. That amusing conflict witnessed so often in the Shavian theater, with its elegant footwork and its flashes of blue steel, is the duel of sex. *Man and Superman,* like Shakespearian and Restoration comedy, portrays this duel. The two conflicts are quite different. The duel of sex can take place only between individuals interested in each other. The war of the sexes is a mass phenomenon of the unacquainted. The duel of sex is all about love, and its action moves toward a settlement. The war of the sexes is all about resentment and hostility, and its action moves toward a victory and a defeat.

Shaw's sortie beyond feminism puts victory and defeat out of the question. In struggling as women must to wrest from an opponent the abstract condition called equality, it is not politic to demand anything more than equality, no matter how sound the logic. But avoiding the battlefield (as no woman of his time could do), Shaw made it possible to substitute for equality a new aim: the emended definition of democracy which he derived from Dean Inge: equal consideration. As he points out elsewhere, equality of opportunity is '. . . entirely and completely and eternally impossible'.

Shaw's disposition to make women a little more than equal in some matters does not result from his infatuation with the vital woman, although that infatuation is unmistakable. In theory as in life, Shaw will not permit his infatuation to come before the serious business of making this world fit for human habitation. His own claim is that he never neglected his work in order to spend 'a gallant evening'. Those who take this to mean that his response to women was deficient, simply do not understand his kind of self-control or have forgotten the importance he attributes to self-control in the evolutionary process. However, when Shaw claims to have had his share of '. . . the masculine silliness and vulgarity on the subject of sex which so astonishes women, to whom sex is a serious matter', one can only conclude that he underestimated that tendency in other men. For one thing, he never flaunted his sexual exploits. In a world so little scrupulous of privacy, Shaw's reticence about one part of his own life has naturally led to misunderstanding. He has said enough, even while saving a little privacy, to show that he was extremely susceptible, easily and persistently fascinated by the kind of woman whom most of his generation would have considered 'fast'. If his love affairs with Jenny Patterson, Bertha Newcombe, Florence Farr, Mrs Patrick Campbell and others leave any doubt about the matter, the recent publication of Shaw's letters to 'Mollytompkins', written between the ages of sixty-five and eighty-seven (at which time he found it necessary to say that 'bodily union' was out of the question), quite clearly show both his need for amorous connections and his refusal to lose his head over them. For all his caution in protecting his wife's feelings and his own exposed position as an eminent man and a radical, for all his horror at Mollykins' fads, manners, spelling, handwriting, accent, her amoral marriage and her anti-maternal motherhood, Shaw still kept her tucked under his wing, and after each new outrage he scolded her without ever breaking off the essentially amorous connection between them.

In his literary work, Shaw was less tolerant. The women are subjected to the same critical and comic scrutiny as the men. It would be misleading to speak of Shaw's amiability toward women without mentioning his amiability towards men, his portrayal of charming rascals, sweet old fools and unsentimental altruists. The essence of Shaw's distinction in respect to women is just this consistently single standard. Perhaps the truth is that the men who are woman-haters are only man-haters and self-haters after all.

If Shaw is almost alone in this theoretical outpost, perhaps it is because he is almost alone in having the strength to make self-control (not to be confused with self-denial) both a private and a public good. Obviously self-control requires strength of character, which ends the matter for some people, but it also requires – if it is meaningful – strength of wit. Shaw's superb strength in both respects prevents him from opening the floodgates of the id with the abandon that characterizes many of his contemporaries. Shaw's whole life and work hold before us the possibility that it may be best to replace the reviled super-ego with a superior ego.

4 RISKS IN READING SHAW

Chesterton says of Shaw, as Faguet said earlier of Voltaire, that his work is 'a chaos of clear ideas'. These ideas are so exquisitely clear, so carefully explained, so consistently maintained and so patiently repeated, that it is strange to find them misunderstood. Yet they are misunderstood, and often so thoroughly that intelligent women who have the average reader's acquaintance with the plays, confess to a prejudice against Shaw and all his works because he is 'a woman-hater'. And this of a man who would be more accurately called a woman-worshipper! No woman who had met Bernard Shaw seems to have made this mistake, yet it is often made by those who know only his books. It is common enough for people to misapprehend the classics, since these are known to most of us by rumor, not by reading. With Shaw, however, many people read what he has said without finding out what he means.

These misapprehensions come from the way Shaw put his ideas together, not in order by any means, but in a convincing chaos in which the reader is sometimes shown a card so rapidly that he may be forgiven for suspecting fraudulence. Part of the conviction of a Euclidean demonstration resides in its deliberate slowness. In Shaw's polemics, both in the prefaces and in discussions within the plays, the speed of the prose is almost overwhelming. Much of the charm of Shaw's theater, in contrast to the slow-stepping plays of American naturalism, lies in his rapid pace. The reader remains fresh and rested, for he is spared the fatigue of waiting for the next thought, which is always in motion before the previous thought has quite come to rest. On the printed page, however, the delightful speed of the prose presents a difficulty, being the speed of light rather than the speed of sound: being, that is, the rate at which our minds are enlightened, rather than the speed at which our ears are assailed.

This speed in Shaw's prose dangerously combines with complication. The complication is not Shaw's fault. Imagine dealing in seventy-four closely printed pages with all the aspects of marriage – historical, political, sexual, sentimental, commercial, anthropological, legal, logical, ethical, genetic, domestic, sadistic and canonical – as Shaw does in the preface to *Getting Married*. Speed is essential. But interest and conviction remain paramount. Deal with this mass of matter systematically, and the reader's interest will sink like a punctured tube. But lead your audience through a well-furnished labyrinth, as Shaw does, so that they can never be wearied by noticing how far they have come, or disheartened by seeing how far they still have to go, and the fascination of the matters at hand will exert its full force. At the end of this intricate race, one is quite convinced on most of the points Shaw has tried to make, but unpossessed, unless one has had another view of the garden, of any systematic scheme of the whole subject. It is when one tries to put this labyrinth together with others – the prefaces, let us say, to *Man and Superman* and *Three Plays for Puritans* – that the sense of chaos may descend. This sense of chaos is merely the reader's illusion. Shaw has a scheme, but the scheme is not what he gives the reader. He offers a new way of looking at things, and certain articles of belief. The prefaces are not meant to be read together. They are occasional pieces of an extremely durable kind and as exegeses of the plays to which they belong are miraculously clear. Chaos is artificially induced when a reader takes bits of various pieces and tries to cram them together into conventional patterns of thought.

For example, one of the great points with which Shaw launched his critical career was an attack on the conventions of romantic love. Yet his characters are prone to fall in love at first sight, as Valentine does in *You Never Can Tell*; and when Shaw came to explain the workings of creative evolution, which was his chief hope for humanity, he put his faith in that instinctive attraction on which the belief in romantic love was originally based. Again, he urged that women sit in equal numbers on all governing bodies, as without them men would never govern properly. Yet he minimized the importance of giving women the vote on the general ground that women are just as idiotic as men. Again, he shocked the world by his outcry against self-sacrifice and the sense of duty and all the ideals of home and family. Yet he pointed out that the search for happiness is self-defeating, that the only real happiness is in being used up in the service of a cause greater than oneself, and furthermore that woman's great function of creating a finer human race must on no account be fulfilled in defiance of the present marriage code of society.

Not one of these three instances is a real contradiction. Anyone who has read Shaw can supply the links and the distinctions I have omitted here, taking them from quite clear statements in the published works. But in Shaw's polemical method each point is made in the way that seems to him most effective, even at the risk of a verbal contradiction.

There is also a confusion that results from interpreting Shaw's statements as though they had been uttered by the ordinary Englishman of his time. Shaw was not separately a socialist, a playwright, a believer in Creative Evolution, a critic of the marriage laws, and so on. Every one of his statements about any of these matters was modified by all his other views. Taken out of context as they so often are, and displayed as witticisms, these remarks lose their depth. Shaw approves Mrs Warren's decision to better herself by becoming a prostitute and by exploiting the prostitution of other women; he approves Andrew Undershaft's decision to better himself by becoming a munitions maker; but we miss his point entirely if we pretend to ignore his deep disapproval of capitalism, prostitution, the munitions industry, the company town and the whole society that faces its members with such choices. By insisting that the madam and the millionaire are right in the choice they make, Shaw is insisting that the pattern of the capitalist economy be seen complete with all its implications, and accepted or rejected for all that it is and all that it involves.

Because questions concerning women are far less clear than those concerning capitalism, Shaw is more likely to be misunderstood when he says such things as: 'Giving women the vote will only double the resistance to change.' That remark will be completely misunderstood, as it frequently was in the days of the suffrage battle, by anyone who ignores Shaw's other comments on the vote and his other comments on the influence of women in government.

In the same way, almost everything he says about women is in effect modified by some implied phrase, such as: 'until the present laws can be changed' or 'under ideal conditions' or 'if there were no such thing as jealousy'. His methods being what they are, Shaw cannot utter these phrases, which are the ingredients of textbooks, dissertations and legal documents, in all of which an overriding object is to avoid saying anything overtly unsound. But for a writer of polemics, the first rule is to arouse interest and keep it alive, and hedging modifications will not do that. Arguments, it is true, depend on the process which fines down disagreement to its essentials by just such modifications. But Shaw's polemical writings (with the exception of *The Intelligent Woman's Guide to Socialism and Capitalism*) are not consistently argumentative, even though they are for the most part logical and consecutive, and buttressed with supporting material that is brilliantly selected. More than once Shaw passed on Owen's advice: 'Don't argue. Repeat your assertion.' He himself did both, of course, but he aimed to convince rather than to systematize. As to the dangers of redundancy, he says, 'Still, a thing that nobody believes cannot be proved too often.'

Much of the piquancy of Shaw's expression comes of this deliberate whetting of interest. 'If you call a man a rascally idealist, he is not only shocked and indignant but puzzled: in which condition you can rely on his attention.' Shaw explains his own method often enough that we need be in no doubt about it. 'I sometimes call it the Irish mind, as distinct from the English mind. But that is only to make the English and Irish sit up and listen.'

Nor can any of these questions be simplified by dividing Shaw's work into the conventional Early, Middle and Late (or Disillusioned) periods. He learned rapidly, one might say instantaneously. In his novels, written between 1879 and 1884, there is a mine from which this fertile but thrifty professional took characters, situations and whole scenes for later and usually greater treatment in the plays. As to his theories, these were so well formed during the period of his novel-writing and his early essays of the 1890's that they remained substantially unchanged and (with one notable exception) quite serviceable during the sixty or seventy years that followed. New phenomena for which the existing scheme would not work were late and few (e.g. Mussolini). In regard to women, there was no strain whatsoever on Shaw's scheme of ideas. Where the situation changed, it merely confirmed his prophecies, and his writings on that subject were henceforth dated, but not invalidated. On this, too, Shaw has, as usual, said the last word and said it first. Writing in 1921 a preface for his first novel, *Immaturity*, he says of his novels: 'They prove too that, like Goethe, I knew all along, and have added more to my power of handling, illustrating and addressing my material than to the material itself.'

Even a division between the imaginative work of the playwright-novelist and the political or didactic work of the Fabian socialist would belie Shaw's consistency. His novels bear out his treatises, and his tracts illumine his plays. There is a difference chiefly in emphasis, and that difference is reflected in the sections that follow, some of which rely more heavily on the essays, others on the plays and novels. However, all dividing lines are false to the unity of Shaw's thought. Without denying the endless contradictions of life, Shaw's ideas have a superb coherence.

Women and the Ideal

CHAPTER 2

Pedestals and Petticoats, Paragons and Parrots

1 THE DOUBLE WOMAN

VICTORIAN England was a fantasia of contradictions, as well as a vale of tears and soot. Incredibly modern and stubbornly antique, its sexual rules unimaginably strait-laced and its sexual aberrations remarkably wide, its women both prisoners and priestesses, the era in which Shaw began his career had already experienced a century of two contradictory kinds of change in the status of women. One led to greater freedom, the other to new restrictions. The results of both trends are accounted for and largely reconciled in Shaw's thought, but our life has not yet caught up with his art in this respect.

The beginning of the campaign for the rights of women was marked by the publication in 1792 of Mary Wollstonecraft's *A Vindication of the Rights of Women*. This beginning was theoretically radical, emotionally intense and historically well-timed, and should have been effective. Insofar as history is a matter of politics, that was the right moment for the birth of feminism. The whole basis of civilized authority had been opened to question by the theories connected with the French Revolution. Theories that went deep enough to find a new and solid basis for the rights of man could hardly fail to give a new basis for the rights of woman.

On the other hand, the ponderous forces of society do not move to the tune of theory alone. Needs that could never have been clearly stated, perceptions that were both deaf and dumb, were changing English manners and ideals in another direction, away from the coarse, bawdy and brutal, toward the gentle and genteel. The English and their critics can now smile at the excesses of this effort, as at a harmlessly neurotic great-aunt, but those who remember certain survivals of the pre-Victorian atmosphere persisting in conservative parts of society like the rural proletariat and the Bank of England, remind us that the need for more gentility was real and the remedy fairly effective.

In this movement toward gentility Woman played an important role, and the emphasis on Woman as a class was paralleled by the negation of woman as an individual. The Romantic movement and these new tendencies interplayed to change the ideal of woman in ways that are complicated to the point of obscurity. The result, however, is clear: an ideal (however imperfectly realized) of sensibility, chastity and obedience.

The change in the ideal of feminine conduct is well illustrated by the difference between Millamant, the woman of the world who is the heroine of *The Way of the World*, and the heroine of Richardson's *Pamela*. Congreve's play represents high comedy at the highest point it was to reach until Bernard Shaw began to write plays nearly two hundred years later. The play bears out George Meredith's theory in *An Essay on Comedy* that comedy flourishes in an atmosphere of equality between the sexes. Millamant, although she is in love with the hero, Mirabell, will accept him as a husband only on conditions which allow her to keep her money, her privacy, her wits and her emotional independence; and Mirabell would only love her less if she were meek and mild and improvident enough to give all for love.

Within forty years the new archetypal heroine had appeared: Pamela, the meek, modest, mild and maidenly. Hysterically resisting seduction by her employer, fanatically humble and conscious of her own virtue, Pamela is at last rewarded by marriage with the baffled seducer, to whom she then presents 'a little prattler' every year. This paragon of all the mechanical virtues was to reign for more than a hundred years. Esther Summerson in *Bleak House* was exactly the same kind of sentimental heroine. The choice between their constricted, priggish personalities and the sprightliness of Mistress Millamant rests on something more solid than personal taste. An unmistakable odor of dishonesty hangs about these sentimental heroines, about the way they preen themselves on their self-abnegation, about the evasion of issues which allows the author to suggest that the reward for abjuring the goods of this world is acquiring them.

This kind of womanly woman is as much a literary invention as a reality, and whatever reality she has is strictly bounded by her social class.

The ideal of the womanly might more accurately be called the ideal of the ladylike, but only if we bear in mind that the ideal was not the same as the actuality. The old aristocratic families whose conservatism makes their women now seem comparatively modern, would never have recognized the mealy-mouthed, virginal heroines of popular fiction as attempts at a ladylike ideal. And yet they were, however misconceived, an aspiration to higher things.

The priggish heroines of fiction and the masculine arguments against emancipation of women, concern lower-middle-class virtues and lower-middle-class living arrangements. Neither the life and appearance of the working-class woman, nor society's provisions for her, bore any resemblance to the womanly ideal. Physical fragility, delicate sensibility, chastity, the sacredness of motherhood and the home, are not easily reconciled with ten-hour shifts dragging carts through the coal-mines or with family life in a one-room dwelling. The sexual implications of poverty, which Zola describes so mercilessly (and Dickens avoids so assiduously), provide the most horrible but not the only evidence that the reality of the working-class woman is ignored by the upholders of the womanly ideal. The most obvious example of this class distinction is the argument about work during pregnancy. The thought of a lawyer with a big belly arguing a case in court, or a doctor seized with labor pains in the midst of a consultation, seemed to many people a telling objection to professional training for women. Aside from the maddening absurdity of these objections, they are a proof that the women who worked under brutal conditions all during pregnancy were not being thought of as women at all.

Even within the class to which this ideal applied we take it for granted that, as one critic reminds us, '. . . Victorian propriety itself is more a convention of public admission than a description of conduct'.

A few women, like Harriet Martineau, author, social reformer and feminist, were immune to the 'combined coercion and bribery' of which Mill speaks. Many other rebellious spirits must have lived and died in silence, like Miss Weeton, an obscure governess whose journal, surviving by chance, tells us that she suffered all her life from her unsuitability to the role in which she was cast.

I often feel as if I were not in my proper sphere, as if I possessed talents that only want awakening – that are ready to bud, did they but find the least encouragement, and . . . that will wither for want of it. . . . I think I could have been something greater . . . had not my natural genius been repressed. . . . Why are not females permitted to study physic, divinity, chemistry, botany, logic, mathematics &c? To be sure the mere study is not prohibited, but the practice is, in a great measure. Who would employ a female physician, who would listen to a female divine, except to ridicule? I could myself almost laugh at the idea.

But spirited persons (and those who want to study) are a small minority in either sex. Most women continued to struggle into their bonds, in the form of corsets, and still do, because flattery is a more noticeable pleasure than freedom.

To the intelligent woman who sensed something wrong with the paragon ideal but was kept in line by her wish to do what was right and becoming, Shaw addressed his paradoxical aphorisms about home and family, duty and self-sacrifice, and even love. His criticism cuts deep because he never fell into the error of simply reversing ideas as he reversed maxims. Every shallow moralist from Arthur Wing Pinero to Tennessee Williams has made the easy assumption that, if Victorian righteousness was an unhealthy sham, then it must be good to be bad. Shaw shocked his early audiences partly because he kept a firm grip on the difference between good and bad. This meant that his revision of principles had to be far more radical than his revision of conduct, and he became himself a paradox of the kind most difficult to accept: a man who went about destroying the simple rules designed to make people behave decently, and at the same time set a higher standard for human behavior than the rules could ever have achieved.

2 MY DEAR DOROTHEA

The ideal which made woman at once paragon, priestess and prisoner was Shaw's first object of attack in his lifelong work on behalf of women. When the prisoner is kept on a pedestal, when her eternal self-sacrifice is (still speaking ideally) not so much exacted from her as assumed to be her own wish, for the nobility of which she is praised and rewarded; when her guard pretends he is both her protector and her slave, all because of her irresistible charm; when, to quell all doubts, the only livelihood open to her depends on pleasing one of these guards whose preferences are so obvious, and all the pleasures of life are in his gift, then it is not easy to persuade the prisoner to step down and put her pretty little feet on the ground.

It cannot have been mere chance that Shaw's first literary work, *My Dear Dorothea*, concerned itself with a little girl, or that its underlying theme was the spiritual management of a woman's life in a badly organized society. In addressing the Victorian little girl, Shaw was approaching society through the being who stood at the bottom of a hierarchy of dominations. Margaret Dalziel, studying the popular fiction of a hundred years ago, finds that the ideal heroine, being very young and beautiful '. . . . had two possible sets of masters. Her primary obligation, established by the law of God and nature, and fundamental to the social order, was submissiveness to authority. This was her duty and her joy'. In a society of such marked inequalities, the weakest person is also the weakest link. Shaw's half-serious half-statements implying that women may save the world are remotely but certainly linked with this early vision of women as a rebellious class, but a class that should have been far more rebellious than it was. Women were not the only ones oppressed in Victorian England. A socialist writer might have been expected to pin his hopes on the proletariat. For Shaw, however, the deprivations of women became a point of intellectual attack (while the deprivations of the poor became a point of practical attack) because the disabilities of women were so clear an expression of what seemed to him false in the ideas which so much of Europe thought it was trying to live by.

Shaw's affinity for Ibsen, who was temperamentally and artistically so unlike him, was based on their similar protests against the large lies of society. The idealization of women is a perfect example of the kind of damage done by these lies. All the talk about the joy of self-sacrifice and the sacredness of the duty of woman *qua* woman, had the desired but dangerous effect of causing women (especially the best women) to embrace their chains. The situation is best described by reversing Tanner's hominist gibe in *Man and Superman*: '. . . she makes you will your own destruction'. Men have made women will their own destruction. It is flattering to be thought nobler than any human being has a right to be, and the temptation to do everything possible to foster that illusion is nearly irresistible. It is equally flattering to be treated as an enchantress, and the tradition of gallantry which is based on this pretense feeds those insatiable plants of egotism which grow in female as well as in male souls.

Clearly, Shaw was an Ibsenite before he ever heard of Ibsen. *My Dear Dorothea*, written in 1878 but not published until 1956, shows an awareness of society's foundation of falsehoods that is subtler than Ibsen's, but equally radical. Just how audacious his advice to Dorothea was at the time it was written, we cannot easily imagine. For all our strictures, we probably underrate the scope and strength of the Victorian convention of propriety. We need the witness of someone like Gwen Raverat, whose *Period Piece* acquaints us with just such a spirited little girl as Shaw had in mind – herself. Although she was a member of the intellectual and often eccentric Darwin-Huxley clan, Mme Raverat says:

> For nearly seventy years the English middle classes were locked up in a great fortress of unreality and pretence, and no one who has not been brought up inside the fortress can guess how thick the walls were, or how little of the sky outside could be seen through the loop holes.

Into this fortress, into the very donjon keep reserved for little girls, who combined in themselves the two sacred and misprized groups, woman and child, Shaw sent his inextinguishable fires.

'Be as selfish as you can.' This is the heart of Shaw's message; and if it sounds impossibly shocking for the day in which it was written, and impossibly commonplace for the day in which it was published, seventy-eight years later, that is because the bare statement leaves out the one element that was an essential part of all Shaw's advice. If we understand that element we can see Shavian selfishness to be a virtue so radical that it is nearly as shocking now as it was then.

> Let your rule of conduct always be to do whatever is best for yourself. Be as selfish as you can. And here I feel that I must stop to explain something to you. In reading this letter, you have been surprised at finding directions quite opposite to those which you are accustomed to receive. It will perhaps surprise you still more when I tell you that what everybody says is almost sure to be wrong.

Therefore she must 'Always strive to find out what to do by thinking, without asking anybody' and '. . . be careful not to give yourself the habit of taking advice'.

Then we come to the element that distinguished all Shaw's comments on the subject of women: an awareness of the primacy of spiritual matters. If that phrase suggests priests and a hypochondriacal concern for one's individual relations with the rest of the universe, the reader will see at once why Shaw does not call it by its name. Spiritual concerns are paramount in all Shaw's major works, but that truth is disguised (to our conventional perceptions) by the fact that he is a realist in religion as in other matters.

Still, we must recognize that the qualities he recommends to Dorothea are qualities of spirit: discontent, proper hypocrisy, pride, individuality, self-control, politeness. These do not prepare a little girl to earn her living or to get the vote or to wear bloomers. They prepare her to be a certain kind of human being and to save her soul alive inside her irrelevant petticoats and corsets.

This spiritual emphasis informs even the reasons given for cultivating politeness: '. . . because politeness is a mark of superiority. . .' . It applies to individuality: 'I am sure you would not like to be called commonplace. Therefore you must preserve your individuality by never imitating others, or pretending to be what you are not.'

How to be selfish: that is the question, and it is given an earnest answer, a little apostrophe to Duty, one of the textual inconsistencies which add to the Biblical quality of Shaw's work. If the following exhortation sounds somewhat prim, that reflects both the earnestness of youth and Shaw's continuing effort to be fully understood. The mature Shaw will also have much to say about the survival of the self-controlled.

When you make up your mind to be very selfish, you must be quite sure that you know how to be so. Some girls think, for instance, that greedy people are selfish. This is not the case. They are only silly people trying to be selfish without knowing how. They make themselves ill, and are disliked by those who live with them; and the bad opinion of those around them makes them so unhappy that they never enjoy themselves except when they are eating. And it is surely very silly to prevent oneself from having more than two pleasant hours in the long day.

You will often be tempted to take things that you want very badly, from people who are weaker than you. But you must not do so, because there are others who are stronger than you; and if everyone were to seize what they desire by force, you would be very miserable. This consideration for the consequences of one's acts is called Duty.

This passage is interesting for the psychological interpretation of gluttony and for the thumb-nail sketch of modern futility: 'people trying to be selfish without knowing how'. Above all, it is a definition of Shaw's kind of selfishness, a term he uses mischievously to alarm and to reform. Such a gloss on 'selfishness' could do much to reduce the cruel bewilderment in which audiences leave *Major Barbara* when it is played as written.

Major Barbara, of course, reminds us that selfishness is not a remedy for females only. In Undershaft, the munitions millionaire, selfishness is bolder in outline and broader in scope than anything little Dorothea or Ibsen's Nora or Undershaft's daughter could achieve. Undershaft will see the world blown apart by his munitions before he will submit himself to the degradations of poverty. None of the women quite reaches this pinnacle of assertion. Yet the actual pattern is not different; and however small the framework, however delicate the tracing, the quality of selfishness in women needs to be emphasized just because it is so difficult to achieve. That remark may sound dubious to readers who know selfish women in life and literature; but these are examples of petty selfishness, not grand selfishness, and of the old-fashioned, not the Shavian new woman.

The grand selfishness Shaw recommends is not self-serving, but self-respecting; it does not result in petty self-seeking, but in a rehabilitation of the idea of the self. Selfishness is the opposite of meekness, humility and self-sacrifice (the womanly virtues), not the opposite of generosity and altruism (the virtues of strength). In a badly arranged world, meekness and acquiescence are dangerous virtues.

In fact, two pieces of spiritual advice sum up this little book and could equally well stand for the whole of Shaw's advice to women. The first is the Johnsonian, 'My dear friend, clear your *mind* of cant.' The second, a comment with reverberations, is: 'Always have the highest respect for yourself, and you will be too proud to act badly.'

Whether this quality is called self-respect, pride or egotism, it has always been most difficult for men to accept in women or for women to accept in themselves. According to Lionel Trilling, it is this quality in the heroine of Jane Austen's *Emma* that dismays the critics and introduces an equivocal note into their judgments of the novel. It is this snag that caused the real and pathetic Miss Weeton in Jane Austen's time to declare: 'I think I could have been something greater. . . .' It is this that is distasteful in the heroine of Charlotte Brontë's *Shirley*, who is a plausible ancestress of Shaw's Lydia Carew: a self-willed, egotistical woman who defies the world to censure her, who feels sure that 'what everybody knows' is wrong and her own unconventional views are right.

One measure of the change in social atmosphere between 1849, when *Shirley* was published, and 1886, when Shaw completed *Cashel Byron's Profession*, is this: that Shirley Keeldar's assertion of her right to certain masculine prerogatives is self-consciously pursued as an end in itself; whereas Lydia treats her feminine self-assertion quite absent-mindedly, with the main force of her attention focused on the objects to which this assertion admits her: interesting studies and rationalized rules of behavior. It may be noticed here in passing, for its implicit comment on two of Shaw's later suggestions about women's rights, that both these symbols of female independence are heiresses, and that each is the mistress of a large house, the superabundant outward sign of a state of being which Virginia Woolf called *A Room of One's Own*. Neither of these women has or needs the vote. Money votes. Money also contributes something essential to the self-assured woman. This is not to say that only rich women can afford to be independent spirits. Women of genius, or women with any genuine calling, have the same ability to live without subordinating themselves to any man. *Love Among the Artists* and *The Irrational Knot* demonstrate this truth with equal effect in a concert pianist and a music-hall singer. Shaw's first major critical work shows his interest in the question of the independent woman.

3 *THE QUINTESSENCE OF IBSENISM*

The Quintessence of Ibsenism, expanded from a talk on Ibsen which Shaw gave before the Fabian Society in 1890, says more about women than it does about Ibsen. Certainly none of the other questions raised by Ibsen's plays engaged Shaw's attention quite so fully. Idealism seems to rival Woman as a subject in the plan of exposition, but not, we must conclude, in the author's mind. The chapter on 'Ideals and Idealists' takes its illustrations mainly from the marriage mores, and is thus a fitting introduction to the next chapter, 'The Womanly Woman'. Ostensibly the latter is '. . . an example of an idealist criticizing a realist'. It does present, in analyzing William Stead's review of the diary of Marie Bashkirtseff, a fine case study of an 'idealist' mind, veering and tacking as the real wind shifts to an inconvenient quarter. What becomes apparent when the *Quintessence* is considered entire, is that this 'example' is the heart of Shaw's book. The elucidations of Ibsen's plays are secondary. Shaw's interest was in the criticism of life, not in the criticism of literature. The classification of idealists, realists and philistines clarifies certain issues, but it is not itself an issue. The image of the two pioneers, one telling people it is wrong to do things previously thought right, and one telling people it is right to do things previously thought wrong, has the prophetic ring that clearly thought insight often acquires. But it is in the discussion of the womanly woman that the book touches life, makes radical assertions, and arrives at the proposals toward which it has been moving. It seems quite probable that, as Stephen Winsten says, Shaw '. . . had toyed with the thought of calling it A Guide to Women'.

In this discussion of the womanly woman, the ultimate point of disagreement, the issue which cannot be dissolved in definitions or in anthropological comparisons, is that of self-love. Womanly roles can be re-defined. It is only too easy to slide along with the real situation and stretch the old ideals to cover the new realities. The 'womanly' has been re-defined in practice to include the self-effacing tasks by which most career women serve some man in an office instead of at home and, conversely, the masculine self-reliance of the middle-class housewife. The new marriage mores have also been partly subsumed under the old ideals, as for example in the concept of divorce 'for the sake of the children'. What must remain intransigeant in the differences between the idealist's view of woman and the actual consciousness of women, was, as Shaw realized in 1890, expressed in Marie Bashkirtseff's exuberant statement: 'I love myself.'

Aghast at such naked egotism, or perhaps only at the audacity of publishing it, William Stead reminded his readers of the womanly taste for self-sacrifice. Shaw's response to this notion is characteristic. He talks of women as though they were commensurable with men:

> No *man* pretends that his soul finds its supreme satisfaction in self-sacrifice: such an affectation would stamp him as a coward and a weakling: the manly man is he who takes the Bashkirtseff view of himself. But men are not the less loved on this account.

This is not the usual way for a man to judge remarks about women. It is Shaw's way, and it raises the ultimate egalitarian question which, for all its laughable disregard of the deep differences between one human being and another, gives the only safe clue to our dispensations for other people: how would it work for ourselves? (Never mind the well-founded criticism of the Golden Rule in 'The Revolutionist's Handbook', which is also true.)*

The idealist critic answers at once that the specifications for the manly man are, in the very nature of the terms, irrelevant to those for the womanly woman. Shaw's response, implicit in all his creation of characters, is based on the assumption that there are – in the soul as in the body – androgynous regions and functions, perhaps more of them than we think.

Shaw also points out that Mr Stead, although he condemns all such women as Bashkirtseff, all the egotists who are females, is enchanted by Bashkirtseff herself. Apparently, in some instances, women too can be selfish and yet be loved.

The right to self-love is not Ibsen's main point, but it is Shaw's main point in explaining Ibsen. The conflict between man and woman in Ibsen's plays is secondary to the conflict between ideals and reality. In Shaw's book, what he calls his 'digression' is in reality his subject, and the discussion of Ibsen's plays an illustrative dénouement. Shaw's explanation of his scheme is significant. He claims to have '. . . traversed my loop as I promised, and come back to Man's repudiation of duty by way of Woman's . . .'. It is true in all Shaw's work that the elucidation of woman's role is also intended to throw a new

---

* 'Do not do unto others as you would that they should do unto you. Their tastes may not be the same.'

light on man's role. Woman is a good starting-point in two ways: first, as the woman's disadvantages give her reason to rebel; second, as her position is a *reductio ad absurdum* of the more general social ideals which Shaw was prepared to attack. That is woman's importance in the first phase of Shaw's work.

Shaw deals with two other issues in *The Quintessence of Ibsenism*: woman's sphere and the paragon delusion.

If we have come to think that the nursery and the kitchen are the natural sphere of a woman, we have done so exactly as English children come to think that a cage is the natural sphere of a parrot – because they have never seen one anywhere else.

Here follows a discussion of philistine, idealist, theological and realist parrots, a little parody on the arguments about woman's sphere, which nicely illustrates Shaw's ability to give his sardonic touches lightness without descending to levity. And, like so many of his disarming sallies, it will not let its audience go away smiling at the end: 'All the same, you respect that parrot [the realist and rebel] . . . and if it persists, you will have either to let it out or kill it.'

Nevertheless, the man who was to coin, 'Home is the girl's prison and the woman's workhouse', warns that 'Woman has thus two enemies to deal with: the old-fashioned one who wants to keep the door locked, and the new-fashioned one who wants to thrust her into the street before she is ready to go.' This is the voice of an anti-doctrinaire, of the author of 'The Impossibilities of Anarchism', of the advanced and daring critic of marriage and conventionality who advises young ladies '. . . on no account to compromize themselves without the security of an authentic wedding ring'. No wonder Eric Bentley celebrates Shaw's inclusiveness in the formula, 'Both/And.' Women have the right to both liberty and protection, to whatever is viable and of value in both the old and the new ways. Furthermore, as Shaw was always a believer in changing society first, he deplored the futility of private gestures of revolt. Besides, he shrank from pain and disaster.

The argument by definition is another trick Shaw defeats in the *Quintessence*. The trick is at its simplest when the definition is a redundancy like 'the womanly woman'. The women whose traits are not acceptable can be defined as '. . . not women at all, but members of the third, or Bashkirtseff, sex'. An extreme example of this frame of mind was the accusation that Sojourner Truth, who crusaded through the United States for the rights of Negroes and the rights of women, was in fact not a woman at all. This explanation of her fortitude and her talent for public speaking was widely believed because, apparently, this was easier than believing that a woman could outwit men on a public platform.*

In this battle of definitions Shaw avoids the facile response of re-definition. There is, as he sees, no hope of defining a term like 'the womanly woman'. At this point Shaw is saying only that we do not know what is womanly until we have observed the creature unchained from her perch. In a later addition to this essay, he makes a statement which cuts deeper, to the very bottom of all the contradictions and dilemmas of emancipation. If I had to choose only one quotation to illuminate the Shavian view, it would be this:

. . . there is no such species in creation as 'Woman, lovely woman', the woman being simply the female of the human species, and that to have one conception of humanity for the woman and another for the man, or one law for the woman and another for the man, or one artistic convention for woman and another for man, or, for the matter of that, a skirt for the woman and a pair of breeches for the man is . . . unnatural, and . . . unworkable. . . .

Yet Shaw, who repudiated the womanly ideal, created for the stage some of the most womanly creatures since Shakespeare, creatures who contrast so sharply in this respect with the heroines of recent plays, that one might almost say womanliness is their chief characteristic. The puzzle, if there is one, is only a word puzzle. Whereas the 'womanly' of Leslie Stephen or William Archer, or any other conventional man of the time, was an ideal, the 'womanly' of Shaw is a quality we feel, one which is like the qualities of real persons who happen to be women and live as women. Shaw's innovation, one which deserves the 'better than Shakespeare' tag, was to do just what

---

* 'What she considered true, and judged right, that she would say, and would do, in despite of the whole world.' This description of the heroine of a Victorian popular novel, *Marmaduke Wyvil* by H. W. Herbert, is judged as follows by another character: 'It is a fine character, truly . . . though not a woman's character; at least not what I think a woman's should be.'

he advised Ellen Terry to do in *Cymbeline* even at a time when
he was fighting against the custom of cutting Shakespeare for
stage production:

All I can extract from the artificialities of the play is a double
image – a real woman divined by Shakespeare without his knowing
it clearly, a natural aristocrat, with a high temper and perfect
courage, with two moods – a childlike affection and wounded rage;
and an idiotic paragon of virtue, produced by Shakespeare's *views* of
what a woman ought to be, a person who sews, cooks . . . and 'always
reserves her holy duty', and is anxious to assure people that they may
trust her implicitly with their spoons and forks, and is in a chronic
state of suspicion of improper behavior on the part of other people
(especially her husband) with abandoned females. If I were you I
should cut the part so as to leave the paragon out and the woman
in. . . .

The importance of sexual prudery to the paragon outweighs
everything else, even forks and spoons. What is mixed in
Shakespeare becomes monolithic in some of Dickens's heroines.
Imagine cutting the paragon out of Esther Summerson! There
is nothing to cut from. Nevertheless, Shaw wrote, late in his
life, '. . . Esther is not only a woman but a maddening prig,
though we are forced to admit that such paragons exist and are
perhaps worthy of the reverent admiration with which Dickens
regarded them.' His effort to be fair even to such an unbearable
artifact is a reminder that the ideal woman had a real historical
function in the transition from eighteenth-century England to
nineteenth-century England, and in the process of civilizing the
English people, no area of life more desperately needed its
brutality softened than that of sex, although we are usually
more aware of the prisons, the executions, the insane asylums
as the blotchy reverse of every Watteau canvas, neither more
nor less real than the lovers in the flowery swing.

In our novels and romances especially we see the most beautiful of
all the masks – those devised to diguise the brutalities of the sexual
instinct in the earlier stages of its development, and to soften the
vigorous aspect of the iron laws by which Society regulates its
gratification.

Shaw's somewhat contradictory (or are they merely inclusive?) remarks about the force of sexuality will be discussed later,

but they belong here also, as the synthesis of 1890 foreshadows *Man and Superman* (1903) and even *Back to Methuselah* (1921):

Tannhäuser may die in the conviction that one moment of the emotion he felt with St Elizabeth was fuller and happier than all the hours of passion he spent with Venus; but that does not alter the fact that love began for him with Venus. . . . When Blake told men that through excess they would learn moderation, he knew that the way for the present lay through the Venusberg, and that the race would assuredly not perish there as some individuals have. . . . Also he no doubt foresaw the time when our children would be born on the other side of it, and so be spared that fiery purgation.

Shaw's reticence often concealed his awareness of the strong sexual component in the attitudes of men (and even women) toward all aspects of the woman question.

The Quintessence of Ibsenism takes into account both lust and the struggle against it.

Therefore Woman has to repudiate duty altogether. In that repudiation lies her freedom; for it is false to say that Woman is now directly the slave of Man; she is the immediate slave of duty; and as man's path to freedom is strewn with the wreckage of the duties and ideals he has trampled on, so must hers be. She may indeed mask her iconoclasm by proving in rationalist fashion, as Man has often done for the sake of a quiet life, that all these discarded idealist conceptions will be fortified instead of shattered by her emancipation. To a person with a turn for logic, such proofs are as easy as playing the piano is to Paderewski. But it will not be true. A whole basketful of ideals of the most sacred quality will be smashed by the achievement of equality for women and men.

Shaw knew the complexity of this sense of duty: the beauty of the ideals on the subject, the unpleasantness of some of the instincts which lent their force to these ideals and turned them into something damaging, the way both were woven into the pattern of society as a support for inequality and injustice, and the impossibility of living without another kind of sense of duty, the kind based on real, instead of ideal requirements.

But predicting the consequences of one's acts calls for intelligence and reflection. The larger and more intricate society grows, the more difficult it is to trace these consequences. Therefore Shaw's preference for the intelligent and unconventional woman.

The accepted idea that a woman's greatest satisfaction must come in sacrificing herself 'for lover or for child', can be used by woman in two destructive ways: to make herself either a dead weight of dependence or an instrument of tyranny. Mrs Dudgeon, in *The Devil's Disciple*, stands for puritan self-denial. Her family must choose between miserable submission and complete rebellion. Mrs Collins, in *Getting Married*, is an example of the other sort of self-sacrificing mother, the kindly incubus. She is a sorry contrast to her mystical and philandering sister-in-law, Mrs George, who knows how to let out her will as a singer knows how to let out her voice, and whose meanderings '. . . certainly made her interesting, and gave her a lot of sense'. Mr Collins says of his womanly wife, 'You see, she's such an out-and-out wife and mother that she's hardly a responsible human being out of her house, except when she's marketing.' Her children have all run away, and her husband is '. . . that fond of my old Matilda that I never tell her anything at all for fear of hurting her feelings'. She is described, in an image that recalls the parrots, as being '. . . like a bird born in a cage, that would die if you let it loose in the woods'.

The other change in the idea of duty is even more fundamental: the duty which is reinstated in *Dorothea* is no longer woman's duty, but simply a human obligation to which distinctions of sex have no relevance.

The idealization of women as somehow 'finer than we' was tightly interwoven with the treatment of women as intellectually inferior and legally subordinate. It is quite consistent with other aspects of the nineteenth-century popular tradition (and indeed with the state of practical affairs) that spiritual refinement should be judged incompatible with business, government, and practical affairs of all kinds. Nothing could have been more unsuitable to the bourgeois world of business than Christianity, either principled or sentimental, unless it were the esthetic sense, which was also consigned to woman's tender care. 'Business is business' was then openly avowed and simply interpreted. Making business and politics nominally the man's world, with amateur esthetics and amateur ethics nominally the woman's world, may have kept it all in the family, but it demanded of the middle-class woman more passion for the chaste, the generous and the artistic than the average person has to give. That is why Shaw's insistence that women are not angels but ordinary fallible creatures, subject to temper tantrums, sexual infatuation and other lapses from decorum, is really a kindness, and certainly a step in preparing men to accept women as their equals.

One source of the general impression that Shaw is a woman-hater is, of course, his mission to free the prisoner from her pedestal. He has not been forgiven for portraying unpleasant women in his unpleasant plays, even though the rages of Blanche Sartorius in *Widowers' Houses*, the sexual infatuation of Julia Craven in *The Philanderer*, the deadly hostility of Mrs Dudgeon in *The Devil's Disciple*, and the courtship of Ann Whitefield in *Man and Superman*, all seem very mild medicine to the readers of Philip Wylie, Jean Anouilh, Norman Mailer and Tennessee Williams. Furthermore, as Shaw pointed out to Janet Achurch, his women are:

the sort of work which, even when it makes them unamiable, at least makes them unamiable human beings, which is better than making them amiable imposters.

This distinction was not always clear, even to such an intelligent and advanced critic as William Archer, on whose point of view Shaw comments as follows:

Now Archer was not such a simpleton as to be unaware that some women are vulgar, violent, and immodest according to Victorian conceptions of modesty. He would probably have assented to the proposition that as vulgarity, violence, and immodesty are elements in human nature, it is absurd to think of them as unwomanly, un-manly, or unnatural. Yet. . . . He reproached me for my apparent obsession with abominably ill-tempered characters, oversexed to saturation.

I shall come later to the real and supremely interesting subject of which the words 'undersexed' and 'oversexed' are a clumsy evasion. The question here is whether Shaw's public statements of the perfectly well-known fact that real women are a mixed lot, as men are, were a service or a disservice to woman. The first and lesser consideration is that Shaw's portraits are by no means savage, not even the most unloving of the early portraits, Blanche Sartorius and Julia Craven. And when we turn from Shaw's portrayal of character at this period to the statements he makes in his own person, these seem equally mild.

Of Wagner's Rhine maidens he says, 'But they are thought-less, elemental, only half-real things, much like modern young ladies.' This flirtatious sally introduces the second and more important consideration about Shaw's attitude: that is, that on the rare occasions when he does say an unkind word about women, it is not their naturalness or their lapses from virtue that he objects to, but their artificiality and their conformity to the womanly ideal. In other words, he places the blame for any apparent inferiorities in women on the whole society and its impossible demands upon women.

Shaw says in another place, 'Strindberg, the only living genuine Shakespearian dramatist, shows that the female Yahoo, measured by romantic standards, is viler than her male dupe and slave.' It will call for a quite deliberate traduction of meaning to ignore 'measured by romantic standards' or to change it to 'measured by my standards', especially in a preface designed to show the impossibility of romantic standards.

Here is another instance: 'The women, who have not even the City to educate them, are much worse: they are positively unfit for civilized intercourse – graceless, ignorant, narrow-minded to a quite appalling degree.' This is the worst Shaw will ever have to say about women, and it is like him, instead of criticizing persons, to criticize society and its institutions. The defects of the homebound woman seem to him the fault of a selfish masculine society. That this society does not, in Shavian terms, know how to be selfish, is irrelevant for the moment. The more interesting fact is that male selfishness in confining woman to her home while condemning her for her homebred defects, had partly freed woman from the illusions of male society. That is one reason for Shaw's tendency to feel that women might be the hope of the world, since even the clever and capable had been given no stake in the titles, uniforms and prerogatives of male society. Therefore, Shaw's belief in the importance of woman rested only partly on the biological energy which he called the Life Force; female politics as well as female instinct might be expected to oppose the standing masculine mode of society.

In the middle classes themselves the revolt of a single clever daughter (nobody has yet done justice to the modern clever English-woman's loathing of the very word 'home'), for an independent working life, humanizes her whole family in an astonishingly short time. . . .

That is the basis for the quizzical character of the Shavian heroine. She takes nothing for granted. She does not rant or make large-scale condemnations. She is aware that things are seldom what they seem. She has the habit of forming her own judgments, but is safe from disillusionment, for she has not formed the illusions of her brothers. She is meant to humanize her whole society almost as she does her whole family. Such changes cannot be wrought by a paragon or, in more modern terms, a conformist. Only a rebel and a realist can accomplish them. That is why Shaw cuts the paragon out and leaves the woman, the ordinary human being, someone rather like himself. Here is the key to Shaw's success where so many have been defeated: for him a woman is a fellow-being, a member of the same species as himself. At a time when women were still referred to as 'the sex', as though to be male were normal and to be female an aberration, this was revolutionary indeed. Here is the key to the furor over Shaw's early plays, to the debate about Candida, to his confusing (i.e. inclusive) statements on sexuality, to his ability to keep all the practical benefits of equality secure while treating Woman as an inspired and saving creature who is in some sense an instrument of the higher purposes of the universe.

Women and Men

CHAPTER 3

The Comedy of Courtship

1 ANA, HUNTRESS CHASTE AND FAIR

Man and Superman does not always appear to be a comedy of ideas. As in most of Shaw's plays before *Heartbreak House*, the framework and movement of the plot are severely conventional.

Ann Whitefield, a modern young lady, is loved by Octavius, a would-be poet. She, however, secretly loves Jack Tanner, a left-wing gentleman who abhors marriage on principle. The play begins just after the death of Ann's father, with the discovery that Jack Tanner has been named as her guardian, jointly with Roebuck Ramsden, a gentleman so old-fashioned that he ' . . . was an advanced man before you were born'. Meanwhile Violet, sister to Octavius, has been secretly married to Hector, a rich American whose father has sworn to disinherit him if he marries any but a titled lady. When Tanner realizes that he is loved by Ann, he flees the country with his chauffeur, Henry Straker. They are waylaid in Granada by bandits whose leader, Mendoza, has renounced the English world after being disappointed in his love for Louisa, sister to Henry Straker. During the night all the characters take part in a strange dream set in a Shavian hell to which the trapdoor in Mozart's *Don Giovanni* is the only other access. The next day Ann and her party catch up with Tanner, and all are released by the bandits. Violet masterfully brings Hector's father to approve their marriage and to make a handsome settlement. Ann entraps Tanner into proposing to her, and 'accepts' him. Both happy couples owe their good fortune to the determination and seriousness of the young women and to their unblushing realism.

Nothing in this plot indicates that the author is a dangerous radical. Even the initiative so adroitly taken by the young ladies is a staple of comedy. On the stage, with the adorably artificial dresses, the coquettish hats, the spats, sticks and gloves of the period, this play may seem even less a comedy of ideas, especially when played with the thrifty omission of Act III. The 'Don Juan in Hell' episode makes demands on time and an even dearer commodity, thought, but it is an essential part of the play, in which the characters appear as the real self of each, abstracted from the period costumes which their bodies and minds have been wearing. Without it the play seems to be a comedy of manners which scarcely mentions the ideas in the preface and in 'The Revolutionist's Handbook and Pocket Companion'.

In another sense, however, for all the conventional plotting, for all the stock characters into whose ready molds Shaw poured the elixir of the unexpected, the play is as philosophical as the preface and more revolutionary than the handbook. The character of Ann as Everywoman is the key to its meaning. Her character transmutes the bitterness of some of the general maxims into the delightfulness of one particular vital genius. Furthermore, it has the less obvious effect of making Jack Tanner look like a dilettante, and his socialism a comparatively shallow doctrine.

Although Shaw acknowledges that every woman is not Ann, yet Ann is Everywoman in the sense that she does what women commonly would like to do. Her success is due in large part to the fact that she is unashamed. A few years later, in *Major Barbara*, Shaw was to make Andrew Undershaft's motto simply: 'Unashamed.' A few years earlier, in *Mrs Warren's Profession*, Shaw had outraged public opinion by showing a successful prostitute who lived by that motto. In both cases, Shaw gifts his strong characters with an awareness that the guilt is society's for having offered them two evils as alternatives, not theirs for having chosen the lesser.

Though it is quite natural and *right* for Mrs Warren to choose what is, according to her lights, the least immoral alternative, it is none the less infamous of society to offer such alternatives. For the alternatives offered are not morality and immorality, but two sorts of immorality.

Ann Whitefield, although her choices are less appalling, has the same kind of choice to make. Like the other strong characters, she does not let her real preference be overruled by false shame. In the play it is Tanner who delivers a diatribe against shame. Yet he himself cries out in a moment of fear, 'You scandalous woman, will you throw away even your hypocrisy'?

As a matter of fact, Ann has nothing to be ashamed of except the hypocrisy that is forced upon her by convention. What is there to be ashamed of in loving a superior man and wanting to consummate that love in the way society approves? Her method, however, cannot be straightforward. 'A cunning and attractive woman disguises her strength as womanly defencelessness: simple men are duped by them.' Shaw's exposure of feminine deviousness is different from most such exposures in that he admires Ann for performing it so well, instead of blaming her for not practicing a disastrous simplicity. She, for one, escapes any genuine charge of hypocrisy by deceiving herself hardly at all, and deceiving others only to the extent that their own hypocrisy forces her to do so. It is as though Shaw were saying, as Tanner says when he drops the game of pretense for a moment: 'Forgive my brutalities, Ann. They are levelled at this wicked world, not at you.'

There are thus two parts to Shaw's judgment of the individual: the first is a test of realism, the second of vitality. The Shavian heroine (or hero) is expected to assess herself and her choices without illusion. And between her alternatives she is expected to choose fearlessly on the side of life. No price is too high for the vital person to pay, even if the irony of life demands that one choose the right to life as Andrew Undershaft does in *Major Barbara*, by dealing in death. Shaw does not encourage self-sacrifice on any terms. Even the deserving poor, he seems to say, deserve just what they get. This very large assumption of the value of life and the individual will, places Shaw at the opposite pole from those religions which glorify death and passivity and the denial of the self. He seems to say that the self is all we have that is human, therefore all we have that is religious. All this is implied in the philosophic background of Ann Whitefield's courtship.

To forestall certain vulgar interpretations of Ann's behavior, Shaw precedes her first entrance with the following description. Its brevity (compared with the way a novelist might convey the same impressions) is saved from cliché by the lifelike complications of character it embraces. Why, except of course that there is no comedy of angels, is Shaw so careful to hedge about with earthly limits this representative of the great forces of the universe?

Whether Ann is good-looking or not depends upon your taste; also and perhaps chiefly on your age and sex. To Octavius she is an enchantingly beautiful woman, in whose presence the world becomes transfigured and the puny limits of individual consciousness are suddenly made infinite by a mystic memory of the whole life of the race. . . .

To her mother she is, to put it as moderately as possible, nothing whatever of the kind. Not that Octavius' admiration is in any way ridiculous or discreditable. She is a well formed creature as far as that goes and she is perfectly ladylike, graceful and comely, with ensnaring eyes and hair. Besides, instead of making herself an eyesore like her mother, she has devised a mourning costume of black and violet silk. . . .

But all this is beside the point as an explanation of Ann's charm. Turn up her nose, give a cast to her eyes, replace her black and violet confection by the apron and feathers of a flower girl, strike all the aitches out of her speech and Ann would still make men dream. Vitality is as common as humanity; but, like humanity, it sometimes rises to genius; and Ann is one of the vital geniuses.

Ann's appearance at once tells us much about Shaw's intentions. She may not even be good-looking. It depends '. . . perhaps chiefly upon your age and sex'. In other words, her attraction is sexual. To say that she is a 'well-formed creature, as far as that goes', is a kind of faint praise designed to direct our attention to a quality that makes it possible for her to be, in Octavius' eyes, a beauty, and to inspire the kind of romantic love of which he is a textbook example. She dresses well, but, in an aside on the nature of vital genius, we are told that even a flower girl could create the same effect – although we cannot help feeling that Octavius would not rise to it. This aside hints that Eliza Doolittle in *Pygmalion* will be another vital genius.

But the fact that Ann's vitality rises to genius and is expressed in sexual attraction might lead to another facile misinterpretation. 'Not at all, if you please, an oversexed person. . . . She is a perfectly respectable, perfectly self-controlled woman, and looks it; though her pose is fashionably frank and impulsive. . . . Nothing can be more decorous than her entry.' Thus is the actress who plays Ann admonished. Shaw knew how the intention of a play could be transgressed against by stage business. The point he intends to make by portraying Ann in this way, is that she is *not* the oversexed person, whom Shaw considered to be a victim and a slave rather than a Dionysian celebrant. Shaw felt for persons in the grip of this compulsion the distaste and uneasiness he felt in the face of any dehumanizing behavior.

Without making her cold or prudish, Shaw has thus tried to show that his huntress is, like Diana, chaste and fair. She is unashamed because the aim for which she works so unscrupulously is something higher than her own pleasure, either the pleasure of physical sensations or the vanity which is so large a sexual motive. Her aim is, as she tells the universe in the last words of the colloquy in hell: 'A father! a father for the Superman!'

Although in our time the sexual notive is likely to be pounced on first, in her own time, Ann would first have been suspected of social and mercenary motives. The husband-hunting combination of girl and mother is another staple of comedy, and the first thing Ann Whitefield does on stage is to invoke 'Mamma'. We see at once that this is a most skillful combination of ordinary good manners with extraordinary strategic sense, for Ann is entirely unmanageable, and Mamma has quite given up; hence the dramatic irony of Ramsden's comment on Ann:

Do you know that since she grew up to years of discretion, I don't believe she has ever given her own wish as a reason for doing anything or not doing it. It's always Father wishes me to, or Mother wouldn't like it. It's really almost a fault in her. I have often told her she must learn to think for herself.

Ann cannot be considered a fortune-hunter or a social climber. All the persons concerned are of the rich gentry; furthermore, to a conventionally ambitious woman, Jack Tanner, with his left-wing sympathies, would seem, if anything, less eligible than the conventional Octavius.

Remember also how Octavius is introduced: 'He must, one thinks, be the *jeune premier*: for it is not in reason to suppose that a second such attractive male figure should appear in one story.' As part of his wily preparation of the audience against error, Shaw has given Ann an attractive, adoring, eligible suitor. Therefore Ann's pursuit of Tanner is lifted a bit out of the usual framework, but not quite. For the simple fact is that Ann is in love with Tanner, and it is not surprising that she should be, considering his audaciousness. On the other hand, so many kinds of feelings are called love that one has to guard against the view of commonplace young ladies as described by Charlotte Brontë:

> With them, to 'love' is merely to contrive a scheme for achieving a good match: to be 'disappointed' is to have their scheme seen through and frustrated. They think the feelings and projects of others on the subject of love similar to their own, and judge them accordingly.

It is part of the play's intention that the 'evolutionary appetite' which Ann so truly represents, be nothing bizarre or even unusual, but perfectly familiar to all of us in the form of the intense individual (not, as Shaw points out, personal) preferences connected with sexual love. This distinction, basic to Shaw's theory of evolution, is a distinction between the personal characteristics which we may think are the reason for love, and the fated, unsuitable, often instantaneous sexual attraction which is supposedly a clue to the demands of the Life Force.

Courtship played out against this backdrop is surely, as the stage directions tell us, 'a drama of ideas'. If one is inclined to forget the ideas while watching the play, that is only because of the deftness with which they are placed among the very events which unthinking life unfolds every day.

2 THE TYRANNY OF WOMEN

Later, in *Major Barbara*, *Saint Joan* and *The Millionairess*, Shaw was to portray masterful women acting directly upon the world. Earlier, however, he had done much to make his attitude clear by writing about the women who control a man's world by controlling men. Of them he said:

> A slave state is always ruled by those who can get round the masters. The slavery of women means the tyranny of women. No fascinating woman ever wants to emancipate her sex; her object is to gather power into the hands of Man because she knows that she can govern him.

In *Candida* Shaw had written a play about just such a woman, with the ironic result that her tyranny was applauded as self-sacrifice, and her calculations as nobility. Shaw's heroine tended to her housekeeping, her husband, and her children, managing them all relentlessly, and encouraged her lover, the young poet,

until the moment when he would have become inconvenient.
Then Candida chose to remain with her husband, a choice for
which she was so admired and sentimentalized that Shaw himself was driven to proclaim her essential immorality. Audiences
have been enamored of this helpmate, this womanly, housekeeping woman. But the play is not in fact '. . . chiefly noteworthy for the depth and beauty of its sentiment', as George
Jean Nathan said. He went on: 'If there is a finer sentimental
play in the whole role of modern drama its name is a stranger
to me.' Here Shaw has created a woman so real that she has
fooled the critics in spite of her author's intentions. They have
taken her at face value as if they were themselves characters in
the play. There *is* a sentimental play on this subject, but it was
written by J. M. Barrie, Shaw's contemporary and for a time his
neighbor, in *What Every Woman Knows*. As Barrie's title indicates,
the power of women is no secret. But a play is to be judged sentimental or not according to its attitude and emphasis. Shaw's
powerful heroine protects and bullies and manipulates people
so instinctively that no line can be drawn between any two of
these methods. She is more candid than Barrie's heroine in that
she plays the role society expects of her without deceiving herself. On the other hand, she is less candid than Ann Whitefield
in that she invites no one (not even her lover) to come inside the
game of pretense with her and relish its little ironies.

In the great scene of resolution at the end of the play, is
Candida's long speech of explanation really a sentimental
accession? And can we not hear overtones in it now that its
early audiences were unprepared to hear?

We go once a fortnight to see his parents. You should come with
us, Eugene, to see the pictures of the hero of that household. . . . You
know how strong he is . . . how clever he is: how happy. [With
deepening gravity] Ask James's mother and his three sisters what it
cost to save James the trouble of doing anything but be strong and
clever and happy. Ask me what it costs to be James's mother and
three sisters and wife and mother to his children all in one. . . . Ask
the tradesmen who want to worry James and spoil his beautiful
sermons who it is that puts them off. When there is money to give,
he gives it; when there is money to refuse, I refuse it. I build a castle
of comfort and indulgence and love for him, and stand sentinel
always to keep little vulgar cares out. I make him master here,
though he does not know it. . . .

Does this sound like the joyous abandon of self-sacrifice? The sound of complaint in it seems to me very loud. If it had been any louder, its self-pity would have drowned out the meanings which Shaw wanted heard above all the clashing emotions of the scene. What is more, it sounds uncannily like Virginia Woolf's bitter and protracted complaint in *Three Guineas* about Albert's Education Fund, and that is a thoroughgoing feminist indictment of the male parisitism which keeps the sisters pinched and penniless at home so that their brother may have an expensive education and all the luxuries that are its normal accompaniment. In the same way, Candida clearly feels that the character and accomplishments of her reverend husband have been plumped out by feeding on the energies of his mother, his sisters, and his wife.

It is obvious that Candida resents the protection she gives her husband, although she does not resent it enough to run out and slam the door of this ironical doll's house. No doubt she resents Morell's illusions about it even more than she does the actual burden of care and sacrifice. But of course the illusions are part of the bargain.

Besides the complaint, there is the arrogance of, 'I make him master here.' We see little of Candida's bullying, but her deft removal of an attractive secretary is a fair sample of her realism and her skill. Moreover the whole scene shows her manipulation. She controls the course of it. She puts the dangerous question, 'I suppose it is quite settled that I must belong to one or the other.' Morell is blind to any meaning beneath the surface, but Marchbanks points out: 'She means that she belongs to herself', a remark which, in a sentimental play, would toss the heroine into his arms; but Candida turns on him in scorn: 'I mean that, and a good deal more, Master Eugene, as you will both find out presently.' And she continues, sparing nothing, 'And pray, my lords and masters, what have you to offer for my choice? I am up for auction, it seems, What do you bid, James?' It is not always observed that, in giving her decision, Candida does not say that she belongs to either one, but keeps the initiative by saying, 'I give myself to the weaker of the two.'

Candida thus does illustrate that kind of relationship in which a woman dedicates herself to the good of a man who needs her, and the man in turn does her the honor of supposing that the sacrifice is natural and joyful. But is this action the sacrifice it is vulgarly assumed to be? How would the most selfish of women decide? One has to remember that there are children offstage. Also, we know that Morell's income will not support two establishments, and might not even support one without his wife's management. Aside from these 'practical' questions, there are others, equally practical. Because her energy and shrewdness are so much greater than her little domestic world requires, Candida is in full control of her husband, her household and – up to a certain point – her lover. Having this easy management of the situation, she is able to do just as she pleases and yet remain, technically, a woman of blameless conduct. Like Ann Whitefield, she can give a perfectly proper accounting for every improper thing she does.

Then why is a lover permitted to build his little nest in the Morell's parlor? Is it because a grand passion has seized this respectable woman, shaking her till her teeth rattle? Not at all; Candida is perfectly cool in her toying with infidelity and '. . . as unscrupulous as Siegfried'. As Shaw points out, 'She seduces Eugene just exactly as far as it is worth her while to seduce him.' When the moment comes for her to make a choice between her solid husband and her fragile poet, Candida shows herself thoroughly practical. It does not matter that the poet is the 'strong' one, for his independence of spirit is risky for a woman, as compared with the solid dependence of the Reverend Mr Morell. Candida knows that the children, the tradesmen, the onions and the lamps, must be attended to, and that by the grace of God and the structure of our society, she has been elected Candida caryatid. And so she stands.

If she were young, childless and classless, like Jennifer Dubedat, the artist's wife in *The Doctor's Dilemma*, Candida might dart about the world attending on an artist man; but for a matron only great passion or inconceivable folly can lead to such a choice, and we know that, in Candida's world, which is not very different from that of Anna Karenina, tragedy must follow.

Real women are not always as practical as Shavian women. Shaw was often distressed to find women rushing into follies inspired by his theories or, as in the following instance, by a misinterpretation of his writings. Some day, I hope, a volume of extracts from Shaw's letters will be issued (with a complete index) under the title, *Sound Advice*. This collection should include a letter he wrote just before leaving London to spend the summer of 1919 in Ireland. Apropos of *Candida*, Shaw says:

... I gather that you wrote to me before, and on receiving no reply revenged yourself by leaving your husband on the responsibility of my ideas. You then came from a play of mine in which you found that the lady did *not* leave her husband, but very deliberately and wisely stayed where she was most wanted.

If you had been 'brave enough to go to your poet', he would certainly have been embarrassed; and he might have taken to his heels. I should advise you to consult some woman who has married a man of genius as to whether she finds her job an easy one. You may discover that she envies you your husband.

... have you considered the notion of simply going home and hanging up your hat in your own hall again before your husband has either become a confirmed bachelor or found a more comfortable sort of woman?

Candida is typical of the women in Shaw's plays in one respect: that is, that she does not need this kind of advice. Whatever her other weaknesses, she sees the sensible course and takes it, even when it happens to be the conventional course as well. Shaw's women may collide disastrously with man-made institutions, as Major Barbara collides with the Salvation Army, St Joan with the Church, and Lysistrata in *The Apple Cart* with Breakages, Ltd., but all three are right in their own terms. They are unworldly in respect of this man-made world of 'how it was done last time'. Therefore they are in trouble with the world, but not with the universe.

3 THE SAVING WOMAN

Lady Cicely Wanyflete in *Captain Brassbound's Conversion* is an interesting variant of the Shavian huntress. As an attractive and commanding spinster whose 'escape' from marrying ends the play, she has most of the characteristics which make Ann Whitefield the mother woman, or Everywoman, but with the sexual elements ostensibly left out. In coaxing Ellen Terry to play the part of Lady Cicely, Shaw declared an intention which he was not quite able to carry out:

I try to shew you fearing nobody and managing them all as Daniel managed the lions, not by cunning – above all, not by even a momentary appeal to Cleopatra's standby, their passions – but by simple moral superiority. . . . Here you get far beyond Candida, with her boy and her parson, and her suspicion of trading a little on the softness of her contours. . . . Here is a part which dominates a play because the character it represents dominates the world. . . . In every other play I have ever written – even in Candida – I have prostituted the actress more or less by making the interest in her partly a sexual interest. . . . In Lady Cicely I have done without this, and gained a greater fascination by it.

Outwardly, this heroine is not unlike other leading ladies. She is '. . . between 30 and 40, tall, very good looking . . .' and, like Ann, attentive to the effect her dress produces. At this moment she is '. . . dressed with cunning simplicity, not as a businesslike, tailor-made, gaitered tourist, but as if she lived in the next cottage and had dropped in for tea in blouse and flowered straw hat'. This tells us that she emphasizes her own femininity and also that she has considerable independence of mind, for 'dressing the part' is a common symptom of uncertainty.

In small matters as in large, Lady Cicely shows spiritual independence. *Captain Brassbound's Conversion*, like *Androcles and the Lion* and *The Shewing Up of Blanco Posnet*, is a modern demonstration of primitive Christianity. Lady Cicely is the only woman and also the only moral instigator among the protagonists of these three plays, the only mind conscious of its own principles, and directing its own destiny. Blanco is a ruffian who learns by accident that a virtuous action can be joyful. Androcles is a Christian by temperament, projecting his own harmlessness so singlemindedly that he wins over (at least in fiction) the lions of this world. But the heroine of *Brassbound* is quite ready for heaven, if we accept the Shavian Don Juan's definition: '. . . to be in hell is to drift: to be in heaven is to steer'.

In other words, the feminine aspect of Lady Cicely's accomplishment is the dominance she establishes through her instinctive management of people. If we simply call this power Moral Superiority or the Triumph of Virtue, we find ourselves in a quagmire of contradictions. Is this not Shaw, the iconoclast? Is he not the diabolonian witness against Christian and capitalist society, who suggests to women that their only hope is rebellion against the virtues which have been their prison?

The difficulty lies no deeper than the inconvenience of our having allowed two quite different kinds of behavior to be signified by one set of terms. As with Duty, so with Moral Superiority: while most people are talking about a superficial and conventionalized virtue, which is actually dangerous because it separates the conscience from real issues, Shaw is talking about an intelligent virtue, a puritan virtue, an aristocratic virtue, which is based on a superb combination of discriminating thought, the responsibility of the individual conscience, and *noblesse oblige*. Strengthened by this kind of virtue, Lady Cicely is easily a match for two theatrical dangers: first, the sinister Moroccans and other savage foreigners including, in a touch of bowdlerized realism, the kings, who always want to marry her; second, the old theme of murderous revenge.

Her first appearance on stage illustrates both her method and her madness:

LADY CICELY Thoughtful man that you are Mr Rankin! . . . and I've arranged everything with your servants; so you must go on gardening just as if we were not here.

SIR HOWARD I am sorry to have to warn you, Mr Rankin, that Lady Cicely from travelling in Africa has acquired the habit of walking into people's houses and behaving as if she were in her own.

LADY CICELY But, my dear Howard, I assure you the natives like it.

RANKIN (gallantly) So do I.

LADY CICELY (delighted) Oh, that is so nice of you, Mr Rankin. This is a delicious country! And the people seem so good! They have such nice faces! We had such a handsome Moor to carry our luggage up! and two perfect pets of Krooboys! Did you notice their faces, Howard?

SIR HOWARD I did, and I can confidently say that I have never seen so entirely villainous a trio. . . .

Lady Cicely's own bland assumption that she will be welcome is both pleasanter and kinder than her brother-in-law's apologetic stiffness. In this small matter at least, Lady Cicely's custom of attributing the most generous motives to others, has a way of bringing about its own confirmation. Obviously this habit can become both foolish and dangerous. Those 'nice faces' and

those 'perfect pets of Krooboys' are more likely to be what the
experienced man of the world expects than what the romantic
and gushy Englishwoman confidently assumes. In a moment
she is off again on the subject of Drinkwater, the wrongfully
acquitted hooligan: 'What a pleasant face your sailor friend has,
Mr Rankin! He has been so frank and truthful with us.' By this
time one wonders whether Lady Cicely is just another of the
breed of silly women who have learned all too well the first rule
for the Victorian lady: never take notice of anything wrong.

Sir Howard takes this view. 'You must not suppose, Mr
Rankin, that my sister-in-law talks nonsense on purpose. She
will continue to believe in your friend until he steals her watch;
and even then she will find excuses for him.' All through the
first scene Lady Cicely shows her benevolent bias. In this she is
like Androcles. Told that the natives are dangerous, she answers,
'Why? Has any explorer been shooting them?' And, 'You
always think, Howard, that nothing prevents people killing
each other but the fear of your hanging them for it. But what
nonsense that is! And how wicked!' And when Sir Howard
objects to a theological note in her conversation, she responds:

> Well, why not? Theology is as respectable as law, I should think.
> Besides, I'm only talking common sense. Why do people get killed by
> savages? Because instead of being polite to them, and saying How
> dye do? like me, people aim pistols at them, I've been among savages
> – cannibals and all sorts. Everybody said theyd kill me. But when I
> met them, I said How dye do? and they were quite nice. The Kings
> always wanted to marry me.

And again: 'You know, really, Howard, all those poor people
whom you try are more sinned against than sinning. If you
would only talk to them in a friendly way instead of passing
sentence on them, you would find them quite nice to you.' There
is more in this vein. Meanwhile, we muse on the nature of the
scenes Lady Cicely describes as the kings wanting to marry her.

It is not until Act Two opens with the firing of guns that we
have a glimpse of Lady Cicely's folly in action. Then we see at
once the nature of her feeling for the pack of villains who are
her escort, for the savages who live in the hills, for the prisoners
in the dock. It is not at all silly or cowardly: it is maternal. In
this Lady Cicely is like many of the women portrayed by Shaw:

like Candida, obviously, and Major Barbara and Hesione Hushabye in *Heartbreak House*, and the sweet-tempered queens, Catherine and Jemima in *Good King Charles* and *The Apple Cart*. Why, for example, are these queens so tolerant of their husbands' philandering? It is because these clever capable kings are seen by their wives as children who are naturally often naughty but must have unfailing love and support.

We have been prepared for Lady Cicely's method in Act One:

LADY CICELY The important thing, Captain Brassbound, is that we should have as few men as possible because men give such a lot of trouble when travelling. And then, they must have good lungs and not be always catching cold. Above all, their clothes must be of good wearing material. Otherwise, I shall be nursing and stitching and mending all the way; and it will be trouble enough, I assure you, to keep them washed and fed without that.

BRASSBOUND (haughtily) My men, Madam, are not children in the nursery.

LADY CICELY (with unanswerable conviction) Captain Brassbound: *All* men are children in the nursery.

Shaw agreed with Lady Cicely. He wrote to Ellen Terry: '. . . no man ever does anything for a woman's sake: from our birth to our death we are women's babies, always wanting something from them, never giving them anything except something to keep *for us*'. A little later in this exchange he avowed: 'Of the two lots, the woman's lot of perpetual motherhood, and the man's of perpetual babyhood, I prefer the man's, I think.'

But in the play, which does not tell us Shaw's own belief, we are left to wonder until Act Two whether Lady Cicely's remark is not mere stylish prattle. When the Beni Siras attack, she wants to talk to them. When a man is wounded she does not, as is confidently expected, faint. She ties him up 'like a bloomin orspittle nass'. We meet her returning with him to the castle, where she proceeds to manage everyone, perhaps not by moral superiority, as Shaw claims, but by the attitude and techniques of a teacher in a progressive nursery school. Like most of Shaw's bosses she knows how to manage without any need to tyrannize. The overbearing Brassbound is beaten only when Lady Cicely caps her series of orders with:

And oh, while I remember it, do please tell me, Captain, if I interfere with your arrangements in any way. If I disturb you the least bit in the world, stop me at once. You have all the responsibility; and your comfort and your authority must be the first thing. You'll tell me, won't you?

One can almost hear the Cicelys and the Candidas comparing notes on the management of men. They are well aware of the phenomenon observed by one of the characters in William Morris's *News from Nowhere*:

And then you know everybody likes to be ordered about by a pretty woman; why, it is one of the pleasantest forms of flirtation. You are not so old that you cannot remember that.

Yet when Lady Cicely high-handedly moves the captain out of his bed to make the wounded man comfortable, she is quite prepared to give up her own bed to the captain and sleep on the floor near her patient. Gradually it becomes clear that, although her tactics involve a certain amount of manipulation, her general strategy is based on a sincere belief in the point of view that seems, as we first try it, so naïve. But Shaw has warned us elsewhere of the abnormality of the average eye. Lady Cicely has the fearlessness of the pacifist and nonresister. Her way is similar to the way of the Taoist and the Friend, to the meekness of person and intransigeance of principle which Shaw extracted from the teachings of Jesus. It has little to fear from the charge of sentimentality, since it does for Sir Howard, the least sympathetic character in the play, just what it does for the poor men who have stood before him to be condemned. He is 'understood'. This is no doubt irritating, but that does not make it wrong.

Bless me! your uncle Howard is one of the most harmless of men – much nicer than most professional people. Of course he does dreadful things as a judge; but then if you take a man and pay him £5,000 a year to be wicked, and praise him for it, and have policemen and courts and laws and juries to drive him into it so that he can't help doing it, what can you expect? Sir Howard's all right when he's left to himself.

But to Lady Cicely, to understand is to plan a reform; it is not to pardon. That is the other pitfall of sentimentality which her ultrapositive approach just manages to avoid. This seems to be the answer to Brassbound's question: 'Have you any feeling? Or are you a fool?'

I have tried to distinguish between the superficialities of Lady Cicely's method, and the reality of her nature. The outward behavior is ultrafeminine. 'Now before I go back to Marzo, say thank you to me for mending your jacket, like a nice polite sailor.' This is silly, even if the actress mixes a little mockery with the coaxing, even if the author wants to show men as babies. But it is typical of a pattern which Shaw recognized; that of women achieving important, common-sense goals by a faultless mastery of the ridiculous weapons in their possession.

In her final scene, Lady Cicely reveals where the strength and the inspiration come from. Brassbound has said, 'I can see that you have some clue to the world that makes all its difficulties easy for you; but I'm not clever enough to seize it.' Her response sounds a familiar note: 'It's quite simple. Do whatever you like. That's what I always do.' The results are as Shaw predicted. Doing whatever she liked has not made Lady Cicely a moral weakling – quite the contrary.

4 THE DUEL OF SEX

Although Shaw thoroughly approved of the huntress, women have often taken his exposure of the subject as a personal insult. For example:

> Mr Bernard Shaw understands women much better than Mr [George] Moore, but we do not like our Bernard; he sees too much with that chill grey eye of his. He would be good to us in actual life, clothe us and feed us and give us good wages, but what woman can forgive 'Man and Superman'?

Cultural lag being what it is, the proper lady whom Dickens described as being doubtful whether it was not indelicate to be present at a christening, considering the implications of human birth, was still a social reality at the time *Man and Superman* was written. A whole set of class and period attitudes toward courtship, birth and all related subjects were outraged by Shaw's frankness. The crowning touch was the use Ann made of ideals, exaggerating them in order to flout them.

All this, in little more than fifty years, has become ancient history. Although a tiny remnant of the once-powerful force of proper ladies lives on in the mountain fastnesses behind modern thought, they no longer dominate. We labor under a new kind of error, the error of assuming that a chase is a battle. And the error is compounded by the assumption that the chase is a skirmish in the war of the sexes. This view is not far from the truth. Tanner, with his bent for abstraction, sees in the chase the eternal struggle between the mother woman and the artist man. But his view is just far enough from the truth to be false. The struggle between mother woman and artist man is a timeless and individual struggle, whereas the war of the sexes is a period piece and a mob scene. It is a period piece of our time because it relates to the liberation of women, to the vindictiveness men feel about it, and to the bitterness released in women when they see by contrast what they have been. It is a mass matter, as markets are mass and media are mass and movements are mass. Where this war is noticed, in magazine cartoons, in newspaper articles, in public events and large gatherings, individuality is either overlooked or apologized to. In the individual instance, or the instance before the First World War, what we find instead is the duel of sex.

That is what takes place in *Man and Superman* between Tanner, our Don Juan, and the woman whose evolutionary appetite is so advanced that it embraces the 'darling object' of life: brains. We see for ourselves that it is a duel: the weapons are refined, the rules formal, the terms equitable, the object honor as much as victory, and the performance skilled. But the delightful thing about this duel of sex is that, as Tanner himself admits, 'They make us will our own destruction.' Therefore we see a struggle without hostility, ending in a reconciliation, not a defeat. Henry Straker knows this when he says, 'I dunno about the bee and the spider. But the marked down victim, that's what you are and no mistake; and a jolly good job for you, too, I should say.'

Shaw's belief in this process was based on observation as well as theory, although these two things are not easily separable. Here, for example, is his report of Ellen Terry's first meeting with her future husband:

Without an instant's hesitation she sailed across the room; put Mr Carew into her pocket (so to speak); and married him. The lucky captive naturally made no resistance. . . . I had not believed it possible for even the most wonderful of women to choose her man at a single glance and bear him off before he had time to realize who she was. Shooting a lion at sight is child's play in comparison, because it does not matter which lion it happens to be: – But it matters very much which man it is when marriage is in question; and so swift a decision by a huntress who, far from being promiscuous in her attachments, was highly fastidious, made me marvel and say to myself, 'There, but for the grace of God, goes Bernard Shaw.'

Although the sporting aspect of this question continues to intrigue us, the motives involved raise a philosophic question: '. . . a woman seeking a husband is the most unscrupulous of all the beasts of prey'.

The beast of prey analogy suits the male combatants in the war of the sexes very well. It may stand up fairly well for the actual stalking, but what happens at the kill? Jack Tanner, even in warning the exasperating Octavius, has to change his metaphor. It shocks Octavius to hear that Ann has patted his cheek as if it were a nicely underdone chop. But when Tavey claims that they take the tenderest care of us, Jack is reduced to: 'Yes, as a soldier does of his rifle.' This metaphor, if just, is far from the bee and the spider or the prey and the wild beast. Instead of being eaten and destroyed, the Reverend Mr Morell is protected and encouraged by Candida, has his way made smooth for him to do the best work he can. Does anyone envisage a different fate for Jack Tanner? The one difference is Tanner's more or less articulate consciousness of being a means to an end, which Tanner feels or pretends to feel as a degradation. But there are two saving truths about the way he is used.

The first is that though woman may exploit man for a purpose not his own, she herself is not that purpose, although it is common enough for the reverse to be true, for woman to be treated as merely a means to man's satisfaction. The woman Shaw is talking about, the mother woman seeking a husband, will sacrifice herself as ruthlessly as she does the man: '. . . all the unscrupulousness and all the "self-sacrifice" (the two things are the same) of Woman'. The deadliness of the struggle between the mother woman and the artist man lies in their identical source of power: '. . . a sublime altruist in his disregard of himself, an atrocious egotist in his disregard of others. Here Woman meets a purpose as impersonal, as irresistible as her own. . . .' This is the second reason for not considering Tanner's capture a degradation any more than it is a death.

Shaw's view does not apply equally to just any woman's ascendancy over any man. He is interested in the courtship in which instinctive motives come first, for this play of instinctive motives is what transmutes one kind of selfishness into another. Shaw's statements on the subject range from: 'Be as selfish as you can', to: 'This is the true joy in life, the being used for a purpose recognized by yourself as a mighty one; the being thoroughly worn out before you are thrown on the scrap heap. . . .' In this there is no more paradox or inconsistency than in any of the subtler truths about human existence. It is easier to believe both things together in the life of a character than in an abstract statement. Blanco Posnet, for example, gives his horse to a woman whose child is dying of croup, even though it means he is certain to be caught and lynched as a horse thief. He does not understand why he has done so, but, having experienced the joy of it, he is '. . . for the great game every time'. The women are better aware of what they are doing. Lady Cicely has always known that she does what she wants to do. Major Barbara has always acted according to her own best lights. She joins her father only when she sees his way is really a fulfillment of her own will. She accepts her lover only when he chooses, without consultation, her way. The Woman in *Buoyant Billions* lives outside modern society very much as the heroine of Eliot's *The Cocktail Party* does; but Shaw's heroine does so because that is what she wants on her own behalf. So does St Joan, whose self-will combines in an odd but authentic way her taste for soldiering, her sense of mission, and her colossal egotism.

Joan is of special interest as the only character Shaw adapted from an established hagiology; and the quality to be extracted from all Shaw's willful women and from some of the men, is saintliness, however diluted, however peculiar. The difference between Shaw's saints and T. S. Eliot's, or, for that matter, between Shaw's saints and the ordinary interpretation of Christian sainthood, is a fundamental dogma of the religion of creative evolution: that 'the great game' is not a result of submerging the will, but of freeing it, that the saintly deed is not an immolation of the self, but a liberation of the self. This is both a humanistic and an optimistic religion.

The Life Force expresses itself through these individual wills which are in harmony with the universe. In Saint Joan, as in some others, it takes the form of celibacy and sainthood. More commonly, it takes the form of the mother woman's determined pursuit of the man who, as instinct tells her, will father the best children. Such a will may be in opposition to habit, to convention, to reasonable compromise, but in the vital person it is never in opposition to the individual will.

There is only one of Shaw's plays in which the women have lost the instinct for this practical and celestial harmony. In *Heartbreak House* we see the Life Force fritter itself away in triviality. Here we encounter the Devil's Granddaughters, women of fated guilt, guilt that seems more trivial than it is.

5 THE DEVIL'S GRANDDAUGHTERS

Of all Shaw's plays, *Heartbreak House* is the one which, in all its artificialities, has the greatest claim to a certain kind of realism. It is realistic in the sense that it treats people according to the immediate social strains behind their behavior, and not according to the eternal principles behind their behavior. In either case the awareness of the characters is artificially heightened and articulated. The difference in *Heartbreak House* is that all but Captain Shotover are limited to a preternatural awareness of their own relation to their own society in their own time. Around the captain's two daughters, Hesione (the cultured idle rich) and Ariadne (the horsey idle rich), the other men spin helplessly. Hector Hushabye, a dashing baby of a liar and philanderer, is indulged most disrespectfully by his wife, Hesione. Randall (the Rotter) revolves piteously around the contemptuous Ariadne. Neither Boss Mangan, the Napoleon of industry, nor Mazzini Dunn, the idealistic businessman whom he has ruined, can cope with these women who go about casually 'fascinating' men whenever it serves their purpose, apparently without any sense that sexual attraction is something one can feel as well as use. These men shift with every turn of the currents because they are anchored only to the floating corpses that are sex, money and ideals as our society knows them. War, this society's ultimate extravagance, is madness; therefore, the captain, looking beyond the values of his time and place, seems mad to all the others. It does not matter that, when the unreality of all their virtues, from Hector's heroism to Hesione's hair, is revealed, the captain's seventh degree of concentration is also unveiled in its prosaic form, as rum. That cannot detract from the dignity of the captain's questions, for they are real questions about human destiny and human responsibility. All the others are mere children, earnestly at play.

That is why the women of *Heartbreak House*, for all their superficial resemblance to the usual Shavian woman, do not fit into any pattern that might lead intelligibly from Mrs Warren, Candida and Ann Whitefield to Major Barbara, Saint Joan and the Millionairess; to account for the competent Lysistrata, the kittenish Orinthia, and the comfortable old cabbage, Queen Jemima. But the fact that does not fit usually has a message for us.

I can think of no other place in Shaw's work where a character can suitably cry, as Hector does while the curtain falls on Act Two: 'Poor Wretch! Oh women! women! women! Fall. Fall and crush.'

There are other jarring notes in *Heartbreak House*. Nowhere else in Shaw's work, for all his active use of Nietzschean ideas, does he even trifle with the notion that whatever troubles a woman can be cured by pregnancy. This is not to be confused with the mother woman's espousal of 'danger and unutterable discomfort' in order to fulfill a purpose not her own, one of which she can only dimly sense the meaning, although this is no doubt the thread of misconstrued evidence on which Nietzsche's assertion is based. He reduces the massive, appalling process of parturition to the petty terms of a cure for restlessness, or 'nerves', to the size of a diversion.

Lady Utterword, who is a storehouse of unexamined conventions, offers this nonsense as a sop to Ellie Dunn's immortal longings. The idea is refuted soundly enough by Hector's introspective criticism: 'Yes, but, damn it, I have the same feeling; and I can't have a baby.' But the fact remains that this view has been uttered (Lady Utterword dreadfully does what her name implies), and has become a factor in the play, just as another, even less Shavian idea obtrudes itself.

In the scene in which Lady Utterword 'manages' her two conquests, Randall (the Rotter) and Hector, who still has some make-believe fight in him, she throws into the battle, which is really her ruthless destruction of Randall, Napoleon's dictum that women are the occupation of the idle man. Randall, by now 'foaming', raves, 'There is no animal in the world so hateful as a woman can be', and so on. To this Lady Utterword makes the sensible answer, 'Cry-baby!' But Randall has sounded a note quite different from anything in Jack Tanner's range. Nowhere else in Shaw's work does the bleat of genuine resentment mar the relations between men and women. How amorously Tanner runs away! With what relish he enumerates the adorable dangers of his flight! But Randall, though avowedly 'in love' (or perhaps because he is), gives off real venom. What does it mean?

It is understood, of course, that a playwright does not hold all the opinions of all his characters. But that is only the first thing to be said about the playwright and his ideas, not the last. It can scarcely be claimed that the playwright is not responsible for all the things his characters say and do. Somewhere between these two limits lies the intention of the playwright and the meaning of the play.

Heartbreak House is set in a world where all the old saws about women, though they may not go unchallenged, are in the air. They hang in the atmosphere, not sardonically as they would in another Shaw play, but quite appropriately. For Hesione and Ariadne are plausibly cast as the devil's granddaughters. The essential difference between them and the heroines of Shaw's other plays, is that they alone conform to the Western literary tradition in which woman exists chiefly to play a part in some man's sexual life.

If this is, as Shaw believes, an artificial and unhealthy situation, it is also one which goes deep enough to account for all the deviltry of these two weird sisters. They are idle women in more than social class. Their very instincts are uncommitted. Their deepest energies are turned to a playful revenge in which the lack of seriousness demeans their entranced victims as much as it does themselves.

At Heartbreak House as at Horseback Hall, Shaw's symbol for the other part of the leisure class, the part which Lady Utterword embodies, this instinctual drought is largely a class matter. Leisure means love affairs. The theory of a leisure class calls for people who have no function – or, to be more exact, no work. Their function is to represent qualities and consume services; and, as Veblen points out, this is a function more largely relegated to women than to men. In the middle class the reason seems to be that men must make the money women spend. *Heartbreak House* implies a more nearly classless and timeless reason: that the woman is seen primarily as a source of gratification for men; that she herself is what the man consumes, even if only his vanity is fed. We are told by Dr Francis L. K. Hsu in *Americans and Chinese* that Chinese women have found it easier than Western women to penetrate into the professions and public life. The author attributes this unexpected finding to the fact that women in the Chinese tradition have been classified as work units rather than as sexual units. Shaw speaks of the contrasting Western view when he says: 'In the Romantic school . . . the whole business was so subtly pervaded by sex instincts that a woman never came amiss to a romanticist. To him she was not a human being or a fellow-creature, but simply the incarnated divinity of sex.'

That is why the sexual revolution of the nineteenth century and the sexual counter-revolution of the twentieth century have made no radical change in the status of women. The divinity may have gone. The dream-world ideal of chastity may have been replaced by a dream-world ideal of lubricity. From the point of view of women's status, it does not matter what the sexual standards may be, for as long as they are regarded as defining her, the real definition of her status is unchanged.

Nowhere, except in the devil's granddaughters of *Heartbreak House*, does Shaw portray women defined entirely by their sexual role. It does not matter that they exist, or in what numbers they exist. A writer chooses his material. Shaw in all the rest of his work chose to write about women in whom, no matter how cramped by circumstance, the fellow-creature lives on.

Naturally, love between men and women becomes quite different when false inequalities are removed. As Yeats wrote to Florence Farr, in a passage which does much to explain the ravishments she inspired in Shaw:

You cannot think what a pleasure it is to be fond of somebody to whom I can talk. . . . To be moved and talkative, unrestrained, one's own self, and to be this not because one has created some absurd delusion . . . but because one has found an equal, that is the best of life.

However, as that kind of love which Shaw considered 'the real thing' is a late-flowering luxury of civilization, it is better to speak first of two aspects of woman's life which come first historically: motherhood and marriage, in that order.

CHAPTER 4

Mothers Married and Unmarried

SELECTIVE breeding, civilized marriage and Fabian socialism are three different matters, but in Shaw's thought they are not separate. His beliefs about the role of women in Creative Evolution depend upon two sets of ideas which have nothing to do with non-human evolution. Shaw moved easily beyond the intellectual snag which caused the neo-Darwinians to assume that evolution in the future must take place according to just those rules which had governed it in the past. In fact, he exactly reversed the neo-Darwinian assumptions about the meaning of life. Whereas they tried to apply the inhuman rules which govern the existence of pond-scum, fruit flies and monkeys, to the conduct of such human affairs as the factory system and international warfare, Shaw made the assumption that human intelligence and human society were also 'hard facts' and could be applied to the evolution of the very species which had brought these new factors into existence. Therefore the most interesting parts of Shaw's theory of evolution are those which concern the human, the intelligent, the social.

In Shaw's reasoning there are two fundamentally simple lines of thought, although their applications are less simple. The first of these is: socialism means equality; equality means inter-marriageability; intermarriageability means the free operation of the Life Force. The second line of thought is not so straight. It begins where we are now, in a society where marriages very largely determine the breeding of the next generation. The first inference to be drawn is that marriages should be determined by genetic considerations. The second inference, in conflict with the first, is that procreation should be separated from mono-gamous marriage for the enhancement of both personal happiness and the genetic stock.

There are two parts to the theory of evolution which Shaw, following Samuel Butler, derived from Linnaeus, Lamarck and Erasmus Darwin. The term Creative Evolution implies a belief in the exercise of will rather than blind chance as the cause of evolutionary change. The more controversial part of this theory maintains that acquired characteristics can, in certain circumstances, be inherited. *Back to Methuselah* is an attempt to dramatize this aspect of evolution. Creative Evolution in this play (or Metabiological Pentateuch) has no special relevance to women, except as it foresees a human species that will have evolved beyond sexual reproduction.

The second and less controversial part of the theory of Creative Evolution gives some fresh turns to the belief that selective breeding can change a species. Here the woman's role is of great importance: it consists in finding and captivating the man most likely to father superior children. In Shaw's view this is by far the most vital responsibility of the mother woman both to her children and to society at large. The weight Shaw gives to this choice is in direct proportion to his despair of political action and the schools, newspapers and so on which are thought to play some part in bringing about changes in human society. 'I leave it to our old parliamentary hands to devise a plan by which our electors can be side-tracked, humbugged, cheated, lied to, or frightened into tolerating such a change. If it has to wait for their enlightenment it will wait too long.' Ultimately, the only way Shaw believes human society can be changed is by changing the human being. 'We must eliminate the Yahoo or his vote will wreck the commonwealth.'

If, as Shaw assumes, 'The mere transfigurations of institutions ... are all but changes from Tweedledum to Tweedledee ...', then a change in breed is the only hope. In the epistle dedicatory which serves as a preface to *Man and Superman*, Shaw says:

There is a political aspect of this sex question which is too big for my comedy, and too momentous to be passed over without culpable frivolity. It is impossible to demonstrate that the initiative in sex transactions remains with Woman, and has been confirmed to her, so far, more and more by the suppression of rapine and discouragement of importunity, without being driven to very serious reflections on the fact that this initiative is politically the most important of all the initiatives, because our political experiment of democracy, the last refuge of cheap misgovernment, will ruin us if our citizens are ill bred.

After some discussion of the haphazard selection already taking place, including '. . . chance attempts at the superman which occur from time to time', Shaw states his proposition: '. . . what is proposed is nothing but the replacement of the old unintelligent, inevitable, almost unconscious fertility by an intelligently controlled, conscious fertility . . .'.

As to the method, Shaw says: 'The matter must be taken up either by the State or by some organization strong enough to impose respect upon the State.' He mentions as possibilities a State Department of Evolution, a private society or chartered company, and 'a general secret pushing of the human will . . .' but the only plan that engages his ironic imagination is a modest proposal for extending the free enterprise system to the field of genetics:

Even a joint stock human stud farm (piously disguised as a reformed Foundling Hospital or something of that sort) might well, under proper inspection and regulation, produce better results than our present reliance on promiscuous marriage. It may be objected that when an ordinary contractor produces stores for sale to the Government, and the Government rejects them as not up to the required standard, the condemned goods are either sold for what they will fetch or else scrapped: that is, treated as waste material; whereas if the goods consisted of human beings, all that could be done would be to let them loose or send them to the nearest work-house. But there is nothing new in private enterprise throwing its human refuse on the cheap labor market and the workhouse; and the refuse of the new industry would presumably be better bred than the staple produce of ordinary poverty.

The mention of state control naturally gave rise to such confusion as this which Shaw related in a letter to Florence Farr:

Miss Murby . . . is a very clever young woman – a Fabian, who is firmly persuaded that my views on the production of the Superman involve the forcible coercion by the State of selected women to breed with the selected men; and she, being a good-looking and clever person, very likely to be selected under such a scheme, fears the worst. Now I protest that I never proposed anything more compulsory than offering, say £2,000 for a satisfactory baby, *à prendre ou à laisser*, as the lady likes.

Coercion by the State is the one way the superman *cannot* be achieved, because regulation by our present understanding can only produce monsters shaped by the errors of our world. This would make evolution as vain a hope as the schools. When Shaw speaks on 'The Case for Equality' he refers again, as in *Man and Superman*, to the breeding of horses, a clear example of the

85

changes to be wrought in measurable time by conscious selection in breeding. But in breeding men, he points out that:

> . . . we should not know where to begin. You see, it is all very well when you come to breed a horse, because when you come to breed a horse, you know the sort of horse you want. . . . You do not bother about the horse's soul; you do not care whether it is a good horse in the pulpit sense of the word. . . . But do you know the sort of man you want? You do not.

Therefore, Shaw argues, you are thrown back on the clue that nature gives you. That clue is instinctive sexual preference: '. . . we shall still have to trust to the guidance of fancy (alias Voice of Nature) . . . for that superiority in the unconscious self which will be the true characteristic of the Superman'. Here Shaw's profound religious sense speaks: 'What is really important in Man is the part of him that we do not understand.' The part we do not understand is the part that writes music and poetry, and, even more important, controls Blanco Posnet and Dick Dudgeon when they prefer the great game to the rotten game. The extent of Shaw's trust in this unknown is shown by his willingness to extend freedom of breeding to 'bad breeding' as well as good, on the ground that it is 'indispensable to the weeding out of the human race'. This suggestion, coming from a man who detested suffering and waste, indicates how deeply Shaw respected the unknown and (by definition) unknowable factor in human breeding. To use the words 'a far more satisfactory arrangement' to describe the birth of 'a great number of children who will all die before they reach maturity', argues some weighty necessity. It is simply that, 'Though more costly than sterilization of the unhealthy, it has the enormous advantage that in the event of our notions of health and unhealth being erroneous (which to some extent they certainly are), the error will be corrected by experience instead of confirmed by evasion.'

That capricious, irrational thing Shaw calls 'fancy' is no more than a clue, and one which will be misunderstood if we forget his stipulation: '. . . the survival of the fittest means finally the survival of the self-controlled . . .'. Hence the sexual impulse is of value in Creative Evolution in proportion to its selectiveness rather than its strength. We have already seen that Shaw considered any instinct so strong as to overcome self-control to be a 'vital defect', and this he applied with particular force to mothers. Furthermore, when Don Juan jeers at Dona Ana's chastity by saying, '. . . it took the form of a husband and twelve children. What more could you have done had you been the most abandoned of women?' Ana replies, 'I could have had twelve husbands and no children: that's what I could have done, Juan.'

Stated as a principle, this comment on the licentious becomes: 'The modern devices for combining pleasure with sterility, now universally known and accessible [read: insofar as universally known and accessible] enable those persons to weed themselves out of the race, a process already vigorously at work; and the consequent survival of the intelligently fertile means the survival of the partizans of the Superman. . . .'

Equality, polygamy, independence and adultery: these are the four principles deduced by Shaw from his doctrine of Creative Evolution.

Equality for Shaw means '. . . human equality; and that, of course, can only mean one thing: it means equality of income'. Equality of income leads to equality of class, and if Shaw had lived in the United States he would surely have advocated racial equality on the same terms. The clue of fancy can hardly make a difference in humanity '. . . until you widen the area of possible sexual attraction; until you make it as wide as the numbers of the community make it'.

Still, in any community where men and women are about equal in number, monogamy means that the inferior person will also reproduce himself. Except, then, where women are scarce, only the practice of polygamy combined with freedom of choice can make any general improvement in the genetic stock. We are assured by Shaw, and also, for the most part, by anthropologists who have studied polygamous societies, that it is not the women who object to such arrangements.

The question, as it presents itself in practice to a woman, is whether it is better to have, say, a whole share in a tenth-rate man or a tenth share in a first-rate man. Substitute the word Income for the word Man, and you will have the question as it presents itself economically to a dependent woman. The woman whose instincts are maternal, who desires superior children more than anything else, never hesitates. She would take a thousandth share, if necessary, in a husband who was a man in a thousand rather than have some comparatively weedy weakling all to herself.

The woman who chooses to have a tenth share in a first-rate man cannot do so happily in our society. She contents herself as well as she can, rather than do without the man altogether, but the motive of which she is aware is the need for a companion and sexual partner, and only in unusual circumstances the need for a superior father for her child. Shaw's comment is an interpretation of the facts known to all of us, not a report.

Far from vitiating the argument, the economic parallel (absent from an almost identical statement in 'The Revolutionist's Handbook') mirrors the genetic advantages of polygamy and will continue to do so until the huge inequalities of income among us are narrowed by socialism or destroyed by war. Naturally, Shaw does not pretend that the man with a thousand pounds a week is a thousand times better than the man with a pound a week, although he taunts his capitalist opponents with just such a supposed theory. Superior income and superior genes are alike only in that they both argue, in flat statistical voices, against the moral beauty of monogamy.

The opposition to polygamy is only, as Shaw reminds us, '. . . the revolt of the mass of inferior men who are condemned to celibacy by it . . .'. The merely sentimental objection to sterilizing, in effect, the inferior male (who tends to desert the children he does have) are far outweighed by the combined sentimental and genetic damage done by sterilizing, as spinsterhood does at present, many of the superior females.

Independence, the third evolutionary principle, refers to the mother's economic independence of the father, and is the only effective remedy for the condition which Shaw refers to as the sterilization of the schoolmistress. It is in the preface to *Getting Married* and in the character of Lesbia Grantham in the same play, that Shaw makes this point most forcefully. Notice that, although the plea for polygamy is theoretical and polemical, the plea for the independent mother is immediate and practical.

. . . the one point on which all women are in furious secret rebellion against the existing law is the saddling of the right to a child with the obligation to become the servant of a man. Adoption, or the begging or buying or stealing of another woman's child is no remedy: it does not provide the supreme experience of bearing the child. No political constitution will ever succeed or deserve to succeed unless it includes the recognition of an absolute right to sexual experience, and is untainted by the Pauline or romantic view of such experience as sinful in itself. And since this experience in its fullest sense must be carried in the case of women to the point of childbearing, it can only be reconciled with the acceptance of marriage with the child's father by legalizing polygyny, because there are more adult women in the country than men.

This, however, is only an introduction to Shaw's argument for independence. He goes on to demonstrate to his own satisfaction that polygyny is impossible in England, first because four out of five men could not support more than one wife and family, second, because the numbers do not come out even! Neither of these objections is quite logical. Socialism would presumably solve the first difficulty. As for the second, polygyny in practice is no more mathematically exact than monogamy. Shaw does not care about this logic for the simple reason that his interest is in another kind of proposal, one which is neither conditional nor remote:

There is no way at all out of the present system of condemning the superfluous women to barrenness, except by legitimizing the children of women who are not married to the fathers.

Shaw's reason for preferring this solution to any other is the existence of Lesbia Grantham and the many other self-respecting women who refuse to marry as long as marriage is what it is. These women are distinguished from the numerically superfluous, who would marry if someone asked them to, by the very qualities that would make the most valuable mothers. Genetically speaking, the voluntary old maids may be the best potential mothers. The character they show in standing out against the mores of society may be just that 'superiority in the unconscious self' which should be the aim of selective breeding.

Lesbia Grantham makes it quite clear that her objection to marriage is not only the barbarism of the laws which regulate it. It is true that when driven to the end of her argument she says, 'There are certain rights I will not give any person over me.' Nevertheless, even reforms which would satisfy all other kinds of women would never reconcile Lesbia to marriage, for she is, as she herself declares, a regular old maid, too independent and too fastidious to allow a man to clutter up her house. One might suppose the lady's name to be a euphemistic hint at the reasons for her intransigeance. It is more likely that Shaw means us to reconsider our judgments of real women who live as she does. For her attitude toward children is not what is usually expected of an old maid:

> I ought to have children. I should be a good mother to children. I believe it would pay the country very well to pay me very well to have children. But the country tells me that I cant have a child in my house without a man in it too; so I tell the country that it will have to do without my children. If I am to be a mother, I really cannot have a man bothering me to be a wife at the same time.

Shaw's celebration of The Old Maids of England proves that he is no admirer of blind fecundity or sexual improvidence, that the clue of sexual attraction and the charm of sexual vitality are no substitute for intelligence and self-control. Shaw makes no reference to the multitudes of women who are prevented, by ignorance or by the bullying of their men, from having any control over the number of children they bear, but the feckless or superstitious women who go on bearing more children while the children they have starve and shiver in poverty, he would certainly term unmotherly mothers. The maternal instinct, as Shaw recognizes, is the instinct for care, protection and nurture.

> The best mothers are not those who are so enslaved by their primitive instincts that they will bear children no matter how hard the conditions are, but precisely those who place a very high price on their services, and are quite prepared to become old maids if the price is refused, and even to feel relieved at their escape. . . .

That is why both the economic and the legal penalties of motherhood, both poverty and illegitimacy, produce an adverse selection, and a counter-evolutionary trend.

The recognition of motherhood as a vocation, and not, as at present, an unpaid and severely penalized vocation, began to be seriously proposed in Fabian tracts about 1900. Clearly, such an arrangement would change the status of wives as radically as that of unmarried mothers. Under modern industrial capitalism, before any of the Labour Government reforms, Shaw could say without exaggeration, 'Everything that can make birth a misfortune to the parents as well as a danger to the mother is conscientiously done.' All medical memoirs of pre-war England, from Somerset Maugham to Ernest Jones, support this statement. George Moore's picture of the life and death of Esther Waters' mother is an epitome of that danger.

As to the economic misfortune, such Fabian tracts as *The Working Life of Women* and *Family Life on a Pound a Week* show that what was economically a misfortune among the middle classes, was a disaster among the poor. The latter tract sets down the statistics that belong to the world of Dickens and also to that of *Widowers' Houses* and *Mrs Warren's Profession*. The high price of poverty is accounted here in shillings and pence: the high relative cost of renting one or two wretched rooms and the high relative cost of buying coal in tiny amounts, are pathetically echoed in the high relative cost of burying dead children. The extent to which these deaths were caused by poverty alone is proved by one interesting set of statistics: families who went hungrier than the others in order to pay a little more for rent (often the difference between rooms in a damp cellar and rooms above ground) had a significantly larger number of children still alive at the time the facts were gathered; and this was as late as 1912.

Facts like these led Bernard Shaw to make his own Modest Proposal, suggesting that the government declare an open season for the hunting of children, so that they could benefit by being '. . . preserved very carefully for ten months in the year, thereby reducing their death rate far more than the fusillades of the sportsmen during the other two would raise it . . . a glance at our pheasants, our deer, and our children will convince the most sceptical that the children have decidedly the worst of it'.

The literally modest proposals which Shaw and the Fabians offered as a first step toward making motherhood a vocation, referred to a class in which a birth meant the loss of the mother's wages for a short time, but no other fiscal event, except the presence of another mouth to feed. Sidney Webb proposed, in *The Decline of the Birth-Rate*, a Fabian tract published in 1907, free medical care in childbirth and free milk and meals for nursing mothers, to put a stop to adverse genetic selection. He used the term 'endowment of motherhood', which became the title of a later Fabian Tract recommending the addition of free universal and non-contributory maternity pensions. The proposals made by Shaw in the years 1910 to 1914 were an integral part of this agitation, in which both socialists and feminists took part. He said, 'Place the work of wife and mother on the same footing as other work: that is, on the footing of labour worthy of its hire; and provide for unemployment in it exactly as for unemployment in shipbuilding. . . .'

Shaw's intensely practical mind was always prepared to treat the immediate questions with the same verve it brought to the making of large and radical proposals. Here is an example, part of a letter written in 1895 to a young woman who seems to have been looking for a more sentimental answer than the one she received:

You call yourself an undomestic woman; but I suggest that your lack of aptitude for household management is too negative a qualification to take an effective stand upon. A positive aptitude for something else is better; but such a positive aptitude gets recognized nowadays. . . . The really hard position for the moment is that of the domestic woman whose enormously valuable services, both to society and to her own household are accepted and even exacted as a matter of course, as though they were the least she could do in return for the privilege of being fed and clothed and housed and protected. Except when the death of a man's wife occurs at such a time that he has to pay a stranger to discharge her household and parental duties until he goes back to the cheaper plan by marrying again, it is very hard to convince him, that his wife is a productive worker; and the woman, unfortunately, is harder to convince that [*sic*] he is, no doubt because she does so many things and does them in such an amateur way (not being directly and avowedly paid for them) that she does nothing well, and therefore has no belief in herself.

If motherhood were treated as a vocation, one result might be a change in the attitude toward unmarried mothers. Economic prejudice being as strong as it is, although stealthy, it would be surprising if an unmarried mother paid by the state for her services, were to remain a pariah. The income itself would make a difference, but even more would be accomplished by the change from viewing the child as a by-product of sexual love, to viewing the child as an asset in the gross national product. Shaw believed that any improvement in the status of unmarried mothers would increase the restlessness of married and marriageable women and lead to the gradual replacement of marriage by a system of settlements and agreements.

It is here that the pattern begins to cloud. For once marriage ceases to be the pin that holds the family together, that provides the children with bread, protection and respectability, its reform can no longer be urged on grounds of the importance of breeding. Marriage then would become, for the first time in history, a personal matter. At the same time, the fourth of Shaw's implied principles, adultery, would become a responsible matter.

Shaw, whose views on adultery as a personal matter are clear, concise and contradictory, does not in so many words recommend adultery as the road to creative evolution, but his proposal to legitimize the children of women who 'are not married to the fathers', is deliberately different from a proposal to legitimize the children of unmarried mothers. What other conclusion can possibly follow from the statement that 'There is no evidence that the best citizens are the offspring of congenial marriages, or that a conflict of temperament is not a highly important part of what breeders call crossing'? The argument which follows here begins as though it were an argument for the abolition of marriage, and concludes as an argument for marriage as domesticity, separated from conjugation. As Shaw says elsewhere, 'Marriage remains practically inevitable. . . .' His clearest statement on the subject is the following:

In short, for all sociological purposes, it may safely be assumed that people are not particular as to whom they marry, provided they do not lose caste by the alliance. But we must not infer from this that they will tolerate any interference with their domestic life once they are married. . . . What we must fight for is the freedom to breed the race without being hampered by the mass of irrelevant conditions implied in the institution of marriage. . . . What we need is freedom for people who have never seen each other before and never intend to see one another again to produce children under certain definite public conditions without loss of honor.

Taking these propositions together, there is no escape from the conclusion that adultery is the technical term for what (in the utopian freedom from jealousy which Shaw postulates) must become the natural arrangement for breeding. In the absence of any indecency or levity, this implication passes almost unnoticed. Frank Harris said: '. . . he is absolutely free from the slightest trace of sensuality and is never offensive. In fact that is what I feel is the whole trouble with him.' This indicates that Shaw's was not only a clean mind but a concrete one. The dramatic ability to imagine real people in the situations of ideal adultery was a factor in his inoffensiveness. Abstraction is the language of scandal. Shaw knew, as almost everyone does, a good bit about the reality behind the gossip columns. He knew how much more vulnerable most lives are to scandalous interpretation than they are filled with genuine scandal. His abilities as a dramatist allowed him to read back from the paragraph to the human reality behind it. The difference between a Shaw play which deals with adultery and the usual hackneyed piece put together out of three or four standard bits of lumber, is partly that the conventional play gives us the tabloid version, which assumes and rather hopes the worst, whereas Shaw gives us the participants' version, which hopes and rather assumes the best.

The utopian adultery which produces superior children has almost nothing in common with the sentimental adultery of the theater. Furthermore, as the conception of a child takes place in a moment, but gestation and nurture fill many years, the interesting change in a woman's life would be not the father's identity but her life with the child. Shaw, being able to abdicate the masculine point of view at will, recognized this proportion and therefore wasted no time in writing about the encounters and adventures that might lead to parenthood. To most male readers Shaw's treatment of adultery was not exciting. There is an abiding interest in what has been called the administrative side of love, and this interest is not satisfied by the dreamlike adulteries in Shaw's plays (excepting, of course, the early and realistically unpleasant *The Philanderer*).

Our didactic author might have been willing to say more about the ideal arrangements for mothers and children, if there had been anything more to say. He knew how to set up in detail the economic arrangements that would replace those of the present; but social custom is not amenable to revolution. It will tinge every reform with the colors of the past. Shaw understood social process well enough to know also that progress in matters like these must be hunted down blindly, like the scent of a wandering creature, not laid out point-to-point like a Roman road. He was able to point out, in the preface on 'Parents and Children', and in many incidental remarks, some of the intricacies of How Not To Do It. Beyond that, there are only hints.

There is one hint in the vision of Lesbia Grantham, the glorious independent old maid in *Getting Married*, who keeps refusing her importunate suitor but admits that she would like to devote herself to bringing up a family of superior children if only she could respectably do so without the bother of a man about the house. Her sense of the emotional superfluity of the husband during the intense times of maternity is no greater than that of the fully domesticated woman described by Enid Bagnold in *The Door of Life* as preparing for the birth of her child and the care of her other children in great contentment at the absence of her husband.

Shaw gives us no portrait of the new woman as a mother, and it would be strange if he had, for to be a new woman under the old rules usually meant renouncing motherhood and marriage in the way Vivie Warren did.

Nor did Shaw approve of mothers who defy convention, pluming themselves on a 'courage' which brings in almost as much as it costs them but must be paid in full, and with compound interest, by their children. Charmed as he was by Molly Tompkins, who thought she could combine motherhood, marriage, lovers, career and 'freedom' in one undisciplined mixture (an illusion common among women who have private incomes), he wrote to her in 1932: 'I think if a woman wants to be a mother she must keep a very regular house and play the game according to the general rule.' The most motherly women in Shaw's plays are the Candidas, the Lady Cicelys, the Queen Jemimas, all diverted to the secondary work of babying grown-up men. The real mothers in the plays are all hobbled by the effects of their status and their period. Perhaps that is why Mrs Warren, whose profession has compelled her to face facts, is the best of an uninspiring lot. If Shaw idealizes mothers, it is potential mothers, not real ones.

Lady Britomart, mother of Major Barbara, has force without discipline or imagination, the aristocratic syndrome. The opening scene, in which she admonishes her spineless son, shows that

Shaw knew everything Philip Wylie would ever know about domineering mothers, and a great deal more besides. Ann Whitefield's fuddled and futile mamma in *Man and Superman* is a fine specimen of the properly domesticated woman. It is reasonable to conclude from the daughters Shaw portrayed and from his comments on the social changes of his time, that Shaw did not attribute either the namby-pamby or the overbearing traits of these women to something inherent in motherhood, but chalked them up to the social expectations which spoiled the average woman as a human being. Mrs Collins of *Getting Married*, who smothers her children under her wings, is an epitome of the conventional as opposed to the instinctive mother.

Two of Shaw's most thoughtful critics nominate Mrs Clandon in *You Never Can Tell* as Best Mother. This choice overlooks, if nothing else, the fact that the play is a comedy. If the estranged husband's humor is ill-humor, the humor of the estranged wife is that she misses the mark by aiming too high. If not a *précieuse ridicule*, Mrs Clandon is a collateral descendant of those ladies who tried too hard and with too much attention to effect. Henry C. Duffin says that this lady '. . . is indeed, perhaps, Shaw's ideal wife and mother, using those terms in the abstract'. Is it safe to call a wife who deserts her husband and turns his children against him, an ideal wife 'in the abstract'?

Augustin Hamon quite rightly gives Mrs Clandon and her ultra-modern methods credit for her children's charm and spontaneity. The twins, especially, are a reminder of a little-known side of Shaw, on whose strong recommendation Sean O'Casey sent his children to Dartington Hall, a progressive, co-educational school. Certainly Mrs Clandon, who gave her children a progressive education of sorts in the 1890's, is far ahead of mothers like Mrs Collins and Mrs Whitefield. But it is a mistake to assume that no one on the side of the angels is a comic figure. On the contrary: the most delicious comedy may be that which does not siphon up the malice in our own spirits, muddying the pleasures of imagination with the rancors of reality. Shaw, in whom a cauterizing scorn prevents political hostility from festering, paints villains nearly as plausible as his heroes, and this somewhat obscures the difference between friend and foe. But the comedy of one's friends is and ought to be real. The Labor stalwarts may be as funny as the Tory stalwarts, the uncritical enthusiasts of progressive education (like Mrs Clandon), as legitimate a butt as the sadistic schoolmaster of Dickens. Mrs Clandon is endearing, ridiculous, wrong and good. She is a sample of the comedy of good will, a woman who has modernized herself ruthlessly, who is to be loved, pitied, admired, laughed at, but by no means emulated. She is, in fact, very much like a critical caricature of G. B. S., a being so rational, self-disciplined, and cool that she cannot possibly understand the rest of us.

According to M. Hamon, this is the heroine of the play: rational, balanced, frank, sincere, and separated from her husband. In his judgment, she is the only mother in Shaw's dramatic work whose children love, value and respect her. It is true that they are fond of her and give her all due credit for her good will and devotion, but they seem to regard her as something of a monster, naively high-minded, perfectionist, and far too possessive. Like Roebuck Ramsden, who '. . . was an advanced man before you were born', Mrs Clandon is an advanced woman preserved intact from an earlier era. It would be unlike Shaw to miss the fun in that.

Her courage and enterprise in dragging her children away from her husband's severity do her credit, but her substitution of noble, sweet and emotional appeals is equally a folly from Shaw's point of view. In a letter written about the same time as *You Never Can Tell*, he said to Ellen Terry: 'I have a morbid horror of any ill-treatment of children; but I believe that love and the more touching sorts of happiness are wasted on them.' Later, in the preface to *Misalliance*, Shaw puts forward the rather Freudian view that the concentrated, conscientious use of love in molding character may be more harmful than plain cruelty. Mrs Clandon, with her 'we' and her domesticated anarchism, is as wrong in her way as the gloomier tyrants. One of her notable failures is that, in her bitterness against men, which is only her bitterness against her own husband, she has not prepared Gloria for the odd experience of falling in love. Gloria's instinctual strength carries her through, but she quite naturally complains, 'Why didn't you educate me properly?' and 'Oh you taught me nothing; nothing.'

In fact, Shaw's suggestions all lead toward the breaking up

of the ingrown small family unit, with its intense emotional relationships and its attenuated social sense. We have seen all this from the point of view of the daughters, but now it becomes apparent that the same tendency to widen and disperse the objects of love and duty is valid for mothers as well. Fabian Tract No. 2, which was written by Shaw, proposed that ' . . . the state should compete with private individuals – especially with parents – in providing happy homes for children, so that every child may have a refuge from the tyranny or neglect of its natural custodians'. This is not the place to enter into the views on parents and children expressed in the preface to *Misalliance*, in spite of their considerable charm and interest and the continued crying need for their decency and common sense, but as an indication of what Shaw did *not* mean in his remark to Molly Tompkins, it is well to remember this comment: 'All one can say is, roughly, that the homelier the home, and the more familiar the family, the worse for everybody concerned.'

Like the ideal mother, the unmarried mother (who may be the same person) is absent from Shaw's work. She is a theory, an extrapolation, not a real character. When we think we are about to behold her in *Man and Superman*, Shaw performs a flick of the wrist, and we see instead the inviolate Violet. Her scandalized family assume she is a fallen woman, as proper people tend so readily to do, but she has been married secretly to a rich American for the very proper purpose of seeing that they keep his fortune. The clever Jack Tanner is the one who looks a fool in this scene, and Shaw intends that he should. Tanner's speeches sound impressive, and they lay a trap for the audience similar to the trap into which Tanner himself is so gracefully stepping when he defends Violet for turning from her frivolous life to the great work of procreation. Shaw knows as well as any woman that it is Tanner who is frivolous in supposing that one can live by abstractions, however true they may be in themselves. In a sense, Shaw is both a talking Tanner and a wise woman. His abstractions may sound as impractical as Tanner's glib speeches, but his vision is concrete, practical and elegant. The unmarried mother of Shaw's ideal arrangements would be no Ellen Terry (although he firmly defended her domestic arrangements, saying that she would always have married the man of her choice if the English marriage laws had been reasonable), no Molly Tompkins wanting '. . . to be an artist and a vagabond, not to say a siren . . .'. She would be a strong-minded 'career mother', probably someone like Lysistrata, the dedicated civil servant in *The Apple Cart*. In fact, of all the illicit unions in Shaw's fiction, not one is fertile, except for the technically illegitimate birth of Eliza Doolittle of *Pygmalion*. The world being what it is, Shaw treats the woman's choice in this matter as no choice at all. Thus, except in the remote reaches of theory, the future of the race still depends on the marriages of the present.

CHAPTER 5

Marriage: The Mystery of the Unhappy Ending

SHAW is a more mysterious and a more poetic writer than is generally supposed. Much of his mystery comes from the use of paradox which transcends the display of wit and deals seriously with serious matters; and much of his poetic quality comes from his sense of the paradoxes which are inherent in human life. On the subject of marriage, in itself a body of inconsistencies and impossibilities, Shaw is in several ways a double man. His hortatory prose pieces are inky tracts full of horrifying information; his fictions about marriage are full of a delightful imagination. According to his theories about instinct and evolution, marriage is the desired and desirable outcome; yet according to his literary theories and his worldly wisdom, marriage is an unhappy ending.

The mystery of Shaw has another ramification: he is an avowed and aggressive anti-romantic who imagines in the arch-romantic tradition. It is not only the endless equivocality of the term 'romantic' which causes this confusion. It is rather a genuine doubleness in Shaw's vision. The best example of this double vision begins with the assumption of romantic comedy that marriage is a happy ending.

Shaw ridicules this tradition in many ways. In the last scene of *Captain Brassbound's Conversion* the captain makes the proposal stage convention demands, but it is a strangely tentative one met by refusal, and the cry, 'And what an escape!' comes from the woman, not the man. It is indeed an escape for both parties, for the attraction between them is not passionate. It is merely the attraction between the woman's strength and the man's weakness. Shaw refuses the demand of audience and critics that any interest between a man and a woman on stage must culminate in marriage. Again in the epilogue to *Pygmalion*, Shaw emphatically denies the assumption of audiences that all unsatisfied questions are to be answered by the great answering enigma of matrimony.

Just as the conventional stage ending echoes an illusion people live by, so Shaw's protest against such endings echoes his protest against the reality of marriage as it is. If this were all, Shaw's anti-romanticism might be argued away as merely his agreement with the universal assumption that marriage is in fact the one great anti-romantic connection possible between man and woman.

The rebellion against marriage as a happy ending is not, however, the only ground for calling Shaw an anti-romantic artist. If it were, one might say that, in rescuing these couples from the knowable, the known, the ordinary thing, Shaw was turning away from a tradition which should really be called the sentimental theater, to the genuinely romantic relationship which remains a shimmer of possibilities and impossibilities, full of the allure of the unknown. The sentimental solution of marriage would ruin the romance that surrounds both Lady Cicely and Captain Brassbound. The very qualities which lend her piquancy as a bandit-nurse and evangelist would make her a dreadful wife and mother, and Brassbound's passive complaints about her domineering would soon make him quite as tiresome as his wife. Yet as long as they remain a dashing lady whose weakness is her strength, whose folly is her wisdom, and Black Paquito, desperado and soloist, these two keep their fascination for the audience and for each other.

The same could be said of Higgins and Eliza. If *Pygmalion* were to end as the sentimentalists think it should, all the starch that charms us in these two warring collaborators would wilt away. The most delicious things about Eliza, aside from the personal charm of the actress, are her realism and her self-respect. Having these, she is not deluded by Higgins's intellect and social position into thinking him a good catch. The very qualities that led Higgins to create a new Eliza make him impossible as a husband. The circumstances of the theater also mislead an audience. It seems that the beautiful leading lady and the impressive leading man must make a rapturous couple. Being infatuated, the audience overlooks the fact that Higgins was a 'predestinate' bachelor and that for Eliza the satisfaction of storming his fortress would be small compensation for having to live inside it ever after. Again, the play that ends without a wedding is the more romantic play. The wary intimacy of these solitary spirits continues with unabated interest, as Shaw himself tells us, through Eliza's commonplace marriage to Freddie.

'Eliza's instinct tells her not to marry Higgins. It does not tell her to give him up.'

In another sense, however, the convention Shaw refused to follow *was* more romantic than his emendations, simply because it affirmed the supreme power and importance of love. For example, in a situation that is a far better test of romantic tendencies than the self-limiting romance of a wedding, Shaw refused to treat the execution in *The Devil's Disciple* as a *liebestod*. The illimitable possibilities of love after death (illicit love at that) might be present in *The Devil's Disciple*. Judith Anderson, like so many tragic heroines, has a husband. Dick Dudgeon, like so many tragic heroes, is condemned to death. Here are the ingredients of an emotional carouse. Yet Shaw's hero dies neither for liberty nor for love. He dies because of the law of his own nature.

The Devil's Disciple is typical of Shaw's plays without weddings. It insists that not *all* interest is love interest. If there were any doubt about this interpretation, Shaw's prefaces explain his rejection of romantic love and romantic marriage.

These assertions seem, of course, to deny the fact that, from *Man and Superman* to *Village Wooing*, the plays treat marriage as woman's aim and man's fate. True, this commonplace is given an interpretation in which a higher purpose takes the place of personal happiness. Nevertheless, the outward manifestations are unchanged. Ann Whitefield would never cry, 'What an escape!' Her marriage is not an unhappy ending. It is not an ending at all. We do not leave the lovers in a self-obliterating embrace; we leave them in a self-asserting discussion. The last line in the play, 'Go on talking', indicates that the engagement is neither an end nor a beginning.

The romanticism of Shaw's view resides in the 'higher purpose' and the mystery surrounding it. In the tradition of revolutionary romanticism, neither happiness nor contentment is a goal. Thus Shaw rejects the vision of marriage as the destruction of two individuals from whose ashes the married couple rises like an ungainly phoenix. We are likely to forget that Shaw held in common with the great romantics of the nineteenth century, including those who seem superficially most unlike him, the axioms that the known is less interesting than the unknown, the reality less interesting than the fantasy, the feasible less interesting than the possible, and so on. In Shaw's plays, although not in the youthful disillusionment of his novels, it is this kind of romanticism that imbues the idea of marriage.

There are two kinds of scene which suggest his peculiar use of the romantic tradition. The first is the scene in which lovers decide to get married. Shaw always affirms the cosmic meaning of that surrender, even though he may do so perfunctorily in the lighter plays, and even though that cosmic meaning is not what the more naïve of the lovers suppose. The second kind of scene is one strange to the theater. In it, married people who have already learned to accept marriage as it is, show their ability to nest among its thorns with ease. The tranquillity such couples achieve, which is not the same thing as happiness, is less important than the elevated kind of humanity required to achieve that estate. In a Shavian utopia, marriage would be neither an unhappy ending nor an end in itself.

The tone in which the playwright comments on marriage could never be predicted from reading Shaw's sociology of marriage. The sources of his two kinds of knowledge, the artistic and the sociological, being different, the conclusions drawn from them are not necessarily conflicting, but neither are they entirely congruous.

Popular tradition quite agrees with Shavian comedy in depicting an eager woman and a reluctant man. The explanation Shaw prefers artistically and polemically is the unconscious working of the Life Force. But conscious, obvious and visible in plain daylight, is one very large fact that may not deny the Life Force but certainly out-faces it: that marriage was for so long the one, the only, the total career for women – livelihood, prestige, accomplishment, all in one. Shaw, as a socialist, explained what this means in a capitalist society by saying that the married woman is '. . . the slave of a slave, which is the worst sort of slavery'.

The force of this statement is not vitiated by its place in a discussion of the labor market. The very crux of the matter of women and marriage is in the nice correspondence of economic, legal and religious sanctions. In *Middlemarch*, for example, an intellectual and daring woman thinks she has found a life that beggars aspiration when she acquires a husband whose intellectual work she can, in humble ways, assist. The intellectual and daring woman who wrote the novel did not content herself with assisting; but most women did. Harriet Taylor, who later married John Stuart Mill, was a woman of unusual abilities, but in spite of his encouragement she remained almost entirely an anonymous collaborator. Among social theorists, it was Mill who most daringly looked the fact of marriage in the face and said many of the things about it which Shaw was later to say more dramatically. Mill also called the married woman a slave: 'I am far from pretending that wives are in general no better treated than slaves; but no slave is a slave to the same lengths, and in so full a sense of the word, as a wife is.' What he meant by this is just what Lesbia Grantham meant when she said, 'There are certain rights I will not give any person over me.' Mill was more explicit: '. . . he can claim and enforce the lowest degradation of a human being – being made the instrument of an animal function contrary to her inclinations'.

Proletarian marriage sometimes dramatizes the implications of the theory of marriage Mill points out that ' . . in the most naturally brutal and morally uneducated part of the lower classes . . . the legal slavery of the woman, and something in the merely physical subjection to their will as an instrument, causes them to feel a sort of disrespect and contempt towards their own wife which they do not feel towards any other woman or any other human being . . .'. Middle class women did not refer to their husbands as 'master' or expect to be beaten regularly, but they had one difficulty which women who grew up in the ferocious conditions of poverty had not. Harriet Taylor described it as follows:

Marriage is the only contract ever heard of, of which a necessary condition in the contracting parties was, that one should be entirely ignorant of the nature and terms of the contract. For owing to the voting of chastity as the greatest virtue of women, the fact that a woman knew what she undertook would be considered just reason for preventing her undertaking it.

Mill took the criticism of marriage into another realm when he called it a school of despotism. 'Any sentiment of freedom which can exist in a man whose nearest and dearest intimacies are with those of whom he is absolute master, is not the genuine or Christian love of freedom. . . .' Lord Acton's observations on power apply nicely to the marriage relation. The repercussions of family life on the conduct of the state also interested Shaw, as did the generally ignored question of what the inferior status of women does to the souls of men.

Shaw, who was as far from being a cynic as any man with his practical experience could be, maintained a perfect cynicism on one subject: the hope of changing society by encouraging a general change of heart. It is true that he portrays some stunning conversions, as in Captain Brassbound, Blanco Posnet and the victims of the wiles of Major Barbara. It is true that he says the will to do so can lengthen the span of human life and change the nature of the human race. It is true that he ceaselessly harangues that small section of the British public whose ear he has, trying to change their minds and strengthen their determination. Nevertheless, where changes in *society* are in question, Shaw's last word is: Legislate.

Reform to Shaw did not mean merely curbing the worst abuses of marriage, nor did it mean abolishing marriage altogether. As we have seen, he considered marriage inevitable but condemned its laws, its economics, its personal relationships, and above all its basic assumptions.

The assumptions most deplored by Shaw and other socialists were those which could be traced to the early commercial nature of the marriage bond, to the acquisition of wives by purchase or by plunder. It is interesting to see with what relish the Victorian iconoclasts seized on every sign of a commercial taint in marriage. These were not difficult to find, but they may have been too simply interpreted.

The connection between marriage and prostitution was drawn with a strong, in fact crude, line. Mrs Warren summarized the whole argument when she said, 'The only way for a woman to provide for herself decently is for her to be good to some man that can afford to be good to her.' This analysis is not peculiar to Shaw. Ernest Belfort Bax, who was as strongly anti-feminist as he was pro-socialist, although perhaps not as seriously, said of marriage and prostitution, 'The one is *purchase*, the other *hire*.' (It was Belfort Bax who wrote so fervently in the nineties about sex favoritism, claiming that the English marriage laws were unfair to men.) When Shaw broached this subject in his own person rather than in stage dialogue, he related prostitution to marriage only as it is supported by men trying to delay marriage until they feel ready to pay its costs and accept its daunting permanence.

Even in stage dialogue, however, Shaw fills out the terms of Belfort Bax's oversimplified equation with a human perception that transforms it. Most reformers treat the subject as mechanically as though the creatures involved were puppets and sticks. We know without stopping to think that there must be more to marriage and prostitution than that, although it is not surprising that critics of Victorian England should have clasped with unmodified rapture a weapon that struck with equal and telling force at their two great *bêtes noires*, cynical capitalism and hypocritical idealism. There was no less fervor and force in Shaw's way of filling out the picture, but there was more persuasion and more humanity. Near the beginning of her long revelation to her daughter, Mrs Warren says just what a reformer like Belfort Bax might say:

What is any respectable girl brought up to do but to catch some rich man's fancy and get the benefit of his money by marrying him? As if a marriage ceremony could make any difference in the right or wrong of the thing! Oh, the hypocrisy of the world makes me sick!

But when Mrs Warren has finished filling in the terms, the equation is no longer simple. She has set in their proper relations such matters as death in the whitelead factory, an old age in the workhouse infirmary, the disagreeables that a prostitute has to put up with in order to earn her living, '. . . just like a nurse in a hospital or anyone else', her scorn for a woman who lacks character, and her adherence to Shaw's great principle of moral choice, self-respect: 'How could you keep your self-respect in such starvation and slavery? And whats a woman worth? whats life worth? without self-respect!'

Even in the twenties, after the great war that punctuated the great revolution in mores which Shaw had done so much to influence, there was no basic change in his explanation of prostitution and capitalism.

In short, Capitalism acts on women as a continual bribe to enter into sex relations for money, whether in or out of marriage; and against this bribe there stands nothing beyond the traditional respectability which Capitalism ruthlessly destroys by poverty, except religion and the inborn sense of honor which has its citadel in the soul and can hold out (sometimes) against all circumstances.

Describing how child labor and the labor of subsidized women had cheapened the market, and how women who engaged in prostitution to eke out their wages had cheapened the market still further, Shaw finds that, 'In certain occupations, prostitution thus became practically compulsory, the alternative being starvation.'

This is exactly the spirit in which Susanna Conolly speaks of marriage in *The Irrational Knot*, the novel which Shaw described as, '. . . an early attempt on the part of the Life Force to write *A Doll's House* in English by the instrumentality of a very immature writer aged 24'. There is no doll's house for Susanna, who is a competent career woman of a class in which respectability is optional. When her lover feels impelled to propose to her, Susanna horrifies him by saying, 'Matrimony is all very fine for women who have no better way of supporting themselves, but it wouldnt suit me.' Later, she expands the same theme, unashamed, like Mrs Warren and Andrew Undershaft:

I confess I shouldnt like to make a regular legal bargain of going to live with a man. I dont care to make love a matter of money; it gives it a taste of the harem, or even worse. Poor Bob, meaning to be honorable, offered to buy me in the regular way at St George's Hanover Square, before we came to live here; but, of course, I refused, as any decent woman in my circumstances would. . . . I can respect myself; and I dont care whether you or your family respect me or not.

Nearly thirty years later, Shaw was still telling his public that until the economic independence of women is achieved, marriage must be maintained as a slavery.

The commercial interpretation of marriage opened the way for an assault on the great fetish of idealism: chastity, a virtue so touted that it could be referred to quite simply as Virtue. This religious ideal, with its history of lip-service through the ages, Shaw expressed in commercial terms at a time when commercial standards were still supposed to be put away on Sunday. He traced both the virginity of the bride and the wife's adherence to 'an inhuman standard of marital fidelity' to their pre-Christian and anti-Christian sources.

At the point at which [the Church] took up marriage and endeavoured to make it holy, marriage was, as it still is, largely a survival of the custom of selling women to men. Now in all trades a marked difference is made in price between a new article and a secondhand one. The moment we meet with this difference in value between human beings, we may know that we are in the slave-market, where the conception of our relations to the persons sold is neither religious nor natural nor human nor superhuman, but simply commercial.

The colloquial phrase, 'damaged goods', has the same implication. Nothing enraged Shaw more than such insults to humanity, as though terms like Woman, Egyptian or Pauper could efface the common validity of human principles. His delectably temperate style does not conceal his feelings about a critic who called Mrs Warren 'ordure'.

I do not like that word 'ordure' . . . to apply it to the woman in the street, whose spirit is of one substance with your own and her body no less holy: to look your women folk in the face afterwards and not go out and hang yourself: that is not on the list of pardonable sins.

The fact that Shaw separated the supposed morality of marriage, that is, its sexual morality, from God and traced it instead to Mammon, must not deceive us into thinking that he ignores the religious questions. Quite the contrary. It is true that his views on sexual purity were thoroughly un-Christian and that he did not take seriously, as some critics still do, hassles over canonical law in a country where civil marriage is acceptable.

For Shaw, the religious aspect of marriage is that in which it touches the old, large questions. How does it affect the life of the spirit; the pursuit of higher values, contemplation, principled action; the exploration of the limits of knowledge, courage and comprehension? To a man for whom the inner life is a reality, intolerable as the physical, legal and economic conditions of marriage may be, its ultimate and unanswerable condemnation is its spiritual danger. He tells us that Jesus saw, '. . . that the effect of marriage . . . was to make the couples sacrifice every higher consideration until they had fed and pleased one another'. It is this kind of sacrifice that women like Florence Nightingale and Joan of Arc decline to make, not the sacrifice of their personal freedom, their legal rights as *feme sole*, or even their physical integrity.

The greatest sacrifice in marriage is the sacrifice of the adventurous attitude towards life: the being settled . . . it is a form of suicide.

Now to say of any institution that it is incompatible with both the contemplative and the adventurous life is to disgrace it so vitally that all the moralizings of all the Deans and Chapters cannot reconcile our souls to its slavery.

The celibacy advocated by the early Christians is as unacceptable to Shaw as it is to the modern world at large. He asserts 'an absolute right to sexual experience'.

Instead, Shaw proposes economic arrangements to safeguard the essentials of religion and save man's soul from marriage: 'Thus, though it would be too much to say that everything that is obnoxious in marriage and family life will be cured by Communism, yet it can be said that it will cure what Jesus objected to in these institutions.' In other words, Shaw's economic analysis of marriage is also a step toward an economic cure, the socialism which will '. . . make the individual economically independent of marriage and the family'. The man's enslavement to his dependents is as destructive as the woman's enslavement to her lord and master. Moreover, the higher the civilization and the more conscientious the partners, the more of an obstacle marriage is to spiritual progress or, as Shaw puts it, individual evolution. This observation is borne out by the renewed emphasis on marriage and the reduced sense of personal freedom in the United States in the last decade, which demonstrates (in reverse) the soundness of Shaw's analysis:

And that is why the revolt against marriage . . . always recurs when civilization raises the standard of marital duty and affection, and at the same time produces a greater need for individual freedom in pursuit of a higher evolution.

Shaw obviously envisioned among the men and women freed from marriage a flowering of mute inglorious souls: those, like his friend Apsley Cherry-Garrard, who would risk their lives exploring the Arctic; those, like his friend Alfred Gattie, who would risk their fortunes on far-fetched brilliant inventions; and those, like the political rebels and religious visionaries of all time, who would risk in the name of an exalted belief their fortunes, their respectability, and their lives. The strongest people take chances in spite of marriage, as Shaw believed the creative artist always would, out of sheer, inspired selfishness. But no one knows what degrees of diffidence, of altruism, of fear, hide the talents of many others. And just as the marriage laws rob society of some of its best mothers, so an unwillingness to drag helpless children through their own dangers and deprivations probably costs society some of its best fathers.

The relevance of socialism to marriage is therefore very much the same as its relevance to breeding. We cannot appreciate Shaw's insistence on social leveling if we lose our sense of the class structure of Victorian England. For one thing, class snobbery in Victorian England was not the joking matter it seems to twentieth-century Americans. It may have been ridiculous to draw the line between old county families and parvenu peers, to make all the petty distinctions of status among the nobility, the gentry, and the self-made classes that were emphasized just because real differences were so slight, but the snobbery that came between the two nations, rich and poor, was by no means so ridiculous, although some of its expressions were both foolish and heartless. This snobbery was based on real differences that put intermarriage almost entirely out of the question. Much has been made, and with justification, of English class mobility and its advantages over the comparative rigidity of class lines on the Continent. This is true as far as it goes, but it has more relevance to Bagehot's political, than to Shaw's evolutionary borderline. For this mobility was usually between the upper middle class and the cadet branches of titled families. Moreover, the chasm could only be deepened by the growth of the city poor, in whom difference went deeper than manners. Class differences based on real poverty affected beauty, size and survival, and might, if allowed to continue unchecked in the way it was going, have bred two races out of the two nations. Concerning size and health we have the evidence of the change in English children after each of the world wars, as well as the evidence of immigrant families in the United States. On the question of beauty we have only the evidence of such artists as Cruikshank, Hogarth and Daumier, but perhaps that is enough. For that matter, in the most inclusive use of the term, manners alone would make intermarriage impossible.

Marriage: The Mystery of the Unhappy Ending

In the mirror of fiction, which though distorted does reflect real things, the classless society of lovers is a very late invention. Margaret Dalziel notices, in *Popular Fiction 100 Years Ago*, that 'Real differences in station between lovers are strangely infrequent. Where they seem to occur, they are almost invariably resolved by the disclosure that the apparently inferior party is in fact of excellent family. . . .' This is the situation at which W. S. Gilbert likes to poke fun: not a real situation, but a literary situation, in which the audience demands a certain kind of relief from the insolubility of real problems. Shaw himself wrote a light-handed treatment of this theme in *Cashel Byron's Profession*. His pugilist hero falls in love with a great heiress of aristocratic manners and highly developed intelligence. She loves him for looking like the Hermes of Praxiteles in his boxing costume and for having a mind unspoiled by books. But although the unequal marriage, the crossing of 'a supersubtle Venetian' with an untutored child of Nature, is the heart of the book, at the end Shaw offers us a revelation. Cashel has always assumed that he is the illegitimate son of an ordinary actress; but his mother reveals that he is his uncle's sole heir, and tells him, 'You are perfectly well connected by your mother's side, Cashel. The Byrons are only commoners; but even they are one of the oldest county families in England.'

Besides the gap between classes, there is another factor we now tend to forget. Writing just before the First World War, Shaw said:

> The biological value of family life in modern England can not be gauged, as differences in income, and, therefore, in social position, render sexual selection impossible. Every individual, male and female, is confronted by the fact that his or her choice of a mate is confined to two or three persons of whom none would have been considered at all had there been a different choice.

. . . .

Fashionable ladies fall in love with acrobats and have to marry colonels. Shop assistants fall in love with countesses and are obliged to marry shopgirls. Kings and Queens have been pitied for their political marriages, but in point of fact the ratio of love marriages in royal circles is probably as large as in other classes of the community.

There are now so many more of us than there were in nineteenth-century England and we cover long distances so casually that 'two or three persons' seems an incredibly small number. Yet the novels of that period remind us what a stir was caused by the arrival of an eligible man in any provincial place. Before he even appears he is talked of as a possible husband for any unmarried young lady in the story. This would be nonsense today, but it was not nonsense then. A small village divided into classes and subdivided into gradations of suitability, offered an incredible poverty of choice among unmarried people, and married people were not then considered to be continuously eligible. Even in London, the more sharply defined circles of the rich and the neighborhood habits of the poor kept the choice fairly narrow. It is not surprising that Shaw should have felt that genuine equality would revolutionize marriage.

So far we have seen, first, that Shaw's iconoclastic treatment of marriage was similar in method and force to those of other nineteenth-century radicals; and second, that he argued more for the genetic results of marriage reform than for the relief of sentimental grievances. Therefore the choice of a mate was more crucial than the nature of the marriage agreement; nevertheless, as everyone knows, Shaw had much to say about the latter. The two beliefs on which all his suggested reforms rest are these: that society must accept many and widely differing forms of marriage with equal tolerance; that divorce must be easily available without stigma. These two derive from the even more fundamental belief that marriage must not abrogate the constitutional rights of either party.

Shaw's own marriage is a good example of the kind of variation which he thought society ought to recognize and provide for. He wrote to Frank Harris:

Do not forget that all marriages are different, and that a marriage between two young people followed by parentage cannot be lumped in with a childless partnership between two middle-aged people who have passed the age at which it is safe to bear a first child.

However, Shaw's marriage to Charlotte Payne-Townshend, which took place in 1898 when he was forty-two and she forty-one, might have remained childless without being sexless. All authorities report, however, that Shaw consistently described his marriage as a partnership of work and domesticity in which sexual relations were ruled out by an explicit agreement. The most recent word on the subject is that of Mrs Shaw's biographer, who says she does not know whether this agreement was carried out. There is, however, absolutely no ground for believing that his unusual marriage implies a warped view of the subject on Shaw's part. Aside from the speeches in his plays and the passages in certain love letters* which would not even have been conceived in the same terms by a man incapable of love in the fullest sense, which excludes the sensual and the sentimental by including both in a more mysterious feeling, there is evidence that Shaw's marriage itself was by no means so simple a project as conventionally-minded readers may suppose.

Shaw refers, for example, to a moment when the relationship *lost* '. . . its inevitable preliminary character as a love affair'. Hesketh Pearson reports also that it was Mrs Shaw who opposed having children, or, as Shaw is reported to have put it, '. . . would never have allowed anything like that'. He is reported also to have said, '. . . but sometimes I have been sorry I was not more insistent on the point . . .'. From all these things I conclude that Shaw's idea of marriage without conjugation was a reasoned belief applicable to couples in many different circumstances, and not an extension of his own idiosyncrasy. The same applies to his view that no marriage should be thought to obviate sexual temperance.

These two suggested limitations on sexual freedom within the married state seem to have been more profoundly shocking to the conventional man than any of Shaw's radical recommendations on divorce, adultery or polygamy. Here, oddly enough, Shaw is in the position of the second pioneer he described in *The Quintessenc of Ibseneism*:

The second, whose eyes are in the back of his head, is the man

---

* Notably those to Florence Farr, e.g.: 'I also am fascinated by your proposal, oh my other self – no, not my other self, but my very self. Now it is all over and utterly dead, as if it had never been. We are mere acquaintances, my dear Mrs Emery, just as we were that day at Merton. And so we are FREE – to begin it all over again. I am a beggar once more; and once more I shall come into my great fortune. I am again an unscrupulous egotist with a remorseless will; and again shall I be moralized and have my backbone sweetly stolen away.'

who declares that it is wrong to do something that nobody has hitherto seen any harm in. . . . The second is treated with great respect by the army. They give him testimonials; name him the Good Man; and hate him like the devil.

Writing in 1890, Shaw declared that: '. . . a guilty society can more easily be persuaded that any apparently innocent act is guilty than that any apparently guilty act is innocent'. He was using Shelley as his example and judging by the reactions to the two statements, 'It is wrong to kill animals and eat them', and 'It is not wrong to take your sister as your wife'. And yet, the changes in society since then seem to indicate that the opposite may be true. Whether it is only that in 1890 the effect of the anti-puritan spirit on the roles of the two reformers could not be foreseen, or whether it is simply that Shaw was overlooking the emotional difference between dietary and sexual rules, the fact remains that society has not been easily persuaded that the 'apparently innocent' sexual freedom within marriage may be guilty.

Shaw's proposals for limiting sexual activity in marriage involve two quite different things. One of these has nothing to do with the kinds of marriage, for it applies to every kind of marital and extra-marital connection.

In the very important matter of sexual temperance a marriage licence is held to dispense with it as completely as is humanly possible. But it is impossible to keep in training for stage work on such terms.

This is a basic tenet of Shaw's, similar to his principles about meat and alcohol, although obviously not the same. Meat and alcohol he considered unnecessary, harmful and disgusting. Making love he considered just the opposite. But he was convinced (hardly the conviction of an undersexed man) that if sexual desire were given a free rein, no one could do his best work on the energy that remained. Here speaks the man who wrote, 'Marriage is popular because it combines the maximum of temptation with the maximum of opportunity.' Besides dispensing with moderation, it creates 'a little Alsatia' within the laws of society. The conference of respectable married men which called forth one of Shaw's great diatribes on his fellow citizens, revealed to him a conception of married life at which:

Peter the Great would have been shocked; Byron would have been horrified; Don Juan would have fled from the conference into a monastery. The respectable men all regarded the marriage ceremony as a rite which absolved them from the laws of health and temperance; inaugurated a life-long honeymoon; and placed their pleasures on exactly the same footing as their prayers.

The point Shaw is really trying to make becomes apparent a little later when he says:

Compared with statesmen, first-rate professional men, artists, and even with laborers and artisans as far as muscular exertion goes, they were underworked, and could spare the fine edge of their faculties and the last few inches of their chests without being any the less fit for their daily routine. If I had adopted their habits, a startling deterioration would have appeared in my writing before the end of a fortnight, and frightened me back to what they would have considered an impossible asceticism.

When Shaw says, speaking only partly from his own experience, that people will marry (or remained married) for the sake of domesticity alone, and when he points out that the connection between marriage and conjugation is an accidental one, he is not arguing this same question, but a new one. His explanation of King Charles, in the preface to '*In Good King Charles's Golden Days*', might serve equally well for King Magnus of *The Apple Cart* or Hector Hushabye of *Heartbreak House* or even for Mrs George of *Getting Married*.

As a husband he took his marriage very seriously, and his sex adventures as calls of nature on an entirely different footing. In this he was in the line of evolution, which leads to an increasing separation of the unique and intensely personal and permanent marriage relation from the carnal intercourse described in Shakespear's sonnet. This, being a response to the biological decree that the world must be peopled, may arise irresistibly between persons who could not live together endurably for a week but can produce excellent children. Historians who confuse Charles's feeling for his wife with his appetite for Barbara Villiers do not know chalk from cheese biologically.

Rougemont says that passion and marriage are irreconcilable and that their co-existence raises insoluble problems. Shaw does not say the same thing, but he recognizes the same difficulty. His emphasis on the impersonality and impermanence of sexual

attraction is a familiar masculine view. But the effect of legitimizing such relations in the manner Shaw suggests would be not
so much to increase their number as to remove their sentimental
sting. Infidelity in marriage as we know it can cause more than
the demeaning unhappiness called jealousy: it can give rise to
the philosophic unhappiness of a disappointed ideal, which
falsifies the marriage relationship on the one hand, and on the
other vitiates the meaning of love.

Shaw finds the lifelong honeymoon exasperating, whether
real or pretended:

> . . . healthy marriages are partnerships of companionable and
> affectionate friendship . . . cases of chronic lifelong love, whether
> sentimental or sensual, ought to be sent to the doctor, if not to the
> executioner.

His sense of something indecent in such relationships is fairly
common, although it is usually expressed in ridicule rather than
repugnance. In relation to his own marriage, Shaw said:

> When one has been married for over forty years there is something
> quite indestructible that grows up between people which has nothing
> to do with emotions in any way.

In a discarded portion of *Back to Methuselah*, he carries the same
point so far as to suggest that:

> . . . when a tie has endured for, say fifty years, it becomes so intimate,
> so sacred, that it establishes, in effect, a relation far closer than the
> relation of consanguinity, and should be placed on the list of degrees
> within which marriage is forbidden. . . .

This whiff of an incest taboo between husband and wife is interesting, but of course Shaw intends nothing so extreme in his
other statements about moderation in marriage.

In these statements a historical moment must be recognized,
as well as a personality. Realistic playwrights like Brieux and
Ibsen had recognized that marriage '. . . may mask all the vices
of the coarsest libertinage with added elements of slavery and
cruelty . . .'. In an extraordinarily interesting passage concerning
the relations of John Stuart Mill and Harriet Taylor, Michael
St John Packe suggests that the spectacle of a barnyard world
in which the lust of men enslaved women and impeded the

progress of mankind, caused 'a carnal disgust' in both of them. At this moment of history the failure of prudery as a safeguard became unmistakeable, and the reaction of man's conscience to inequality had begun with some advanced spirits, although less conspicuously than the reaction of woman's instinct. In these circumstances, the bold, huntress woman becomes quite naturally a clean expression of instinct. On the other hand, the Tennysonian, 'Man is the hunter; woman is his game', comes to seem entirely too gross a *Realpolitik* of sex, carrying into the sexual realm the 'nature-red-in-tooth-and-claw' concept which so many civilized men felt impelled to adopt. However, men who rejected the neo-Darwinian values of capitalism and nationalism were, by logic or by temperament, inclined to reject primitive male dominance as well. In men of special sensitivity, like Mill and Shaw, it is not surprising that their reaction against brute conquest went so far that they preferred not to be in possession of any predaceous powers over any other human being. There is no way of knowing the part this diffidence played in Shaw's elaboration of his theory of marriage.

Just as Shaw declines to choose between the reform of fertile marriage and the separation of marriage from procreation, so he declines to choose between the reform of permanent marriage and the establishment of contingent marriage. Obviously, the permanence of marriage is its greatest drawback, but far less in the marriage of companionship than in the marriage of passion. Shaw is doing no more than he claims society has already done when he countenances many kinds of relationship under the name of marriage. This is both pluralism and pragmatism, the natural result of being aware of both the complexity of the world as it is and the rapid changes of an unpredictable age.

Few things in Shaw's discussion of marriage are more significant than the fact that, although he recommends many kinds of marriage, he believes in only one kind of divorce, granted unconditionally, '. . . whenever it is desired, without asking why'. Every word Shaw says about divorce is plain and unequivocal. He proposed, '. . . to make marriage as easily dissoluble as any other partnership . . .'. Of the eight recommendations on divorce in the long preface to *Getting Married*, the first two are a revolution in themselves:

1. Make divorce as easy, as cheap, and as private as marriage.

2. Grant divorce at the request of either party whether the other consents or not; and admit no other ground than the request, which should be made without stating any reasons.

Later, Shaw went even further, claiming that divorce might be justified without the request of either party:

Should not divorce of the separated be made both compulsory and secret so far as the names of the parties are concerned? In China the State has power to dissolve marriages on its own initiative even when the couple are living together and bringing up their children in perfect concord. When a thief marries a prostitute and their children are being brought up to follow their parents' callings, should not the Home Office intervene and cancel the union? Why should a marriage licence be held more sacred than a driving licence?

The logical flaw here is that if the state could take such children away from their parents, the divorce would not be necessary. As we do, however, lump marriage and parenthood together in our laws, it is clear enough what Shaw intends by his example. His proposals seem extremely simple because, being concerned with the social results of divorce, they abandon the unavowed punitive element that exists in even the most liberal divorce arrangements in our society.

It is interesting to see how the sense of guilt can affect the most valiant efforts of reform. Packe prints the draft of a letter by Harriet Taylor in which she proposes that, pending the time when the whole community (properly educated) could disregard the marriage laws, divorce should be '. . . attained by *any, without any reason assigned,* and at a small expense . . .'. This is a perfectly extraordinary idea for a young lady to propose in the 1820's. And yet she proceeds to one of those safeguards against abuse which soon become abuses in themselves: '. . . but which could only be pronounced after a long period'. Having the wit and courage to grant so much, why make such a stipulation? No comparison with what was done seventy years later by one of the world's great revolutionaries can denigrate the courage of Miss Taylor's statement. It is interesting precisely because it shows how a certain kind of weakness can penetrate so much strength. The concession appeases not only something in the outside world, but something lurking in the corners of the soul.

The freedom from just this kind of self-distrust is one of Shaw's great qualities. He takes his stand on divorce without apology, but also without the bravado of *mauvaise honte*. He tried to keep his own life 'blameless' – free, that is, not of passion but of scandal. His relations with Mrs Patrick Campbell, which made his wife so painfully jealous, may seem to contradict this view, but he never threw caution away in this or any other amorous encounter. He kept himself free in another way of the need to hedge divorce about with safeguards which were becoming more and more a protection for the woman. Both socialism and the right to a career would ease the practical problems of divorce for women, and Shaw worked for both. But the wounds to vanity, the social stigmata, and the complications of *ménage*, which fall so unequally on the two parties of divorce, are as real as the need for housekeeping money. These difficulties too would be mitigated if woman could achieve the sense of self which includes but surpasses self-respect, as Shaw encouraged her to do.

With woman's economic and emotional independence as part of his program, Shaw is justified in urging divorce at the request of *either* party. This particular knot is cut by his explanation that we do not force people to marry if only one of them wishes it, no matter how many threats of suicide are entered. The argument indicates how precisely marriage is defined by divorce. It indicates also Shaw's willingness to accept a degree of contingency in marriage that might seem to deny the term all meaning. During the thirties he wrote:

> If he were alive today St Vincent would probably propose a clean sweep of all our difficulties about marriage and divorce by forbidding people to marry for longer than a year, and make them renew vows every twelve months.

Both Shaw and this first of the modern social saints prefer the hope of responsible loyalty to the insurance of formal loyalty.

One amusing example of Shaw's realism about this subject occurs in his answer to one 'Proteus', who had written a letter to the *Westminster Gazette* warning that if Shaw's proposals on divorce were granted no household would be safe from the 'divorce-him-and-marry-me' approach, and society would end by having to segregate men and women. Shaw began: 'DEAR

PROTEUS. You are a hopeless fool – probably unmarried.' He himself foresaw quite a different result.

The familiar libertine's opening 'You are not happy in your marriage. Forgive me; but I cannot bear to see you suffering. I also am unhappy. I love you, &c., &c., &c.,' would be at once met by the inquiry whether the sympathiser's intentions were honourable, that is, whether he or she intended marriage after the divorce. Many ladies and gentlemen who now play the cuckoo in indissoluble households in an entirely selfish spirit would be unmasked if the legal obstacle to the happiness they profess to long for were removed.

We come, finally, to the old question of personal happiness. From first to last, as we know, Shaw scorned the search for happiness as weak, foolish, self-indulgent and self-defeating. The best justification for calling Shaw a puritan is in such statements as:

This is the true joy in life, the being used for a purpose recognized by yourself as a mighty one; the being thoroughly worn out before you are thrown on the scrap heap; the being a force of Nature instead of a feverish selfish little clod of ailments and grievances complaining that the world will not devote itself to making you happy.

And yet Shaw's proposals on marriage and divorce, for all their socialist and evolutionary arguments, can be read as arrangements to increase personal happiness. 'Any tolerable western divorce law should put the sentimental grievances first.' It would be the merest word-worship to treat this contradiction in terms as though it were something more. Shaw's ethic is not to be comprehended in a phrase or a slogan. If his belief that the human being has a divine responsibility to society is a departure from individualism, it is not therefore collectivism. The hatred of the individual which characterizes fascism was so foreign to his nature that he could scarcely perceive it when confronted with it. If he was out of sympathy with individualism as a cult and happiness as an end, it was not that he distrusted the human soul and its deepest instincts. It would be more accurate to say that Shaw believed in the possible harmony between individual will and social values. He could honestly believe, for he had his own feelings as evidence, that a life of hard work and self-denial, if it is freely chosen and successful, may be more joyful than any form of self-indulgence or happiness-seeking.

But to speak only of theory is to miss almost entirely the benevolence of Shaw's observations. Marriage as an institution, marriage as an abstraction, has been so shamelessly overrated that its critics dare not concede one theoretical inch. But while Ibsen, Brieux, Tolstoy and other critics of marriage were writing on this subject stories full of disillusionment and bitterness, Shaw was projecting on stage a remarkable series of marriages in which any oddness was compensated by an astonishing amiability. This amiability was entered, moreover, as a credit to Woman.

Devotion, solicitude, maternal self-effacement, fierce protectiveness and unlimited indulgence – these are the sentiments of the typical Shavian wife. She is not inspired by amorous passion or beglamorized adoration, not deluded by idealization or blind possessiveness. These are for young, marriageable girls, whose power comes from instinct, not from knowledge. Wives are something else again. They are the voice of experience, the voice of civilization. Shaw refers to them as 'the only women who know what womanhood really means'. And Mrs George, in *Getting Married*, is the voice of the married woman.

Getting Married is a problem play, a navigator's chart showing all the dangers of a wide sea, everything wrong with marriage under the existing laws. And yet, consider the wives who are supposed to illustrate the fatal effects of matrimony. There is Mrs Bridgenorth, of whom we know little except her husband's gratitude and her placidity on stage. There is Leo, a silly and selfish girl who nevertheless, being a wife, fusses maternally over the elderly husband she is trying to divorce, and longs for a sensible bigamy that would allow her to continue to take care of him. There is Mrs Collins, 'a regular old hen', whose husband would like to run away from her but cannot, for fear of hurting her feelings; still, he is not running away from mistreatment, but only from an excess of love and self-sacrifice. Edith is only a bride, Lesbia only a 'glorious strong-minded old maid of old England!' The remaining woman, Mrs George, personifies wifehood. Collins describes the marriage of his brother George this way:

He married a very fine figure of a woman; but she was that changeable and what you might call susceptible, you would not believe. She didnt seem to have any control over herself when she fell in love. She would mope for a couple of days . . . and then she would up and say . . . 'I must go to him, George'; and away she would go from her home and her husband without with-your-leave or by-your-leave.

To clarify her relation to her husband Shaw tells us that her great venture in spiritual love is with the bishop, not her husband, although her profane love rushes out to the many men who later return her to him like an embarrassing lost package. For the essence of being married, in other words, there is no classification like spiritual, sensual or conventional. Mrs George explains it to her new lover this way:

> Oh, I dont know that I love him. He's my husband, you know. But if I got anxious about George's health, and I thought it would nourish him, I would fry you with onions for his breakfast and think nothing of it. George and I are good friends. George belongs to me. Other men may come and go; but George goes on forever.

This explains nothing and tells everything. It is bootless to pretend that hers is only the self-protection of a permanently married little bourgeoise, although anyone is free to claim that in Mrs George's everyday equivalent it is no more. Shaw has clearly intended to put Mrs George beyond all that by giving her supernatural gifts which make her impossible to classify. He said as much himself in a letter written in 1908:

> Love costs a man so little, and brings him so much, that his light-heartedness on the subject degenerates into comic mischievousness. I cannot escape altogether from the vulgarity of my sex in that matter, though I make an effort now and then to shew that I know better. In order to do this in Getting Married, I was forced to resort to the device of clairvoyance, in order that I might for the moment obliterate Mrs George as a comedic personality, and substitute the entire female sex crying to the ages from her lips.

Furthermore, this wife of a coal merchant is expressing the same principles which, in other plays, guide the wives of two kings (*The Apple Cart* and '*In Good King Charles's Golden Days*'), a clergyman (*Candida*), and a gentleman of the leisure class (*Heartbreak House*), as well as a number of women in minor works. These women are not economic puppets. They are affectionate human beings, protecting and cherishing a man, but protecting even more their own sense of responsibility and self-respect. Candida's choice of the man who needs her more is the simplest clue to this relationship. Here is the motherly woman again, placing that role above passion, romance and even independence. 'We are all women's babies', Shaw wrote to Ellen Terry. Yet a great amiability persists. The uncompromising device on Shaw's banner has always been legible: 'The attack on marriage is an attack on property.' More faintly to be discerned, in the dramatic form of motherly wives and grateful, admiring husbands, is the rejoinder: 'But not an attack on love.' Only, Shaw would specify, that love must be the Real Thing.

CHAPTER 6

The Real Thing

SHAW had great confidence in his own understanding of love. He explained that in his plays '. . . when the question of passion arises, it is the real thing . . . .' He defended his own view of the subject against both prudes and sensualists, and referred his critics to the impressive but ill-defined authority of the sex whose 'whole existence' love was said to be:

> When I began, Archer complained that my plays were reeking with sex. Now that I am ending, you complain that I am an anchorite. Women have never complained of me either way. *They* know that I know what I am talking about.

At first this statement seems to be a little drama of obsolescence. Attitudes that had seemed daring to the verge of depravity when Shaw began to write, began in the twenties to seem as old-fashioned as the bustle and the bosom. The public manners of sex, if nothing else, were changing radically, although the evidence of a change in private sexual behavior is less reliable. At any rate, Shaw's difficulty with the hobgoblin of little minds was not that he failed to move with the times. To a large extent, it was he who had caused the times to move. And yet his attempts to assimilate the new order of Woman into his later plays are feeble, and it is to lack of sympathy as much as to failing dramatic powers that I attribute the blank creatures who fill the place of women in so many of the later plays. Neither feeling nor memory had failed him, as we learn from the powerful sermon on sexual love in the otherwise slight *Village Wooing*. Although he has been called the father of the flapper, Shaw found her difficult to believe in – and impossible to portray in depth. His Z., his Sweetie, his Begonia Brown, all show a lack of characterization which reveals his bewilderment, unless of course this total absence of individuality is all there is to portray.

Deep reading might be attempted here. Names like Prola, She, Z., take the place of names like Lady Cicely Waynflete and Ann Whitefield. Families and milieux vanish; names are the symbols of these, as they are of history and tradition. Their absence symbolizes an era in which, for the first time, detached young women began to turn up in society, confronting men with a formless moral situation. Females in whom the Shavian self-confidence has degenerated into petulance, stand on a confused and universal stage. Instead of being able to escape pursuit by darting into Air Street, as an early Shaw heroine could do, the new woman stands on a featureless tropic isle which symbolizes her lack of modesty as her name symbolizes her lack of individuality. Until Shaw returns to the traditional woman with *Good King Charles* in 1939, we miss all the comforts of home: London, money matters, social strata, sexual intrigue, and fashionable clothing. *Good King Charles* is in more ways than one a Restoration comedy.

These observations, however, do not explain Shaw's supposed transition from reeking with sex to freezing with asceticism. While the women in Shaw's plays dwindled in realism, his treatment of forbidden topics became more open, and bold conversations about the 'lower centres' replace the sexual overtones which sounded so discreetly offstage in the earlier plays. The literary conventions had outdistanced him, of course, but such conventions are not the issue here. There is in Shaw, early and late, a delicacy on the subject of love which he himself simplifies by distinguishing between the Real Thing (love as portrayed by Shaw) and every other interpretation known to art and legend; but the real-and-unreal division does not explain the matter any better than the early-and-late division.

Shaw began as a crusader against the cant of love. This cant was a literary tradition which had become also a business tradition in publishing and the theater. Bellamy and H. G. Wells had to add 'love interest' to their utopian and scientific fantasies. In the theater the situation was made more difficult by the fact that the love interest, which was assumed to be the only infallible interest, '. . . must proceed upon genteel assumptions'. This dreadful dilemma resulted in what Shaw called the romantic play. He attacked with scorn the assumption that love conquers all and that love ennobles all. Of the former he said:

Since most people go to the theatre to escape from reality, this convention is naturally dear to a world in which love, all powerful in the secret, unreal, day-dreaming life of the imagination, is in the real active life the abject slave of every trifling habit, prejudice and cowardice, easily stifled by shyness, class feeling, and pecuniary prudence, or diverted from what is theatrically assumed to be its hurricane course by such obstacles as a thick ankle, a cockney accent, or an unfashionable hat.

And Shaw's rejoinder to the assumption that love is an ennobling motive is: 'When we want to read of the deeds that are done for love, whither do we turn? To the murder column; and there we are rarely disappointed.' This particular sally is intended to justify Dick Dudgeon's sacrifice of his life to satisfy '. . . the law of his own nature . . . .' but Shaw has a two-edged axe to grind. Dudgeon, like Blanco Posnet, plays the 'great game' without sanctimonious reasons. Furthermore, he does so without sentimental reasons. This the critics found hard to believe, especially with an attractive leading lady in plain sight.

In spite of his accurate observation about the murder column, Shaw impartially disbelieves in love as an ennobling motive and love as a tragic flaw. He goes further than Voltaire, who said, 'If love is not tragic, it is insipid, and if it is tragic it must rule alone.' He rejects the nineteenth-century revival of the Tristan legend in favor of the seventeenth-century tone of self-possession, which says: 'I could not love thee, dear, so much / Loved I not honour more.' That is the mood behind the following statement:

Besides, I have a technical objection to making sexual infatuation a tragic theme. Experience proves that it is only effective in the comic spirit. We can bear to see Mrs Quickly pawning her plate for love of Falstaff, but not Antony running away from the battle of Actium for love of Cleopatra.

Shaw's heroes, in this respect, have a good bit of seventeenth-century stuff in them. Tanner loves philosophy more; Marchbanks loves poetry more; Cusins loves power more. It is only the spaniels who are all for love. Poor, abject Octavius in *Man and Superman*, Randall the Rotter in *Heartbreak House* – these are the Tristans of Shavian drama. No clever woman wants them; instinct tells her that their lack of self-control implies a lack of substance. When Cusins has his great decision to make, he and Major Barbara do not, like modern young couples, consult each other democratically before deciding what they think and what they are. Each prefers the risk of finding the other unworthy; and the concomitant joy of finding the other worthy independently. Shaw speaks of this same kind of strength from the dramatist's point of view when he says:

> . . . people who sacrifice every other consideration to love are as hopelessly unheroic on the stage as lunatics or dipsomaniacs. Hector and Hamlet are the world's heroes; not Paris and Antony.

When some years later our author points out the lack of '. . . modern English plays in which the natural attraction of the sexes for one another is made the mainspring of the action', he is not contradicting himself, for such plays would not be liebestodal tragedy, but social comedy. In the latter genre the love-death is only another milestone on their way. Ann Whitefield may faint dead away, but only for a tactical moment. Tanner may say, 'Let it kill us', but that is only his way of rising to the rhetorical moment without quite proposing marriage. What Shaw proposes to do in *Man and Superman* is to extract from the complex of love the kernel of meaning. 'You propound a certain social substance, sexual attraction to wit, for dramatic distillation; and I distil it for you. I do not adulterate the product with aphrodisiacs nor dilute it with romance and water. . . .' Those who consider Shaw an anchorite fail to see how closely he connects these two forms of adulteration. Before discussing Shaw's idea of prudery, it might be well to mention one quality in his work which is of the utmost importance in judging his views.

This subtle element in Shaw's work is a comic amiability which is probably unique in the theater. Goldsmith's unequal gentleness, for example, is not at all the same thing. It is Shakespeare whom Shaw most resembles in his ability to treat his comic characters without venom. Shaw's characters represent a higher sort of comedy than Dogberry and Verges, are more pertinent to our own follies than Bottom and Quince, for instead of thrashing about blindly in the medium of words, they thrash about blindly in the medium of ideas. As comedy enters the period of the Restoration and again the period between the two world wars, the note of savage pain grows louder in the laugh which Shaw says we give to keep from crying.

This quality can only be obscured by calling Shaw the twentieth-century Molière as one French critic has done. Certainly the parallels to be drawn are many and instructive. But such parallels should always alert us to the differences hidden among the similarities. A twentieth-century Molière is almost as impossible as a seventeenth-century Shaw, for history is a magic wood in which the self must lose itself and find instead a contemporary shape. Through the tangled forest of two complicated, radical centuries, the mind of the artist could hardly maintain its old shape. Shaw details all this with his kindly explicitness whenever the question, 'Better than Shakespear?' arises.

The salient distinction of Shaw's comic types is that theirs are not deep-dyed follies or detestable souls. He does not pretend that their follies are 'human nature', a delusion which embitters the mixture by allowing self-hate to leak into it. These follies are a part of *social* nature. The fools are teachable beings. They need not learn their lessons by being beaten over the head, unspeakably humiliated at the bedroom door, or drenched by the perpetually poised chamber-pots of a simpler and less sanitary age. They learn in a way for which we must not deny our own preference: by conversation. That is one reason for the recurrent complaint that in Shaw's plays talk supplants action. There is plenty of action in the plays, of course, but it is usually a sideshow. The real events take place in an invisible arena. That is why, as in opera, stage business can spoil but cannot save a play by Shaw.

But the social critic in Shaw is not so sunny as the dramatist. The dramatist creates beings of innate goodness and perfectibility, flawed by weaknesses which allow the corruption of society to enter. The social critic recognizes that there are some human beings whom he must consider, for all practical purposes, incorrigible. These people do not appear on stage. The true prude or lecher is absent from Shaw's plays for this reason. A lampoon appropriate to his faults is not appropriate to the Shavian theater. The prefaces, however, are chocked with these indigestible remnants: explanation, condemnation and horrible examples. It is there that Shaw's understanding of prudery is made clear. In 'The Revolutionist's Handbook', prudery is described as '. . . only a mere incident of popular squalor: the subjects which it taboos remain the most interesting and earnest of subjects in spite of it'. We are told that sex becomes offensive where poverty makes cleanliness impossible. Although he does not remark upon it, poverty also makes sex offensive by making privacy impossible. To the gourmand of sexual experience, this demand for certain minima of civilization may in itself stamp Shaw as a prude. There is, however, a difference, deeper than it is wide, between prudery and fastidiousness. Shaw's fastidiousness is too obvious to need expatiation and too unusual to gain general sympathy.

The prudery of contemporary discussion he attributes to the fact that only one in a million can speak of sex without 'wounding our self-respect'.

The prudery of the newspapers is like the prudery of the dinner table, a mere difficulty of education and language. We are not taught to think decently on these subjects, and consequently we have no language for them except indecent language. We therefore have to declare them unfit for public discussion. . . .

Prudery as a class phenomenon is depicted but not analyzed by Shaw. As a socialist he thinks of the poor; as a satirist he thinks of the middle class; as a playwright he takes aristocratic standards for granted. Even Mrs George, the coal-merchant's wife in *Getting Married*, conducts her amours as if she were a duchess. The freedom that money and an assured social position made possible for upper-class women, was quite comparable to the freedom which Shaw believed the new era should grant to all women. But the class idea remains implicit in his plays. It is explicit in the horror of the *nouveau riche* Mrs Tarleton of *Misalliance* at the coarse talk of titled ladies.

When Shaw disclaimed prudery for himself, he did so in a tone of badinage. Speaking before an international meeting on sexual reform in 1929, he claimed to be an expert in sex appeal, and when the audience laughed he replied:

I do not in the least know why that remark of mine has elicited laughter; but as a matter of fact I am an expert in sex appeal. What I mean is that I am a playwright. . . . The theatre . . . has to deal in sex exactly as a costermonger has to deal in turnips. . . . One very important function of the theatre in society is to educate the audience in matters of sex. . . . Being a born artist I have always been specially impressionable by sex.

These are typical of Shaw's remarks on the subject of his own sexual attitudes, remarks which manage always to claim and to substantiate the claim of the utmost sexual liberality, yet do so in a manner which raises doubts. The doubts, however, are unjustified. On the subjects which Shaw treats seriously (as he does not treat an audience's relation to himself) he is more thoroughly liberal than most of those who laugh at his old-fashioned reticence.

'Taboo in the Schools', part of a preface contemporaneous with the pioneering work of Havelock Ellis, makes a clean sweep of the whole rationale in support of innocence. Shaw's claim is that children given no sex education have nothing of the subject concealed from them but '. . . its dignity, its honor, its sacredness, its rank as the first necessity of society and the deepest concern of the nation'.

On the subject of *Lady Chatterley's Lover*, still a test of tolerance, Shaw takes an extreme view:

> If I had a marriageable daughter, what could I give her to read to prepare her? Dickens? Thackeray? George Eliot? Walter Scott? Trollope? or even any of the clever modern women who take such a fiendish delight in writing very able novels that leave you hopeless and miserable? They would teach her a lot about life and society and human nature. But they would leave her absolutely in the dark as to marriage. Even Fielding and Joyce and George Moore would be no use: instead of telling her nothing they would tell her worse than nothing. But she would learn something from Lady Chatterley. I shouldn't let her engage herself if I could help it until she had read that book. . . . *Lady Chatterley* should be on the shelves of every college for budding girls. They should be forced to read it on pain of being refused a marriage licence.

The case becomes even more emphatic when we realize how strongly Shaw disapproved of Lawrence's language. Even in the act of protesting against the mangling of Shakespeare, he makes an exception of '. . . the obsolete Elizabethan badinage which is and should be cut out as a matter of course'. His verbal delicacy went so far as to cause him to bowdlerize for publication a letter he had written to Frank Harris about his own experiences, changing 'whore' to 'mistress' and 'copulations' to 'gallantries'.

This whole field is so mined with inelegancies that Shaw himself, for all his innate dignity, could begin a sentence, 'I liked sexual intercourse because. . . .' (See page 142.) No wonder euphemism has its appeal!

Shaw's old-fashioned courtesy of expression was not the only thing that kept him from writing like Lawrence, of whom he said, 'Lawrence had delicacy enough to tell the best, and brutality enough to rub in the worst.' There was also his clearer grasp of a historical pattern. He had watched the emergence of a spate of plays and novels purporting to be 'new' and hoping to succeed by sharing the notoriety of writers like Ibsen and by exploiting the taboos which serious writers had defied for other reasons, but he deplored the rash of fashionable and sentimental plays which were based on the simple plan of making the heroines of these plays 'naughty ladies'. By the time Shaw wrote his preface to *Three Plays by Brieux*, this tradition had taken another step.

Sexual irregularities began to be attributed to the sympathetic characters in fiction not as the blackest spots in their portraits, but positively as redeeming humanities in them.

A note of irritability creeps into this preface, perhaps because the audacious Shaw of the nineties had dared only on the strength of a self-discipline to which the audacious writers of the twenties did not submit. These writers, he said, '. . . assumed that unmentionability was an aim in itself – that to be decent was to be out of the movement'. In that sense, certainly, Shaw was not in the movement.

Shaw was delighted when a lady of his acquaintance told him that his most shocking play, *Mrs Warren's Profession*, was a great favorite of her children. Why the children found this play so interesting is not clear, except that the lovers turn out to be brother and sister; but it is easy to see why, after his painful encounters with official and unofficial censorship, the author said: 'Thank goodness, they found nothing but purity in the play.' There is nothing in any of Shaw's plays that is unsuitable for children. Even the burglars are reassuringly manageable, just like the lion in Androcles, if only you go about it the right way. And yet many of the assumptions still scandalize adults. But that is to be expected when an author disregards certain social conventions without losing his respect for the realities from which they originally grew. No one could accuse Shaw of catering for his audiences as he said the theater managers of the nineties did, '. . . with coarse frankness as a slave-dealer caters for a Pasha . . . .' Nor has his explanation of his restraint, although it is intended to reassure, the common touch:

I found that the whole business of stage sensuousness, whether as Lyceum Shakspear, musical farce, or sham Ibsen, finally disgusted me, not because I was Pharisaical, or intolerably refined, but because I was bored. . . .

The fact that others seem not to have been bored, he attributes to the convention of 'celibacy' in the arts: '. . . the English novelist, like the starving tramp who can think of nothing but his hunger, seems to be unable to escape from the obsession of sex. . . .' Meredith says much the same thing in his essay on comedy: 'Where the sexes are separated, men and women grow, as the Portuguese call it, *afaimados* of one another, famine-stricken. . . .'

On the other hand, Shaw was perfectly free from the conviction that there is something inherently sinful about sex. When he first came across the writings of Freud, about 1911, he boasted, 'I have said it all before him'. It is impossible to compare literary and medical methods, but the conclusions of these two dissimilar men of genius, who were born in the same year, show interesting similarities. In *The Quintessence of Ibsenism*, which appeared four years before Freud's first psychoanalytic work, *Studies in Hysteria*, Shaw makes a statement which seems to express metaphorically Freud's view of the genital origin of all erotic feelings in the broadest sense:

Tannhäuser may die in the conviction that one moment of the emotion he felt with St Elizabeth was fuller and happier than all the hours of passion he spent with Venus; but that does not alter the fact that love began for him with Venus. . . .

And in 1911 Shaw declared that the treatment of sex as an obscene thing was the most dangerous of early Christian excesses, '. . . because it is a blasphemy against life. . . .'

The sense of something anti-Freudian in Shaw's work may spring from the literary Freudianism of the critics. But their method is retrospective. It may some day become clear that Shaw created an early literary parallel of Freudian psychology. In a paper published in 1908, Freud drew some quite Shavian conclusions about the morality of marriage, the capacities of women, and the need for social reforms. However, according to Ernest Jones, Freud never came to like Shaw's writings, '. . . probably because of their widely differing conceptions of womanhood'. There Freud's biographer leaves the matter.

In one way Shaw's drama seems a world apart from Freud, and this no doubt goes deeper than statements of principle. In all the plays, even though they are problem plays, sex is never a problem. Sexual attraction may raise difficulties in the course of serenely fulfilling itself, but these come from outside; whereas Freud demonstrated the sexual origin of a mass of obscurely related ailments. Shaw assumes that, whatever else may go wrong, in sexual relations all will be well, and a great depth of well-being is implied in the amiable relations between men and women in his plays.

Even the presence of subjects ordinarily treated as problems seems to pass unnoticed by author and audience. Shaw claims that his plays are full of '. . . all sorts of terrestrial things except adultery . . . and when the question of passion between the two sexes arises, it is the real thing, not the convention which holds its stead on your modest boulevards'. But if the relations in *Candida, Heartbreak House, Overruled, The Apple Cart* and *Good King Charles* are not adultery, what are they? To call them polygamy, as Shaw does in the preface to *Overruled*, is rather skirting the issue. Augustin Hamon also claims that Shaw is like Molière in eschewing the subject of adultery: 'Ce qui distingue encore son théâtre de celui de tous ses contemporains et de celui du XIX siècle, c'est l'absence presque complète de l'adultère. Par cela encore il rappelle Molière. . . .' Another critic, Mina Moore, also calls the sexual relations in the plays a violent reaction against the false idea of the theater in France that love is the only subject-matter and adultery an inexhaustible mine of dramatic situations. Shaw's way of treating adultery does foster an illusion that this is by no means the same subject we are accustomed to meet as a profound event on stage and a casual routine in city and suburb; and, in effect, it is not the same subject. Adultery for Shaw is a social problem, not a sexual problem, and he assumes that institutions must be adapted to serve instinctual demands.

Overruled, playing upon all the emotional disadvantages of monogamy, and ignoring marriage as an institution, argues for adultery on the ground that it constitutes a *de facto* revision of the marriage laws.

In *Heartbreak House*, Shaw's study of the clever rich, adultery is the chief sport and interest, replacing the stables which Lady Utterword so regrets. He does not condemn this sport, in part because it is only a symptom, but in part because he seems to find it one of the pleasanter perquisites of an idle class. The exception is Randall (the Rotter), a Tristan made ridiculous by an uncooperative Isolde. Shaw had pictured this kind of relationship, one illegitimately descended from the idea of courtly love, in *Candida* and again in *Man and Superman*, but it is only here that we see its unpleasant implication realized. Ann, who playfully tempts Octavius to become '. . . a sentimental old bachelor for my sake', and Candida, who might enjoy that power immensely but has a less pliable poet for her lover, keep the relationship pleasant because of their own sensible personalities. In the cynical keeping of Lady Utterword, the relationship shows its full potential of unpleasantness. But in Randall, as in more fortunate adulterers, irresponsible love affairs are only a symptom of a more crucial irresponsibility.

In the later plays, especially in *The Apple Cart* and *Good King Charles*, adultery is condoned not only by the all-seeing author, but even by the injured wife. In the design for living of these two royal households, the most striking part of the pattern is the part that is absent. This, too, gives the impression that the subject is not adultery: jealousy has vanished. It vanished from Shaw's plays near the beginning of his career, after *The Philanderer*, which the author himself came to consider revolting. Shaw's comments seem to imply that it is the tangle of amorous relationships he finds objectionable, yet these relationships, a fairly accurate reflection of Shaw's own difficulties when an old mistress grew jealous of a new one, are in some ways less unpleasant than those in the later plays which Shaw never disowned. The one painful difference in *The Philanderer* is the presence of jealousy, and it is present simply because the play is realistic. Whenever Shaw created a world for the theater, he created it without jealousy. He expressed his loathing of this emotion in a review of *Little Eyolf*:

Of course the wife in her jealousy, hates the sister, hates the child, hates the book, hates her husband for making her jealous of them, and hates herself for her hatreds with the frightful logic of greedy, insatiable love.

In his utter scorn for such emotions, Shaw implies that it is jealousy that is furtive and disgraceful, not adultery. To adultery, in fact, Shaw adopts simply the old attitude of the aristocracy. King Charles, we are told, was 'the best of husbands'. His relations with his queen, like those of King Magnus with Queen Jemima in *The Apple Cart*, are a model of tenderness, appreciation and respect. These queens ignore their occasions for jealousy in a bland, absent-minded manner indicating clearly that their calm is not the result of self-control. They simply do not feel jealousy, for their love is a maternal, protective, selfless love. Whatever is good for the king is good. This is indeed a dream. Augustin Hamon speaks of the way woman's love, in Shaw, is always tinged with maternal feeling. Sensuality, he says, is mingled with the need to protect and is even, at times, almost completely eclipsed by that need. No wonder Shaw preferred the man's role of eternal baby to the woman's role of eternal mother. The wife's recompense is the reverence and tenderness expressed by King Magnus when he tells his mistress: 'Being my wife is something quite different. The smallest derogation to Jemima's dignity would hit me like the lash of a whip across the face. About yours, somehow, I do not care a rap.'

It is not only the world's great men, its rulers and its artists, for whom wives like Jennifer Dubedat of *The Doctor's Dilemma* pour out devotion without reserve. Hector Hushabye, who is a liar and a parasite besides being a philanderer, has his wife's indulgence and protection simply because of the fathomless store of good-will left behind by their receding passion. The lineaments of gratified desire show themselves this way in *Heartbreak House*:

We were frightfully in love with one another, Hector. It was such an enchanting dream that I have never been able to grudge it to you or anyone else since. I have invited all sorts of pretty women to the house on the chance of giving you another turn. But it has never come off.

If this sounds like a self-sacrificing ideal woman of the nineteenth century, the impression is corrected in a moment, when

Hesione stops caressing his arm and says, 'Now I am going off to fascinate somebody.' The idea that real love rules out jealousy is given a Shavian twist in a two-minute playlet called 'Beauty's Duty'. The beauty claims that falling in love with her has improved her husband so much that she ought to use her genius in the field to 'improve' men by the dozen. Another lady of similar genius varies the argument by saying,

Every good wife should commit a few infidelities to keep her husband in countenance. The extent to which married people strain their relations by pretending that there is only one man or woman in the world for them is so tragic that we have to laugh at it to save ourselves from crying.

In sum, the woman's word on adultery is: 'You make too much fuss about it.'

Other sexual irregularities (ruling out, as a matter of course, all forms of exploitation and abuse) perturbed Shaw just as little. He was one of the few to stand by Oscar Wilde, although he said, 'I have all the normal violent repugnance to homosexuality – if it is really normal, which nowadays one is sometimes provoked to doubt.' He also defended the publication in England of Havelock Ellis' *The Psychology of Sex* in 1898, and referred to the English laws on sexual aberration as 'abominably superstitious'.

Shaw's tolerance of deviations from convention, his rhapsodies on love, his reliance on the freeing of instinct, mingled with his demand for sexual moderation and his scorn for people to whom love affairs take precedence over public affairs, do not seem to him his own inconsistency, but the inconsistency of the sex instinct. He makes a distinction which indicates that for the individual this is not so much an inconsistency as a conflict.

Sex is an exceedingly subtle and complicated instinct; and the mass of mankind neither know nor care much about freedom of conscience . . . and are concerned almost to obsession with sex. . . . In our sexual natures we are torn by an irresistible attraction and an overwhelming repugnance and disgust. We have two tyrannous physical passions: concupiscence and chastity. We become mad in pursuit of sex; we become equally mad in the persecution of that pursuit. Unless we gratify our desire the race is lost; unless we restrain it we destroy ourselves.

Love is even more complicated than sex. That elusive emotion, the Real Thing, includes not only the impersonal sex instinct, but also personal feelings in themselves extremely complicated. Late in his career Shaw simplified this bubbling cauldron by distinguishing two elements: the lower centres and the higher centres. Since we allow philosophers to separate in theory primary qualities and secondary qualities which are in fact inseparable, perhaps we may allow Shaw, who infers no moral hierarchy, to distinguish these two 'centres', even though we have no reliable way of separating or defining them, even though Shaw and the rest of the literary tradition seem to hint that it is in their inseparability that the Real Thing finally resides.

In *Too True To Be Good*, Shaw not only gives a microbe a speaking part, but gives a name and, indirectly, a voice, to a force that had previously been distilled before presentation: Aubrey, who loves below his station, in the thrilling Victorian style, explains it thus:

> Would you believe it, Mops, I was in love with this woman: madly in love with her. She was not my intellectual equal; and I had to teach her table manners. But there was an extraordinary sympathy between our lower centres. . . .

Shaw will not allow 'this woman' any of the redeeming traits which the Victorians commonly threw across the trail in such cases to confuse the scent. Sweetie is neither good nor clever, although she is not therefore to be considered bad or stupid. She is just an ordinary woman. The only interesting thing about her is her high degree of sexual vitality and the attraction which it radiates. This vitality is not, as it is in Ann Whitefield, contained within a perfect propriety and self-control. Sweetie is what would ordinarily be called promiscuous. But Shaw does not allow the use of this term in referring to a woman who merely changes men twice a week. She is a 'varietist'. In his remarkable will to give everyone the benefit of the doubt, Shaw does not ask himself at what point varietism begins to imply promiscuity, although he had much earlier hinted at the possible limits:

> If we are to judge by the utterances of some of our Moral Reform Societies, the members when they walk down Oxford Street, are so

wildly and irresistibly attracted by every woman they meet, young or old, that nothing but the severest and most stringent laws restrain them from instant rapine. I cannot imagine how any man gets himself into such a deplorable condition of mind as to believe this is true of himself, much less of any other human being . . . and they will in any case be fortunate (because I like the sensation when it comes to me) if, on the most crowded day and in the finest weather, they meet two women for whom they feel that curious physiological attraction which we all recognize as the sex attraction.

Here is the clue to some of Shaw's own contradictions. It explains why his tolerance of other people's varietism was compatible with a good bit of restraint on his own part.

His refusal to condemn Sweetie as promiscuous, however, is not made on such relative grounds. Theoretically at least, if she had changed men twice a day, Shaw might have considered her no more promiscuous than the woman who changes twice in a lifetime – as long as she keeps her self-respect.

AUBREY You had acquired an insatiable taste for commercial travellers. You could sample them at the rate of three a week. I could not help admiring such amazing mobility of the affections. I had heard operatic tenors bawling Woman Is Fickle; but it always seemed to me that what was to be dreaded in women was their implacable constancy. But you! Fickle! I should think so.

THE COUNTESS Well, the travellers were just as bad, you know.

AUBREY Just as bad! Say just as good. Fickleness means simply mobility, and mobility is a mark of civilization. You should pride yourself on it. If you dont you will lose your self-respect; and I cannot endure a woman who has no self-respect.

From first to last, Shaw made self-respect the standard of moral judgment. That made it possible for him to move without any unseemly shifting of moral gears between Mrs Warren and St Joan, between the virginal Lady Cicely, the huntress Ann Whitefield, and the susceptible Mrs George. That made it possible for the same man to abhor a woman who is the slave of her passions, who loses her self-control and in that degree her self and her humanity in the dominance of the 'lower centres', and yet to declare that, '. . . in all the life that has energy enough to be interesting to me, subjective volition, passion, will, make intellect the merest tool'. For to negate part of the self, especially to be ashamed of it, is also a lack of self-respect. He partly agrees with Sweetie when she says,

> Who are the good women? Those that enjoy being dull and like being put upon. They've no appetites. Life's thrown away on them: they get nothing out of it.

Under the infinitely shifting sands of custom, period, class and personal preference, self-respect stands like a rock, for it is equally valid in all worlds. Mrs Warren has her self-respect, and with reason. Shaw scolds Pinero for the sentimental assumption that the second Mrs Tanqueray hates herself, explaining that:

> . . . a woman of that sort is the same at three as she is at thirty-three, and . . . however she may have found by experience that her nature is in conflict with the ideals of differently constituted people, she remains perfectly valid to herself, and despises herself, if she sincerely does so at all, for the hypocrisy that the world forces on her instead of for being what she is.

The standard of self-respect is a profound one which has nothing to do with the surface question of what is and what is not shocking. Here Shaw's reticence is sometimes confusing. His reluctance to use blunt language seems sometimes to be a condemnation of the writer who does, and sometimes to be a comment on the spade he declines to call a spade. But remember that Shaw was born in 1856 into a shabby-genteel family and had grown up before he left the provinces. Hence the contrast between his restraint of manner and his intensity of revolt, which made possible the witticism: '. . . Wells was a cad who didn't pretend to be anything but a cad . . . Bennett was a cad pretending to be a gentleman . . . Shaw was a gentleman pretending to be a cad.'

Shaw was by nature a gentleman of the old school, so that when the cad became the sexual hero of modern fiction, Shaw's style began to seem a trifle old-maidish. The difficulties of living through this transition were felt by Gwen Raverat, who, without having a single good word to say for the Victorian hypocrisy which she had experienced, came to realize that it had one advantage: she found it easier to pretend to be shocked when she was not, than to pretend not to be shocked when she was. It is equally difficult to pretend to be a cad.

But modes of expression are not everything, and Shaw in his own way gives extravagant expression to the real thing in many passages. If the terms in which he does so are not vulgar, that is for reasons deeper than verbal reticence. The experience to which these passages referred, the consciousness in which they took shape, were not vulgar: why should the expression be at odds with the thing expressed? When Shaw does give vulgarity its due, as in the following speech by Sweetie, the intensity decreases in proportion:

Take this tip from me; one man at a time. I am advising you for your good, because youre only a beginner; and what you think is love, and interest, and all that is not real love at all: three quarters of it is only unsatisfied curiosity. Ive lived at that address myself; and I know. When I love a man now it's all love and nothing else. It's the real thing while it lasts. I havent the least curiosity about my lovely sergeant: I know just what he'll say and what he'll do. I just want him to do it.

The lady, revolted, declares that she cannot bear this talk, but she makes an effort which might be Shaw's own effort to accept the writers of the twenties and thirties:

No doubt its perfectly true. It's quite right that you should say it frankly and plainly. I envy and admire the frightful coolness with which you plump it all out. Perhaps I shall get used to it in time. But at present it knocks me to pieces.

Compare this with the elevated tone of Mrs George acting as medium for the spirit of Woman:

When you loved me I gave you the whole sun and stars to play with. I gave you eternity in a single moment, strength of the mountains in one clasp of your arms, and the volume of all the seas in one impulse of your soul. A moment only; but was it not enough? Were you not paid then for all the rest of your struggle on earth? When I opened the gates of paradise, were you blind? Was it nothing to you? When all the stars sang in your ears and all the winds swept you into the heart of heaven, were you deaf? were you dull? was I no more to you than a bone to a dog . . . we spent eternity together . . . we possessed all the universe together . . . I have given you the greatest of all things. I gave you your own soul. . . .

Here, shorn of its comments on the institution of marriage, is Shaw's apostrophe to sexual love. It is impossible to pretend that this is the love of the 'higher centres'. It is a love that the married bishop understands and the celibate chaplain does not. Its mystical duration is '. . . a single moment. . . . A moment only. . . .' Mrs George compares it with the grace she received from the bishop when he spoke to her soul years ago from the pulpit, but says clearly that when she is the messenger of grace for men she is '. . . their prey; and there is no rest from their loving and no mercy from their loathing'. When she protests against the roles of devil, saint and pythoness which men put upon her, she redresses the balance by reminding them: 'I am a woman: a human creature like yourselves. Will you not take me as I am?' On behalf of the human creature, Shaw again rejects the mode of society, the convention of literature, the style of love, which sets woman up as a prisoner-priestess. He need not deny or even modify the mystical raptures of sex in order to assert the androgynous nature of a large part of human life; he merely puts sex in its place. In *Village Wooing*, the courted man explains to the huntress, 'I am a woman; and you are a man, with a slight difference that doesnt matter except on special occasions.'

Shaw's androgynous beings are neither undersexed nor are they members of an intermediate sex. They are simply people, none of whom fit the stereotypes as conveniently as might be:

> You will find that the grandchildren, like all children, have the qualities conventionally ascribed to old age. The ideal old person is a child, the ideal child is forty, the ideal woman is a man, though women lie low and let that secret keep itself.

In *Village Wooing*, Shaw extricates sex from its vulgarisms and sends it again into orbit among the heavens. To Z.'s colloquial euphemisms her newly-won lover responds with a shriek of outraged reasonableness. Declaring his senses sufficiently gratified by pepper, mustard, fresh lavender, medieval buildings, Beethoven and hot-water bottles, he proclaims himself a poet, not a materialist, and points out that '. . . the bodily contacts to which you are looking forward [are] neither convenient nor decorous'. For a moment it sounds as though some of our clever contemporaries had worked over this poet's consciousness, but his gloss on this statement bursts out in directions which would seem to them utterly deplorable:

> Your secondhand gabble about gratifying my senses is only your

virgin innocence. We shall get quite away from the world of sense. We shall light up for oneanother a lamp in the holy of holies in the temple of life; and the lamp will make its veil transparent. Aimless lumps of stone blundering through space will become stars singing in their spheres. . . . An extraordinary delight and an intense love will seize us. It will last hardly longer than the lightning flash which turns the black night into infinite radiance. It will be dark again before you can clear the light out of your eyes; but you will have seen; and for ever after you will think about what you have seen and not gabble catch-words invented by the wasted virgins that walk in darkness . . . the world of the senses will vanish; and for us there will be nothing ridiculous, nothing uncomfortable, nothing unclean, nothing but pure paradise.

Here is Shaw's distillation of the Real Thing, and a letter he wrote to Frank Harris indicates that it is a distillation of his own experience. The tone is pedestrian, for Shaw was not at ease being so explicit, but he subtly teases Harris by his conclusion.

I liked sexual intercourse because of its amazing power of producing a celestial flood of emotion and exaltation of existence which, however momentary, gave me a sample of what may one day be the normal state of being for mankind in intellectual ecstasy.

One might argue, with all the world's idealists, chemists and amorists, that the distilled product, freed of the irrelevancies and imperfections of its natural state, is the real thing. One might also argue, with all the world's realists, geologists and clinicians, that the natural substance, fresh, salt or brackish, frozen or volatile, polluted by sewage, chemicals and fall-out, is the real thing, and the distilled product artificial and unreal. Shaw uses the phrase, the Real Thing, in its colloquial sense, meaning love in its purest and most concentrated form. He does not assert that it is common or enduring. It is the real thing while it lasts, as Sweetie says.

Traces of this Real Thing are to be found in two kinds of love between men and women which do not reach the height of stones singing in space. In these two kinds of love the sexual element becomes at once unproductive and undestructive; it is transmuted by the social atmosphere into a civilized, not a primordial force. The primordial force, the 'something stronger than either of us', is not in control here. It is either past, as in the established marriages, or potential, as in the flirtations which furnish a kind of esperanto for male and female strangers. Considering the extremely old-fashioned nature of both these relationships, Shaw must have feared for the affectual bonds between men and women in the brave new world. Both the seasoned marriage of companionship, consideration and respect, and the use of flirtation as a provisional kind of rapprochement between the sexes, have been falling into disuse in the ideal culture even more than in the real culture. The ideal culture only *seems* to be following Shaw's teaching of greater tolerance in sexual matters and greater freedom for women. In fact, Shaw wanted to remove from the sexual imagination its stodginess, its prudery and its brutality, all in one transformation. The popular impression, on the other hand, was that prudery was the only difficulty. Shaw's theoretical separation of the personal and sentimental element in sex from the physical and unreasoning element was not adopted and could not be adopted in a political atmosphere that required every practical change to be bought with an ideal concession. Instead of separating personal from impersonal, the idealist's excuse for the new forms of sexual morality became an even closer connection between the two. The new rationale of divorce cast upon marriage an even greater obligation of continued passionate love. The new tolerance of love affairs armed itself against criticism by asserting that a squalid intrigue was quite different from a glorious affair, because in a glorious affair the personal and sentimental feelings came first and remained as the protective coloring of the whole dishonest procedure.

It should surprise no one that Shaw, whose personal life was circumspect, was able to accept the entirely physical nature of some attractions, whereas H. G. Wells, for example, whose personal life was indiscreet, insisted on making moral distinctions among illicit affairs according to their personal and sentimental nature. In *Ann Veronica*, when the heroine declares herself to the man of her choice, he resists for reasons quite different from Jack Tanner's. He mentions as disadvantages the existence of his frigid but otherwise blameless wife, the danger of ruining his career, the danger of discrediting his scientific work; but the great drawback in his own estimation is his own amoristic unworthiness, proved by his affair with another man's wife, an affair based on physical attraction only. This appalling sentimental secret heightens the affirmation of the new love affair. The new affair, being a 'glorious affair', is good for the self-esteem, and leads to an ecstatic holiday in the Alps, later to marriage, overwhelming success as a playwright, exquisite furnishings, and the utter capitulation of Veronica's cast-iron father. What makes the difference? Love. We see by its excesses that this is a fairy tale, but it is not oracular enough. Its moral is: young ladies, elope! You will grow rich, famous and respectable watching your friends and relatives eat crow. On the other hand Shaw, in his loudest avuncular voice, warns young ladies never on any account to compromise themselves.

When D. H. Lawrence later treats the same situation without any of the euphemism and optimism which now cause Wells' novel to seem so girlish, his lovers also decide to elope. The difference is, first, that neither one expects any return from society except trouble, and, second, that the feelings which make them willing to undertake these troubles are so largely and unashamedly sexual feelings, no matter how much they may symbolize or reflect the vitality that opposes the factory system and the cash nexus.

Although Lawrence's affirmations may have affected popular notions of sexual freedom, it is the more superficial and more sentimental perceptions of writers like Wells that have affected popular ideas about marriage. That is the result of the changing class patterns of the last century, above all the conversion of the Western world to the love match. The result has been that, instead of separating the passional and the domestic aspects of marriage increasingly, as Shaw recommended, the patterns of social change, which sometimes seem to roll backward like the wheels in a badly timed film, have tied these two aspects of marriage more tightly than ever and imply that their first moment after noon is night.

Shaw's idea of domestic marriage contains more kindness and more realism. Its stability is greater because it is not founded on passionate love alone; and yet it is neither loveless nor sexless. If its love has a strong maternal element as we have seen, it has also something else which exists only between husbands and wives and has no name at all, so that Mrs George has to explain it by a willingness to fry her lover with onions for George's breakfast. Whatever this peculiar bond may be, it is certainly unique and therefore need not be threatened by any other attachment, spiritual or sensual. But to call any love sexless which does not include copulation, is a piece of dreary Neanderthal reasoning. Shaw's chaste marriages, chaste adulteries, chaste engagements, also his religious conversions, dentistry, speech lessons and political arguments are, although not reeking, quite decidedly flavored with sex. The sex may be residual, as in the marriages, or potential, as in the flirtations. In either case, the women are always well aware of being women, and the men are always aware of them as women. They talk to each other in a special way. Their oppositions are lyrical.

This atmosphere of flirtation is not a mere parlor game, although it serves that purpose admirably. It is a *modus vivendi*. Whether it belongs to Shaw or to a period or whether it still goes on in a changed way, is impossible to say of anything so ephemeral as this atmosphere. Virginia Woolf thought it was the period before the First World War that produced, '. . . a sort of humming noise, not articulate, but musical, exciting, which changed the value of the words themselves'. After the war she felt that this musical interchange between men and women had gone. This very change of tone can be heard in Shaw's late plays: after St Joan, the women's speech is no longer a recitative flowering into occasional arias; it is prose, flat-tongued and documentary.

Yes: you are like the great European Powers: you never fight except in self-defense. But you are two stone heavier than I; and I cannot keep my head at infighting as you can. You do not suit. . . . Mr Sagamore: arrange the divorce. Cruelty and adultery.

Shaw himself never ceased to hum the tune, as women who met him in his old age testify. He called himself a male flirt, and in this sense, this delicate amorous undertone to all speech, he certainly qualified. We have no reliable record of such conversations, although anecdote breeds where Shaw and women are concerned. Instead we have hundreds of delectable letters to women, in which the tone of flirtation hardly ever breaks, even for business, even for reprimand. His letters to men are a contrast – sensible, Shavian, informative prose. All the playfulness, all the fireworks of wit and buffoonery, all the homages, all the gold-hatted, high-bouncing letters go to women.

From the vantage point of the years after the war, the years when Virginia Woolf felt the lack of something at luncheon parties, Shaw deplored his own early gallantry as a part of the old slave-relations between men and women. The courteous man's pretense that he was every lady's slave and, as far as it was proper, smitten with her charms, was the civilized gloss of some otherwise uncomfortable facts. Its relation to the idea that woman is primarily valuable as a sex-object is quite plain. It imports the style of a potential love affair into meetings in which the very notion is otherwise ludicrous. And yet it serves to grease the wheels and to reduce friction in a confrontation of which no one quite realized, as long as the pretense went on, the potential awkwardness. The new woman, if only to show she could be a gentleman, made it a point of honor not to take advantage of her sex. No doubt the determination not to flirt has made her seem rather cross at times and unduly self-conscious. While this limitation of sex in ordinary friendly contacts was taking place, the sex in amorous approaches was becoming more direct and instantaneous. This meant that the milder and more intense forms of flirtation were dwindling simultaneously. But in all Shaw's major plays before 1930, the music of flirtation and sentiment between men and women goes on without pausing, and only occasionally grows tiresome. There is no need to concur in Shaw's self-condemnation and put him down as a renegade romantic with the image of a pure angel-woman painted in his heart. Something of the kind was there, something in Woman which he went on reverencing and wooing all his life. But as it did not lead him to say, 'Why do you want the vote, my dear, when you have something so much better?' or to worship at the altar by seducing impressionable girls, we are not bound to condemn him for his susceptibility. By some simple magic, he was able to give woman due credit as a human creature very like himself and at the same time to make her a free gift of his charming estimate of her charm.

Women and the World

CHAPTER 7

Bread and Circuses: The Career Woman

1 THE ECONOMIC WOMAN

THE Shavian career woman is many things nested in one, like a Russian wooden doll. Each of these stout painted women contains her smaller twin. Thus the career woman depicted by Shaw is an image of the great hidden potential of Woman, who is pregnant of something more than infant posterity: her grown-up self. This Shavian career woman is a criticism of society, is an embodiment of the divine spark, is a Bernard Shaw, is a dominant protective mother, is a vestal virgin to whom sex is given for safekeeping. These are not contradictions nor even consonant differences; they are the same substance again and again like the layers of an onion. Nevertheless one can and must separate these layers, especially as debates on the subject of careers for women lose so much clarity when they muddle together the quite different issues raised by two different motives.

Women go to work for two unrelated reasons: to earn and to achieve. Most arguments on the subject muddle the two together, although each has its own sphere, its own justifications and its own opponents. Most women, like most men, work for a combination of these two reasons, but the women who work to earn their bread are always a potential menace to male superiority, and those who work to achieve have found, like most athletes, that high achievement and professionalism are almost indistinguishable.

In the realm of theory, however, a distinction can and should be made, especially in reading Shaw. In the collected works of a socialist, one of the earliest defenders of the New Woman, one might expect to read problem plays dealing with the suffrage and with unfair hiring practices. One might expect to meet some of the helpless victims of injustice and a great many women like Vivie Warren – women who, although they need not all smoke cigars and reject lovers, would exchange the fripperies of femininity for the armor of feminism. Instead, we see on the stage in almost all of Shaw's plays a leading lady who is feminine to the tips of her feather-boa, whose sexual attraction is irresistible, whose occupation is captivating men, whose talent is for managing people, whose method is coquetry, whose power is moral realism, whose greatest conquest is the playwright who created her. She is Woman incarnate.

The reason is simple. Shaw is not avoiding the implications of his own ideas. He is merely separating the bread from the circuses. He never denies the importance of the bread-winning job for the sake of the bread itself, for the sake of liberating the women enslaved by their husbands and fathers, for the sake of the self-respect involved in doing useful work, work that is recognized as useful by the universal badge of cash payment. Shaw fought the cash nexus by joining it. He knew that no medieval monastery ever built could withstand the blast of modern commercial power. His crass uncompromising socialism is an attempt, like Wright's Imperial Hotel, to move with the power that moves the earth and so survive. That is the lesson of *Major Barbara*.

Shaw dealt once, notably, with the dilemma of the economic woman, in *Mrs Warren's Profession*. His fearful realism about money and his fearful realism about sex combined to put this play beyond the pale. Shaw's assertion that the play is perfectly decent can be accepted only in its most profound or its most naïve application. What is really shocking in this play is its reminder of one of the world's most resolutely ignored facts: that is, the sexual exploitation of women who are *not* prostitutes, which is probably the most repugnant feature of all societies which have treated money as a privilege, whether capitalist or pre-capitalist. Shaw's socialism, or any other plan to distribute the goods of a society reasonably, would end a state of affairs which respectable conservatives simply refuse to consider: like the babies in 'A Modest Proposal', girls in any society which refuses them work at a living wage have only one capital asset.

After Mrs Warren, Shaw does not deal with the economic woman dramatically. In the *Intelligent Woman's Guide* Shaw analyzes thoroughly the way the wages of the subsidized woman (partly supported by her husband or father) beat down below subsistence level the wages of all women in a *laissez-faire* economy. But characteristically, the woman question is, for Shaw, only part of a larger question. Equality, for Shaw, means equality of income, and in his analysis, the existence of a 'woman's wage' is as great a menace to the man's bargaining position as to the woman's. But because of his belief that socialism would automatically solve the bread-winning difficulties of all women, Shaw's dramatic treatment of this aspect of woman's work is conceived very much in the spirit of a character from William Morris's *News from Nowhere*:

'Well,' said he, 'of course you will see that all that is a dead controversy now. The men have no longer any opportunity of tyrannizing over the women, or the women the men – both of these things took place in those old times. The women do what they can do best, and what they like best, and the men are neither jealous of it nor influenced by it. This is such a commonplace that I am almost ashamed to state it.'

Shaw is not so naive as to suppose that such a utopian state can be reached without a struggle, but the struggle is not complicated enough for him to find it dramatically interesting. It is the kind of external, two-sided conflict that has given the problem play its bad name. To the simple-minded playwright every conflict may be a problem, but to Shaw not every social problem is a dramatic problem. Two points of view make a debate, not a play. The conflicts that interest Shaw are those in which a variety of subjects play upon each other, particularly those in which the subject is so complicated that each of the human wills involved is in some degree divided against itself. This is the state of affairs 'when it is complicated by the genius being a woman . . . .' In woman's work the instance that interests Shaw is the one in which, whether or not the woman is a genius, the career is a calling. Shaw's career women work for a purpose larger than the self, just as his huntresses pursue fathers for their children, while the huntresses of other authors pursue husbands for themselves.

In this, as in so many of his ideas about women, Shaw is consistent with his views in other fields. The notion, endemic in our letters columns, that women have a right to some work with more egotism to it than housekeeping, is among the unwritten apocrypha of our Constitution. It is a part of the pursuit-of-happiness plant which, in its vagueness, sends forth such a muddle of unpruned conflicting branches. To separate the strands tangled in the idea of happiness we have to turn back to Shaw's conception of the self.

First, an assertion so obvious, intangible and basic that it bears repeating: Shaw grants to woman as the first of all her rights, the right to a self as absolute as a man's. But Shaw's conception of the self, as we have seen, does not lead to the simpler forms of selfishness. He opposes for men as well as women a life dedicated to the pursuit of personal happiness. Arguing craftily from the example of the idle rich, he demonstrates that happiness is to be achieved only in the effort to achieve something else. Arguments about happiness travel in the same interminable circles as arguments about altruism, or the old evasion, 'enlightened self-interest'. We need not quarrel with Shaw over every contradiction in terms. His attitude towards abstractions was cavalier, of course, but only because he preferred to meet the demands of the particular and concrete first. In this instance Shaw has used 'happiness' to refer to the unconsidered, selfish idea of happiness which treats the maximum of food, drink, fornication and idleness as the optimum. 'Selfishness' he has used, where it suits his purpose, in just the opposite way: to refer to the best expression of the self, to exclude undisciplined greed in favor of self-esteem, self-assertion and the kind of purposeful self-discipline which justifies them. With his usual explanatory passion, Shaw helps us to the meaning of his term. Misunderstanding is inevitable only when some commentator wrenches a few witty words from their context, forgetting that in Shaw even the joys of aphorism pale beside the joys of argument.

Careers for women, then, as Shaw considered them, could be considered selfish only in the most exalted sense. His interpretation, if women could live up to it, might even now clear the air of some of the masculine uneasiness about female intrusion into the working world. About one cause of this uneasiness the male is inarticulate because abashed. He knows intuitively, although he would argue against it rationally, that (apart from the brutal conditions of deep poverty) 'working' is self-indulgent compared to keeping house and rearing children. About another aspect of his uneasiness, the male is highly articulate. He feels (and in this instance knows he feels) that the working woman is indulging in an unpleasant competitiveness simply by entering and taking part in his world. The vulnerability implied in this complaint is quite pathetic, especially in the extreme form that claims man is castrated by the successful competition of women. Are women really tougher competition than other men? If so, what conclusion follows?

Shaw's approach to the working woman avoids all this by treating the social rather than the individual issue. It was, of course, easier for Shaw to be Olympian than for most men. He was invincibly attractive to women and so sure of the value of his own work that he could receive female bullying as the form of flirtation it so often is. Nevertheless, his approach is more a result of method than a result of personality. Like his pleas for socialism, for capital punishment ('extermination') and for educational reform, his support of the working woman is based on the good of the whole society. If we sense behind these proposals a heart that bleeds for poor people in the workhouse, for men in prison, for children in school and for women at home, it is only by peering through tiny chinks in the barricade of unsentimentality Shaw has built up around himself.

2 CARDINALS ON STAGE: A PORTRAIT OF THE ACTRESS

The real drama, in brief, is that of the woman whose interest goes beyond the right to work and embraces the work itself. When Shaw began to write in the eighties there were only two careers in which women could be found in sufficient numbers to have established a pattern: writing, a detestable career to dramatize, in which the woman sits at home, ink-stained, and neglects the family she cannot ignore; and acting, a career full of motion and daring and glitter. As Shaw says, 'If the Examiner were to refuse to license plays with female characters in them, he would only be doing to the stage what our tribal customs already do to the pulpit and the bar.' But the Examiner had not done so and real women were taking the parts of imaginary women on stage. It is no wonder Shaw so frequently chose to write about actresses, including the musical performer, the acrobat and the evangelist. As John Stuart Mill had pointed out:

Women artists are all amateurs. The only field in which they are generally professionals is the histrionic, and in that they are confessedly equal, if not superior, to men.

In addition to this ready-made evidence of the abilities of women, Shaw needed the technical assistance of a milieu in which social classes mingled, and the artistic world provided that. Furthermore, Shaw's interest is in the working woman who is a successful and dominating person, not a drudge. Harris reports:

> Indeed, he remarks somewhere that those women who, if they were men, would have been cardinals, king's counsellors or ambassadors, go on the stage instead where they are more highly paid than men and enjoy an undisputed equality of opportunity and esteem with them. He sees, except for rare instances, that the male actor is at the bottom of the professions open to men, whereas the leading lady is at the top of those open to women.

Shaw had personal reasons also for attempting the portrait of the actress. He was stage-struck and very soon stage-centered. The scathing of his dramatic criticism is largely the fury of a disappointed lover. I emphasize the love rather than the experience because Shaw's first portrait of an actress was written before he was intimate with any actress or professionally involved in the theatrical world. It is difficult, in fact, to say whether his various love affairs with actresses, his experience as a dramatic critic, even his intimate place on the rehearsal stage as a strong-minded and practical playwright, had any effect at all on his depiction of the career woman. Shaw was one of those who learn by knowing.

The novels in which so many of the portraits of actresses appear were written in the 1880's. At that period Shaw was in love with the excessively proper Miss Alice Lockett, a hospital nurse. Nor were any of his other love affairs in this period connected with the stage. The only close personal connection on which Shaw could then base the portrait of the female artist was his sister Lucy, who sang with moderate success and bore a striking resemblance to Ellen Terry. Lucy must have been, with variations, a model for Susanna Conolly of *The Irrational Knot*, as Shaw himself was a model for her brother Ned. But the great actresses with whom he was for so long on intimate terms, came into his life later.

Perhaps the explanation of Shaw's seeming to learn by knowing is partly that his own apprenticeship in writing had taught him much about the process of becoming a professional. Another explanation may be that he knew women as well as he knew men and perhaps, being a flirt, a little better. Of course he fully understood only the intelligent women, but that is natural for an intelligent man. With his sense of art and his sense of intelligent androgynous personality, he was well equipped to portray in advance the women he would later meet and fall in love with, and this he did in Madge Brailsford and Aurélie Szczymplica of *Love Among the Artists*, Mrs Byron of *Cashel Byron's Profession*, and Lalage Virtue (Susanna Conolly) of *The Irrational Knot*.

The result is that in Shaw's imaginative works, the rational, egalitarian subject of women's rights is dressed, not in tailor-made tweeds and sensible shoes, but in the languishing dramatic garments of the leading lady.

The actress appears only incidentally in *Cashel Byron's Profession*. She is Cashel's mother, the woman who inspired the historic cry, 'I hate my mother!' She is second only to the intellectual Lydia in calling forth Stevenson's famous comment on that book: 'I say, Archer, My God, what women!' Mrs Byron is certainly no flowing fountain of maternal love or family lore, but this is a lack for which Shaw will later value the artist woman above the womanly woman: that is, for having real interests of her own. Without these real interests she might smother her children with love and bore them with domestic brooding, like Mrs Collins in *Getting Married*. Yet in Mrs Byron there is undeniably a hint of the justified but far from bitter resentment that Shaw must have felt toward his own neglectful mother, who was too deep in the excitement of music to see that her children's food was properly cooked in the damp basement of the house on Synge Street.

Neglectful or not, Mrs Byron was outwardly Shaw's vision of the actress: graceful, lovely and commanding. Her beauty, now modified by a complexion somewhat wanting in freshness, is less interesting to him than the skill with which she manages her body and her voice, and even this, as we come to realize later, interests Shaw as much for the training and dedication it implies as for the beauty of the result.

Susanna Conolly, in *The Irrational Knot*, reveals the artist woman more fully. Although she ends melodramatically as a drunkard, Susanna shows the advantages of the actress as a Shavian heroine. Professionally she is only Lalage Virtue, a music-hall performer, and not an attempt to put the lady-like Ellen Terry into a novel. If Conolly represents Shaw, the brilliant young man who comes up from poverty with finer artistic tastes than those of the cultivated classes, Susanna represents his sister Lucy, who had, for a time, a promising career as a singer. But Shaw takes off from the genteel Lucy and her respectable songs, to create the first of his attempts at the down-to-earth woman. In portraying any woman but an actress, these effects would have been impossible. For her, respectability is optional. Because she earns her own living she can choose the honorable independence of living 'in sin' with the gentleman who loves her, even bearing an illegitimate child without any artificial horrors. All this she does, as we have seen, on principle, because she has the clear perceptions of those who see society from backstage, where all the works of illusion are exposed. She is the same sort of woman as Nell Gwyn in *Good King Charles*: generous with sex, careful with money, unaffected, unilluded and affectionate. She has one other trait which Shaw admires in the working woman: she is tough. Susanna explains her acceptance of separation from her little daughter (reminiscent of Mrs Byron's detachment from her son) by asking how she could have survived so far if she had been thin-skinned.

In her day, to be thin-skinned was a doctrinal necessity, almost a religion, for ladies. Shaw's insistence on the imperturbability of his heroines is a reaction from that folly. He knew all that weakness and sensitivity must be a sham, since these same ladies, who supposedly could not carry a parcel or endure the sight of blood without fainting, were still bearing children in the immemorial way. Furthermore, the sham was a dangerous one. It might be useful to the individual woman at times, but for women as a group it had the double disadvantage of feeding the fires of male superiority and of crippling female self-confidence. Therefore the grit of the working woman was an essential part of the New Woman as Shaw imagined and observed her. The dumb endurance of the poverty-stricken factory drudge can never produce this kind of grit. The quality above all that distinguishes any Shavian protagonist is will.* It is the one thread that ties all his successful characters together – the great and

* '. . . in all the life that has energy enough to be interesting to me, subjective volition, passion, will, make intellect the merest tool'.

the small, the just and the unjust, the male and the female, new-fangled and old-fashioned, sweet and sour. To labor out of necessity may harden the soul but cannot strengthen it. To choose to live by one's wits, especially by that strange wit (country of origin unknown) which art in any form requires, both strengthens the soul and implies a certain strength already within it.

Susanna learns this suppleness of will in the hard work of studying her parts, in the self-discipline of improving techniques and meeting competition, and in rebounding from all the hard knocks which, at the rough edges of society, draw blood. The lady amateur cannot compete with this kind of woman. When Conolly first accompanies his future wife and learns that she cannot tell what key she requires, and '. . . can sing A sometimes – only when I am alone', he learns some of this:

Conolly sat down, knowing now that Miss Lind was a commonplace amateur. He had been contrasting her with his sister, greatly to the disparagement of his home life; and he was disappointed to find the lady break down where the actress would have succeeded so well. Consoling himself with the reflection that if Miss Lind could not rap out a B flat like Susanna, neither could she rap out an oath, he played the accompaniment much better than Marian sang the song.

Far from being thin-skinned, the Shavian heroine has the hide of a rhinoceros. Lady Cicely remains as placid under gunfire as at the tea table. Major Barbara confronts an enraged hoodlum with unfeigned calm. Saint Joan comes back at a military man who tries to warn her of the horrors of battle, 'You must not be afraid, Robert'. Every one of these pieces of intrepidity is part comedy, part polemics, part simple fact. Shaw has in mind exceptional women like Florence Nightingale and Beatrice Webb and Octavia Hill and the Pankhursts, but he also had in mind all the ordinary women who willingly faced childbirth before either anaesthesia or the statistics on maternal death rates could offer them much comfort.

Other kinds of toughness, especially the toughness of standards that is called professionalism, were only potential in most women. Shaw was not so infatuated with the spectacle of Woman, the enchanting love-object, as to deny that most ladies, their minds sharpened on needlework, were perfect fools.

But he did have the fairness to point out that if men had been cut off artificially from intellectual and public interests as women were, the father-in-law would be as deplorable a figure in popular tradition as the mother-in-law. Conversely, the revolt of a single clever daughter can, according to another of Shaw's early prefaces, humanize her whole family. In *Love Among the Artists*, we see just such a daughter in revolt.

Madge Brailsford is an affectionate daughter, but she is also a new woman, obeying like a man the law of her own nature, instead of obeying like a dutiful daughter the law of her father's nature. In her we observe the toughening and refining process of stage training as it affects a young woman aspiring beyond the craft, to the art. Madge, as an apprentice, is set off against the unshakable aplomb of the complete artist, Aurélie Szczymplica. Aurélie, her Polish positiveness sharpened by competence and success, is completely credible as a dainty rhinoceros. The only weak thing about her is her husband, Adrian Herbert, a watery artist already overshadowed by his clever mother.

There is, however, in this novel, a prototype of the artist man, who redresses the balance. He is Owen Jack, a modern Beethoven, who has '. . . all the unscrupulousness and all the self-sacrifice (the two things are the same) . . .' which Shaw attributes to the man of genius. Dubedat, who poses *The Doctor's Dilemma*, is a later example of the same type. This kind of man, with his disrespect for clean collars and the individual ownership of silver spoons, fits into Leslie Fiedler's category of anti-Oedipal men who flee a motherly civilization because it seeks to suppress instinct in favor of cleanliness and respectability. Surely the arbitrary narrowing of the meaning of instinct to refer only to the forces which bind us to savagery, simplifies a real question to the point of mythical abstraction. The issue is not one between the primitivistic male, untutored child of instinct, and the civilizing female, schoolmarm to an unwilling world. Civilization – cleanliness, self-control, moral decency and all its other unachieved aspirations – cannot have arisen except in answer to other instincts, now so rigidly institutionalized that we tend to forget their human reality. Such observations as Mr Fiedler's symbolize and therefore simplify the tug of individual instinct against collective civilization. Up to a certain point this division of wills agrees with Shaw's statements about the opposition between the artist man and the mother woman. Beyond this point, the point at which we leave abstractions and come down to cases, Shaw, like life, grows more intricate.

This intricacy is of value not only in the important instance of the woman who is a genius; it is even more significant as a reminder of a general principle, that which affirms the existence of Eros in two guises and denies any theoretical need to associate one guise or the other with Thanatos. Shaw is doing justice to two valid life forces when he says that, in the man of genius, '. . . Woman meets a purpose as impersonal, as irresistible as her own. . . .'

Shaw is, moreover, more interested in what his artist accomplishes and affirms than in what he flees and denies. In this respect, Owen Jack and Aurélie Szczymplica are alike: their unconventionality is no mere fancy-dress costume; it is a working garb. The similarity of artist man and artist woman proves that sublime assurance does not belong only to Woman and that it therefore need not derive from some mystical value in being Woman.

The first important career woman in the plays is Major Barbara, whose kinship with the actress is less in the public performance she gives as a Salvation Army lass than it is in her personality and purpose. She, like all the career women who take Shaw's interest, need not work to earn her bread, but does so to spend her ideas, her daring and the energy bounding in her veins. Like Florence Nightingale she finds the boredom and stagnation of the drawing-room more terrible than the battle-fields of the Crimea.

Shaw created the counterpart of Aurélie a quarter of a century later in *Misalliance*. Lina Szczepanowska is an acrobat who has more in common with Aurélie than just a name which Englishmen pride themselves on being unable to pronounce. She too is modelled to some extent on Marie Bashkirtseff, but Shaw makes one subtle adaptation. By making his characters Polish instead of Russian, he invokes the spirit of Chopin and Mickiewicz, of art and the spirit of romantic revolutionary nationalism, and also an incisiveness, a medieval European iron which is not believed to characterize the Russian ambience. Lina, the later creation, has all these qualities to an even greater degree than her predecessor. Her career as an acrobat calls even more sharply for discipline, for self-making, for rising above the mere woman, than do even the demands of fine art.

3 CAREER WOMEN IN LOVE

There is a paradox about the commanding Lina which illuminates the contrast between male and female ideals. Shaw combines in her two legendary masculine traits which he had ridiculed in *Arms and the Man*: coolness in the face of physical danger, and fealty to abstract honor. The androgynous point of view proves its value here. This heady mixture, which causes men to make, from a modern point of view, such fools of themselves, provides just the piquancy needed in the bland context of the womanly woman. Any *man* in a Shaw play strutting about and saying, 'You cant cover me with that pistol. Try,' would be an inflated fool, remnant of a dead era. A woman doing the same thing is not just a novelty, but a realignment of moral forces. For Shaw is doing more than freshening old values by transposing them into a new gender. We know we are faced with a completely new synthesis when the woman also *admits* that she knows all the men want to make love to her, when, like a cad, she talks about it and does so without any pretense of dismay. Like Marie Bashkirtseff, but also like Yum-Yum in *The Mikado*, she does not deny her majesty. The Slavic scenery should not blind us to the general application of this point, any more than the japanned ware of W. S. Gilbert does. Professional acrobatics should not deceive us either, whether they involve the trapeze or the calculus.

Yum-Yum is only a little maid from school, not a great artist or a financial genius or a saint who hears voices. Yet she mocks the sham of the womanly woman:

> He don't exclaim
> 'I blush for shame,
> So kindly be indulgent.'
> But, fierce and bold,
> In fiery gold,
> He glories all effulgent!
> I mean to rule the earth
> As he the sky –
> We really know our worth,
> The sun and I!

Bread and Circuses: The Career Woman

The Mikado dates from the year 1885, from Shaw's novel-writing period. Both writers are dealing with what was unmistakably a reality of the period. It would be strange if Gilbert's perpetual social comment had ceased for this one aria. Instead we have in Yum-Yum a marionette little version of Ann Whitefield. 'Art and nature, thus allied / Go to make a pretty bride.' All the arch and adroit young ladies of Gilbert's libretti, who are as essential to the Gilbertian scene as the blathering major-generals and lord chancellors, are semi-Shavian women. Gilbert, as always, curbs his criticism before it cuts to the bone, but what he observed was certainly the same spectacle: shrewd realists and contrivers blushing and fluttering to order. The firm young ladies in Wilde's plays also give the lie to the sentimental convention of the Victorian heroine. All this reveals something about the confident Lina, the knightly circus-performer, the desirable female, the placid domineeress.

If professionalism, with all that it implies of discipline, accomplishment and range, were the source of the Shavian career woman's poise and calm, would we encounter the same kind of assurance in that merest confection of a creature, Yum-Yum? Dare we overlook the fact that all Shaw's career women are as successful in the lists of love as they are on the flying trapeze? The exception is obviously Saint Joan, but it is just as obvious that for once the rule *can* be tested by its exception. Unlike any other Shavian heroine, Saint Joan is not in the arena, not wholly of this world. The ordinary working woman is best represented by Vivie Warren, who turns her back on men and love affairs for reasons connected with men and love affairs. Her work is a result, not a cause. The men are not irrelevant to her life; in a negative way they shape and determine it. But Joan, to whom sexual love is irrelevant, is the only one of Shaw's geniuses, large-scale or small, who is not an outstanding success in love as well as in art, business or evangelism.

Is her poise, then, only the poise of an attractive woman who can manage the world because she can manage the men who control it? Is the assurance of the female saint and artist only the assurance of the minx? As we have seen, Shaw considered his portrait of Candida to have been weakened by her use of feminine wiles. He terms such dealings 'unprincipled'. Nevertheless, as we observe Lady Cicely in *Captain Brassbound's Con-*

version, to whose greater glory the criticism of Candida was made, we go away convinced that no man could have done what she has done – not without being knocked down. My conclusion is that Lady Cicely blatantly trades in a quite different commodity: if not sex, then surely femininity. The lady is good-looking, but she is an old maid in more than status. She has all the tricks and cranks of uncontrolled independence, and she has reached the decided years. She is served less by her winsomeness than by her weakness, although the two together are formidable. The power of weakness is one we have already seen that Shaw fully understands.

Had Shaw been less an artist, less an accurate observer of human reality, he might have cleared away all possible misunderstanding by constructing his pantheon of the successful career woman with Eros omitted. That is the penalty the masculine world in general tries to impose upon intruding females. Lysistrata, in *The Apple Cart*, is one of the few portraits Shaw ever attempted of such a woman. To accept this penalty would, however, have been untrue to Shaw's conception of the vital genius and equally untrue to his polemical intent, which is to combat the idea of the formidable woman as a 'sexless virago' by putting in her place the complete woman, in whom all qualities are at the optimum. He scorns the choice given to Fanny by the complacent Trotter, who says, in *Fanny's First Play*:

And now let me warn you. If youre going to be a charming healthy young English girl, you may coax me. If youre going to be an unsexed Cambridge Fabian virago, I'll treat you as my intellectual equal, as I would a man.

Trotter considers being treated as an intellectual equal, which is exactly what Fanny would like, to be a punishment. Shaw knows that being treated as an intellectual equal does not exclude being treated as a woman. He ridicules the assumption, less common now than it was in the nineties, but far from extinct, that a woman active in public life is made of some peculiar stuff.

[Pinero] has fallen into the common error of supposing that the woman who speaks in public and takes an interest in wider concerns than her own household is a special variety of the human species

. . . and that there is something dramatic in her discovery that she has the common passions of humanity.

Shaw's successful career women make this point by being invincibly attractive to men in spite of being obtrusively bossy creatures. The source of female success is clear enough in any case, and by being real instead of simple it gains the advantage of teaching two inextricable facts together.

We have only to ask ourselves whether these career women succeed *because* they are attractive to men. Does Lina become a first-rate performer because all the men want to make love to her, or do all the men want to make love to her because she has the vitality which has made that first-rate performance possible? Does the millionairess make her fortune with the help of the Egyptian doctor she has captivated, or does she overcome his resistance to her wooing by the sheer surplus of her own will to succeed? Obviously, Shaw's career women do not need the help of men in their careers, and they are always represented as bosses, not subordinates. All along the scale – madam, artist, saint – the career woman is an entrepreneuse and an equal. Again, Shaw is making, not the minimum, but the maximum claim for women. In defending his portrayal of Mrs Warren, he says:

These critics must know, too, from history if not from experience, that women as unscrupulous as Mrs Warren have distinguished themselves as administrators and rulers, both commercially and politically.

The woman who works as a secretary, as a research assistant, as a dietitian, holds no interest for Shaw, partly because, like her male equivalent, she lacks dramatic power, but even more because she represents a new kind of female subjection. The career woman in Shaw's plays may be Queen of Egypt, Empress of Russia, Powermistress General (a significant post), Salvation Army major, saint or boss.* The preface on bosses belongs to a play in which the boss is a female – and what a female! Epifania Ognisanti di Parerga (*The Millionairess*) is a woman overpowering enough to call forth the same sort of horror from twentieth-century man as Lydia Carew drew from R. L. S. But neither

* In *Caesar and Cleopatra*, *Great Catherine*, *The Apple Cart*, *Major Barbara*, *Saint Joan*, *The Millionairess*, respectively.

her ruthlessness nor her domineering dismays our author or the men he allows to drop into her jaws like paralyzed birds. In other words, while most were humbly urging women's right to work humbly, Shaw was urging women's right to succeed and to be loved for eminence instead of for insignificance.

4 IS WOMAN HOUYHNHNM?

The saving woman was a familiar literary figure who vanished from the scene during Shaw's lifetime. He himself was one of the strongest of the forces that brought her era to an end. Something remained, however: a margin of meaning to which Shaw attached a new interpretation. In the old tradition, the saving woman was characterized, unintentionally, as a prig. She was artificially constructed without selfishness, without animal instincts, without the weaknesses of common humanity. Shaw, in asserting the strength of these weaknesses, seemed at first to be offering only disenchantment with 'the female Yahoo', a mistake which many intelligent women have managed to maintain over half a century of headlong change.

From Pamela to Esther Summerson the chief quality of the sentimental heroine was artificiality. The male novelist of this period may write 'character' parts that show he has actually seen real women, but the leading lady is *all* leading lady, as in the theater; she is always the same creature of fashionable dress, fashionable coiffure, fashionable accent, fashionable grimace. She is not supposed to act: she is supposed to embody an ideal. The leading lady is supposed to embody West End fashion or Broadway fads. The heroine of the Victorian novel was supposed to embody something considerably more valuable and hence more dangerous: the virtues which real women could only approximate. In other words, she was a paragon. On stage she was the kind of paragon of convention that Shaw was deprecating when he advised Ellen Terry to 'cut the paragon out' of the part of Imogen and 'leave the woman in'. And yet, in his intense reaction against all that was implied in the paragon, Shaw did not become a part of the movement (which extends in growing vacuity from Strindberg to Philip Wylie and Tennessee Williams) to attribute man's ills to the destroying woman. On the contrary, as he goes about, decade by decade, removing more and more of the Victorian surface from his heroines, the conviction oddly emerges that Shaw does believe in the saving woman. This conviction may even be, in some ways, stronger than the purely conventional one it has replaced. This need not, on reflection, astonish us. The danger of the destroying woman did not begin with emancipation. She seems to be equally menacing to man whether she is that epitome of the old regime, the repressive mother, or the voracious consumer of sexuality who is so absurdly hailed as a new invention. In the same way Shaw's belief in the saving woman survives the apparently profound change from Lady Cicely's exquisite spinsterhood to the promiscuity of the cheerful vulgarian called Sweetie. It is Sweetie's play, *Too True To Be Good*, that ends with Shaw's strongest statement on the saving woman:

The author, though himself a professional talk maker, does not believe that the world can be saved by talk alone. He has given the rascal the last word; but his own favorite is the woman of action, who begins by knocking the wind out of the rascal, and ends with a cheerful conviction that the lost dogs always find their way home. So they will, perhaps, if the women go out and look for them.

The progression of saving women in the plays is an interesting one. It might be said that Shaw deliberately removed one after another of the elements which were not essential to the saving quality, in order to isolate just that one element which saves. The process begins with *Candida*. To her husband, she is the wife who remains behind the scenes, making his eminence possible by her vigilance, her wit and her hypocrisy. To her lover she is a personification of ideal womanhood, a pre-Raphaelite madonna. To her author, however, she is the paragon revealed; unselfish by necessity, arrogant, domineering, dishonest and unscrupulous. To her charm, her craft and her usefulness, he quite obviously pays tribute. Yet Candida represents, in a sense, the worst of both worlds, for she acts the part of the prig-paragon without believing in it. Shakespeare's Imogen and Dickens' Esther Summerson, in so far as they are frauds, deceive themselves as intently as they do others. That, in fact, is required in order to render a prig as a heroine. Candida, however, is the very spirit of the middle-class married woman. Part of her understanding of the world is expressed by Shaw's millionairess, in the play written forty years later, when she says, 'Besides, it is convenient to be married.' In this sense Candida is the only fraudulent saving woman in Shaw's plays. She is succeeded by Lady Cicely Waynflete, who converts Captain Brassbound, saving both his soul and his skin.

In Lady Cicely the somewhat cloying apogee of the saving woman is achieved. But it is only the manner, probably imitated from his sister-in-law, Lady Cholmondeley (to whom *The Intelligent Woman's Guide to Socialism and Capitalism* is dedicated), that is cloying. No doubt this manner had its charm in the person of an actual Edwardian lady, and no doubt this charm, so dubious to the modern reader and so alien to the modern leading lady, was conveyed by Ellen Terry, for whom the part was written, although St John Ervine's comments on her performance raise some doubt about that. Still, the word cloying applies only to the outward manner, for Lady Cicely's will does not war with her deeds. According to Shaw, she is free of any suspicion of 'trading on the softness of her contours', although the reader is not quite so sure of that. She does not do so by calculation, at any rate, and perhaps that is all Shaw means. She does not, as a woman in a man's world, advance *herself* by her wiles. They are merely a part of her strategy, her use of all means at her command to advance an ethical purpose. Her work is evangelical, as surely as Major Barbara's or Saint Joan's. Yet it contains that purely Shavian element which is so unlike the old-fashioned saving woman: the boss. After Lady Cicely, the boss emerges more and more strongly in Shaw's heroines, but Lady Cicely herself establishes the fact that we are dealing not by any means with more-of-the-same-thing, but with a new departure in the old tradition. Woman could save in the nineteenth century because, in Hector Malone's phrase, her moral number was higher than a man's. Now, although Lady Cicely's moral number may be demonstrably higher than that of 'Black Paquito' or the hanging judge he so closely resembles in her eyes, Shaw does not muddle us into believing that the higher moral number is effective in itself. The effect is achieved by the shrewd maneuvers of a managing genius.

In the next of Shaw's saving women, Major Barbara, management is more essential an element than ever before. Her moral number, although quite sufficiently high, is no higher than a man's – not, at least, in any sense a modern realist would find important. She has the moral attributes of devotion, self-sacrifice, *et cetera*, which have often been dubbed 'womanly' and yet lacks a moral quality far more important in Shaw's universe. Her father, representing realism, and her fiancé, representing classical values and sublime masculine uselessness, are her teachers in this matter. They do not make their moral contribution by playing at the alleviation of poverty. They do so by understanding the way of the world and working with it in a shrewd although abstruse harmony. The quality that Barbara Undershaft possesses to the point of genius is the skill (and the special kind of energy) required for managing people.

This skill is of the greatest importance because it is part of the talent for government; and this rare and ill-defined talent was to become for Shaw increasingly a subject of argument and alarm. From the Lady to the Major, the line of the saving woman has moved far in the direction of the public personage. The nineteenth-century saving woman is called upon only to save some lucky man. The twentieth-century saving woman is called upon to save society, to save the world. In some sense Shaw seems to have hoped that Woman, this eternal mother of baby-men, this finder of lost dogs wandering without orbit in a fearsome universe, this bitch-goddess who must surely know (if only because man so obviously does not) a way home among the senseless stones that move in space, might at last save the human race. This, however, he did not look for in women's adoption of men's methods: leagues, associations, committees and all the other manifestations of how-not-to-do-it. He looked for salvation, with a mixture of seriousness and playfulness, to something that might be called a modern spiritual method.

Major Barbara, when we first meet her, is still saving individual souls by the old handicraft methods of the nineteenth century, but she has taken a huge step ahead in that she is not saving souls which stand in a personal relation to herself, but souls in large numbers, through an organization, souls from whom she herself has nothing to gain. She moves from the nineteenth to the twentieth century at the moment when she realizes that souls cannot be properly saved by piece-work or by charity, but only by the one benefit that can be mass-produced: that of living in a well-run society. This play, in the crisis of its leading character, in her being forced to recognize that good will and good works are not enough for a heroine, but must be guided by a realistic understanding of the world as it is, is a forerunner of Shaw's late plays on the difficulties of statesmen, *The Apple Cart* and *On the Rocks*.

Lina Szczepanowska in *Misalliance* is such a saving woman. She is not in the direct line – Lady to Major to Saint – in the sense of being a public personage. All her saving is done in one idle-rich household, a foretaste of Heartbreak House. Yet Lina is real. No one can say of her, as Ellie Dunn says of the mistress of Heartbreak House: '... there is nothing really strong and true about Hesione but her beautiful black hair . . .'. Lina's grip on reality comes of facing death and responsibility together: 'On the flying trapeze there is often another woman; and her life is in your hands every night and your life in hers.' When this pretty piece of dialogue sends Tarleton, the underwear king, into sobs, Lina reveals the spiritual meaning of muscle-work: 'Come. You need a few exercises. I'll teach you how to stop crying.' This 'man-woman or woman-man whatever you call her' is unmistakably sent down from the skies (a *dea ex machina* whose airplane crashes into the greenhouse) as a spiritual leader to the lost tribe of the underwear manufacturer. Risking her life once a day as a point of honor, praying to remind herself that she has a soul, shunning marriage as a degrading slavery (although accepting as reasonable the proposition that, '. . . all ambassadors make love and are very nice and useful to people who travel'), Lina shows the strength and unconventionality which in another vocation might qualify her for sainthood.

Saint Joan is the ultimate saving woman in the line of the public personage. There is another line of development, the line in which Woman removes more and more of her 'womanly' trappings without ever losing the magic they were believed to contain, but in that line Saint Joan is far from the ultimate. She is, however, far beyond Major Barbara, who saves the souls in one mission or one model town. Joan saves a nation and does so in the light of the highest religious principles. In her, for the first and the last time, Shaw does get completely away from sexual appeal. The girl is armored both physically and psychologically. It is still a girl, with the audacity and the charm of girlhood; but the essence of its power is ageless and sexless.

Again, in Joan, a genius for managing people is joined to an energy that will not admit defeat. Again, Woman, as an out-sider, is free from the cant, the rigidity, the ambitions, the commitments, of the male insider. Princes, bishops, and generals are imprisoned by the world because they own the world. This farm girl, like the millionaire's daughter and the duke's sister, has little to lose by being bold and imaginative and even destructive.

Again in Saint Joan we see, more clearly than ever before, how bossy this saving woman can be. In her, as in all Shaw's strong-minded women, we meet the unbending quality of saints and martyrs, a quality based on their immoderate assurance of being right against all opposition and all evidence. Except for Joan, these women are invincible. Her story being more or less history, Shaw could not pretend that she had, beyond a certain point, managed them all as Daniel managed the lions, by sheer cunning. The relation between female cunning and female rightness was one Shaw dealt with by faith and love, not by ratiocination. For his entirely fictional heroines, the moment does not arrive when the world, simply by its bulk and weight and its imponderable stupidity, destroys the vital woman, whatever her cunning or her convictions may be. This flirtatious, kind, unusually old-fashioned man would never have allowed that to happen. His heroines are protected by a kinder providence. Even when they are blindly aggressive, when they behave in ways that would, in real life, repel all human sympathy and especially man's love, their magic in the theater and in their author's mind is such that all opposition falls before them. These heroines seem to act insidiously upon the nerves of those about them. 'I cannot resist her will' is the universal cry of the subordinate characters.

This magic is seen quite naked in the last of the great saving women, the millionairess. She is the descendant of all the strong saving women, and in the male line, of the unashamed millionaire, Andrew Undershaft. By boldly putting away everything connected with woman's higher moral number, by denying all the social-service mummery with which women craftily disguise their rightful will to succeed and to dominate, by removing even the eternal justification of the mother animal, Shaw reveals at last the bare bones of the androgynous boss; and even on the strength of pure bossism, the creature still can save.

The coward does it with a kiss, the millionairess with fists, blackmail, a ruthless expertise, and the power of her father's money. Her husband is able to save himself physically by being a boxing champion, and mentally by taking refuge in a womanly nonentity known as Polly Seedy-stockings. The heroine's lover goes downstairs in a clatter of broken bones when he casts a few well-founded aspersions on her late father. She has guile enough, however, to throw herself down at once and cry, very much as Ann Whitefield does in the last scene of *Man and Superman*, 'You have killed me!' Her unwilling employer is forced, in a matter of minutes, to become her subordinate in the new enterprise she hatches in his nest. The shabby hotel she takes over becomes a dashing success. Its manager rises with it by turning out the owners, his parents, to a premature and unhappy death, and by averring the essential soundness of his act and of all such acts.

Of such is the kingdom of Undershaft's true daughter – money-minded, succeeding because she is in tune with a money-minded world, and free of all the old-fashioned principles and qualities which are dissonant in that world. She is a strange heroine but a revealing one, for in her, during the Realpolitik decade of the 1930's, Shaw displays the female wolf which had been hidden in the sheep's clothing of Candida's domestic virtues, Lady Cicely's meekness, Barbara Undershaft's social service and Joan's sainthood. According to Shaw, the capitalist arena in which this woman wins over all comers is purely incidental to her meaning. Speculators and exploiters would disappear under communization, 'But the decider, the denominator, the organizer, the tactician, the mesmerizer would remain. . . .' In his 'Preface on Bosses', Shaw attributes the existence of tyrants to the existence of slaves. He admires those who rightly assess the chasm and leap to the side of success. In his millionairess Shaw flaunts success, quite like a Calvinist businessman, as the outward symbol of an inner grace. Her best opponent, the Egyptian doctor, is finally added unto her as a husband. Even in love, she can succeed against the wish of the beloved. This woman, who dismisses her first husband with the words, 'You do not suit', acquires her unwilling second because she has, in Shaw's euphemistic terms '. . . a pulse in a hundred thousand'. Thus the curtain goes down on the millionairess, boxing champion, business champion, pulse champion, and still undefeated.

Anyone inclined to dismiss Epifania Ognisanti di Parerga as the sport of a senile imagination, need only compare this ripened hoyden with an earlier heiress, the Victorian heroine of *Cashel Byron's Profession*. Shaw is more than consistent in this case. He is downright repetitious. Lydia Carew has also a deceased millionaire father of decided and unconventional views. Both heiresses have been groomed for that role by their fathers, who represent the one great emotional tie of their lives. Both are strong-minded, strong-willed women who marry boxing champions much their inferiors in wit and character. Epifania explains her marriage by saying, to her solicitor's dismay, 'He stripped well, unlike most handsome men.' Lydia, as a Victorian virgin, finds a way to say essentially the same thing, comparing her accidental glimpse of Cashel in his tights to a statue by Praxiteles. The differences between these two women are absurdly small compared to the romping revolution in mores that took place between the 1880's and the 1930's. The more recent heroine, now already a shade quaint, uses plainer words, rougher wooing, and more worldly studies – financial instead of philosophical speculation. Yet the two are otherwise twins – twin daughters of Shaw's insistence that will and intelligence *must* be entrancing in Woman, that the mothers of tomorrow must *not* be the mere kittens of today.

Between *Candida* and *The Millionairess* the saving woman has traversed a long road. That road is quite parallel, however, to the social changes of the same period. The difference between Shaw and the popular culture at large is simply that Shaw's modernized woman has still, in all her unwomanliness, the power to save and, tightly bound up with that, the power to exact love. The conquering hoyden and crass business woman represent all those characteristics traditionally deplored in women, characteristics for which Shaw sought to establish respect and even relish. If one can love a kitten, he seems to argue, how much more exciting a lioness! Perhaps he could admire Epifania partly because he could still believe in Nell Gwyn.

Nell makes her appearance in 1939, only three years after the lady with the remarkable pulse. The play in which she exudes womanliness is called (or at least its name is called) '*In Good King Charles's Golden Days*'. If Epifania and Lina mean discomfort and excitement, Nelly means comfort and peace. Her lover's soul is not dying of linen draperism like Johnny Tarleton's in *Misalliance*. He does not need more awareness or more excitement; as a King he needs exactly what Nelly can give: the advantages of the courtesan – sexual availability without moral issues or emotional demands – combined with the advantages of the mother – interest, solicitude, tenderness and defense. Unlike Orinthia, the royal mistress in *The Apple Cart*, Nelly is the guardian of her lover's peace. Orinthia is a kitten, but Nelly has the grave, responsible maternalism without motherhood that is sometimes seen in little girls. One feels that her seriousness, compared to the mature dignity of the Queen, is a child's seriousness, none the less real, none the less sensible for that. A mention of the Queen should remind us that King Charles is twice-saved, for, unlike the philanderers of cheap fiction and cheap conversation, he has a wife who is a perfect treasure. King Magnus in *The Apple Cart* is another great man who is saved in duplicate. Shaw apparently felt, as other great men have felt, that great men deserve (or perhaps need) to be at least doubly saved. All four of these royal blessings are intensely womanly in a non-Victorian way. They are tender, self-sacrificing and, Orinthia excepted, sensible.

The word 'sensible' calls up the country of the Houyhnhnms, Swift's country, Shaw's country, out of Ireland, out of England, out of this world. These heavenly horses, whose virtues stand as a reproach to our simian society, are in many ways as unlike the Shavian woman as possible. Yet in the meaning that lies under the surface, Woman is sometimes for Shaw what Houyhnhnm is for Swift, the chief difference being that Woman, being real instead of mythical, is by comparison an ill-defined and doubtful hope.

Swift's fastidious, formal, vegetarian, nonviolent beasts are as great a contrast to the female Yahoo as to the male. When Shaw referred to the mass of voters as Yahoos, he did not in any degree or any way exempt the females. As to fastidiousness, Shaw pointed out (ignoring certain specialized conditions like army life) that if women were as fastidious as men the race would perish. There is no doubt about Swift's belief that women are likely to be physically more disgusting than men. Shaw, who lived among the benefits of the 'nice' nineteenth century, could not share this view, but he did not make the opposite mistake. He knew that his heroines were clean simply because they were members of the clean classes, as Eliza Doolittle proves, and that their habits, where custom gave no lead, might be far from pleasing. In one important respect, that of feeding, à la Yahoo, on the flesh of dead animals, women were quite as bad as men. During Shaw's lifetime the reek of tobacco and alcohol also became part of woman's standard equipment. As for the gentle formality and sweet tempers of the Houyhnhnms, we have only to recall Shaw's implicit and explicit defenses of the female temper tantrum and the uncensored female tongue, to see that woman, in this respect is anti-Houyhnhnm. In this case, however, we are dealing with the historical happenstance of the literary conventions Shaw had to resist.

Nevertheless, screaming with rage, devouring bloody beef, tearing the veil of decency from all her cherished secrets, the Shavian woman is still, in a sense more important than all these, her author's equivalent of Swift's sensible horses. It will not do to say she is rational, for Shaw insisted, as an artist and as a thoughtful observer of life, that the rational has its limits. He admired woman for being, if anything, less trammeled by rationality than man. At any rate, although the Houyhnhnms are rational beyond human aspiration, one is struck even more by a quality in them which might be better called reasonableness. Yet even this does not satisfy the sense of Shaw's implied values. In general, the most reasonable of men, Shaw was in some matters, right or wrong, a crank. Only the lesser magnitude of these matters – vegetable food, woolen clothing, alphabet reform – in relation to his other concerns, saved him from being a fanatic. In 'The Revolutionist's Handbook' he pays tribute to the unreasonable man:

The reasonable man adapts himself to the world: the unreasonable one persists in trying to adapt the world to himself. Therefore all progress depends on the unreasonable man.

It is significant that, in the plays, the unreasonable man is so often a woman. None of these saving women is quite reasonable. If she were reasonable, Lady Cicely would stay out of those dangerous mountains and would see the need for avenging one's mother and punishing criminals. If she were reasonable, Joan would pray for the soldiers and perhaps run a little canteen behind the battle line, and would certainly agree to that little formality asked by the Inquisition. If she were reasonable, Epifania would work in the sweat shop and save her pennies while writing a book on social conditions, renounce the resistant doctor, and work to win Alistair back from Polly by visits to a marriage counselor and mannerisms copied from the hortative monthlies. No, none of these ladies is reasonable, but all, for their author, are right.

The adjective that links Swift's Houyhnhnm and Shaw's Woman best is: sensible. There is no nonsense about either species. Their most irrational behavior, their most unreasonable expectations, all are the most suitable means to common-sense ends. For both these hypothetical groups, the fine points of ratiocination, the abstract claims of reason, must yield to the dicta of good sense – in fact, horse sense. War, as Gulliver describes it to his master, is not so much unreasonable as it is insane. Faction, as mocked in the Big-enders and the Little-enders, is not so much irrational as it is nonsensical. The sensible animals apply the pragmatic test to all such little follies. They waste no time in trying to justify their conviction that a decent life in a decent society is desirable.

This parallel has, of course, strict limits. As men and women are divisible groups, while Yahoos and Houyhnhnms are inseparable elements in each of us, Shaw cannot pretend, as one can in writing fantasy, that sense belongs to one group and nonsense to the other. All he can do is to give woman a slight edge over man, and even this only in his works of imagination, never in a factual analysis of society. His grounds for doing so are nebulous, but not altogether specious. They are based probably on the realization that this world of injustices, atrocities and falsehoods is largely a man-made world. There is some possibility, at least in theory, that women might have done better. Shaw, looking at his city and his century, would say they could hardly have done worse.

Perhaps we cannot explain at all Shaw's faith in a Something about Woman; but we can rule out certain simplicities. Shaw's boyhood friend, Edward McNulty, for example, thought that

Shaw's views on the subject sprang from '. . . the spectacle of Mr Shaw struggling ineffectually with bills and ledgers. He despised his father's weakness and inefficiency, and began . . . to admire his mother as a masterful woman who knew how to solve her problems and settle her affairs.' This, I submit, is woefully insufficient to color the impressions of eighty subsequent years, unless it is supported by so many other exhibits of the same kind as to make the original quite superfluous. Shaw paid close attention to life for a long, long time, both with the conscious, analytical mind and with the playwright's conscious and subconscious faculties for soaking up personalities and relationships. Shaw cannot be explained by trauma.

Nor is Shaw alone in feeling this way about Woman. A glancing sidelight on his notions in this field occurs in the memoirs of the psychoanalyst, Ernest Jones, who says:

> Incidentally, I would express the opinion that, whatever the average may be in the two sexes, that indefinable quality called 'vitality' reaches on occasion a higher pitch of intensity, amounting to true genius, in the female sex than it ever does in the male. . . .

The curious thing about this assertion is that Jones supports it by examples drawn from the London theaters of the period of Shaw's dramatic apprenticeship, including two of Shaw's close personal attachments, Ellen Terry and Mrs Patrick Campbell. Some suspicion of bewitchment hangs about the whole matter.

Hostile comments, on the other hand, are usually so vague in their venom as to offer no clarification at all. C. S. Lewis, normally a precisian, says:

> You may add that in the hive and the anthill we see fully realized the two things that some of us most dread for our own species – the dominance of the female and the dominance of the collective.

Whether this means that Shaw and Jones are indeed old dreamers seduced by the memories of the gaslit theaters of their youth, or whether this means that they are right about the vital genius of the female, since it seems to be strong enough to threaten the entrenched power of clever men, no one can say.

One other dubiety remains. There is more of a mystical aura about this faith in Woman than the comparison with the Houyhnhnms would suggest. One senses this in the affinity between Saint Joan's voices and the instincts of the other women who are vital geniuses. It is hinted in incidental remarks like this one from a letter to Ellen Terry:

Curious, how little use mere brains are! I have a very fine set; and yet I learnt more from the first stupid woman who fell in love with me than ever they taught me.

Even though this admission is a standard ploy in lovemaking, it is so resonant with the same tones heard in the love scenes of the plays that it cannot be so easily dismissed. Beyond common sense and beyond social observation, there remains in Shaw's partiality to women a small but irreducible mystique.

CHAPTER 8

Emancipation and its Discontents

SHAW's attitude toward the struggle for women's suffrage, which was at its height in England about 1910, seemed inexplicable to many women at the time. Now, fifty years later, we can see in our own political and personal lives the justification of his peculiar views. I am speaking only of those countries in which women have had the vote long enough to have tested its advantages, as they have in England and the United States. In these countries, just because society offers so much in the way of personal choice, mobility and excitement, a sour trace of discontent exists among women who have even a little more than the minimum of money and education. Below the irregular line which defines this minimum, women have neither the attention to spare nor the concepts to use in formulating a discontent so generalized. Above this dividing line, the rebelliousness that follows an incomplete revolution is widespread, although often repressed. We – let me neither pretend to view this group from the outside, nor grant the view from outside to be any clearer than the view from within – are like guests at a lavish banquet who find ourselves forbidden to touch half the dishes. One is not hungry under these circumstances, but one may well feel insulted. We have reached that stage of liberation which Major Barbara, in the radiance of her final scene, describes this way: 'My father shall never throw it in my teeth again that my converts were bribed with bread. I have got rid of the bribe of bread. I have got rid of the bribe of heaven.' Now that women can earn a living wage, often at congenial work, they may leave a cruel father or a brutal husband whenever the provocation is great enough. Hence cruel fathers, especially, have been going rapidly out of style. Husbands are less threatened by this new freedom. We have got rid of the bribe of bread, and even the bribe of heaven, but we have not got rid of the bribe of love. Consider the plaint of Mme Gwen Raverat, a perceptive observer of the change in woman's status from the Victorian Age to the wonderful post-war world: 'Why mayn't we have pockets? Who forbids it? We have got Women's Suffrage, but why must we still always be inferior to men?' This question would have seemed like an abominable frivolity to the women who faced ridicule, imprisonment, torture and even death for the right to vote. Yet the fact remains that, although women's suffrage removes a gratuitous insult, it has done less than it was expected to do about the intangible differences of which pockets may be a symbol. If it were not true that women are still inferior to men, why should there be, a generation after Virginia Woolf's *Three Guineas* and *A Room of One's Own*, works of broader condemnation and deeper rebellion, the obvious great example being Simone de Beauvoir's *The Second Sex*? The vote may at times be a safeguard against unfair legal measures, but it is the intangible matters which are the burden of the modern woman's discontent, and these remain untouched by the practical results of the franchise, and only very slightly altered by the abstract justice it represents. All this is as Shaw predicted. Hence his peculiar stand on the suffrage issue.

There was never any reason to doubt Shaw's support of political rights for women. If some of his utterances, especially the later ones, raised some doubts, that was the fault of the reader, not the writer.

Fabian Tract Number Two, issued by the Fabian Society in 1884, asserts: 'That Men no longer need special political privileges to protect them against Women, and that the sexes should henceforth enjoy equal political rights.' The proposition is Shaw's. It turns upside-down the usual assumption that women were demanding a high privilege in demanding the franchise, and it includes a gibe ('to protect them from women') aimed with Shavian adroitness at a vital part of the masculime myth – male strength. All this is done, moreover, with the air of having done nothing of the sort, of having made a plain statement in the plainest possible way.

All the rest of Shaw's utterances on the franchise itself are restatements of this one. Propositions, however, are one thing, and political action another. For various and quite sufficient reasons, Shaw's work on behalf of women's suffrage was limited to three kinds of support: first, he successfully fought to have women's suffrage included in the Basis of the Fabian Society. (This was one of the chief points on which he opposed H. G. Wells in the struggle over the composition of the Basis.) Second, he wrote occasionally to reprove the government for its worst excesses in dealing with the suffragists. Third, and most important, he was constantly creating dramatic images of women whose ability was combined with great personal charm. The New Women of Shaw's creation are all ultra-feminine feminists.

Among the excuses Shaw offered for not taking a more active part in the suffragist cause was the rather specious one of not being a woman himself. Yet a newspaper interview which he rather reluctantly granted to Maud Churton Braby in 1906, after an exchange of playful letters, contains a clear incitement to revolution:

'The suffrage is nothing to me,' he began. 'I have no opinion on the subject. I'm not a woman; I've got the suffrage.'

'But if, for the sake of argument, you were a woman——'

'Of course, if I were a woman, I'd simply refuse to speak to any man or do anything for men until I'd got the vote. I'd make my husband's life a burden, and everybody miserable generally. Women should have a revolution – they should shoot, kill, maim, destroy – until they are given a vote.'

'And what would you consider the proper qualifications?'

'There's none necessary; the qualification of being human is enough. I would make the conditions exactly the same as for men; it's no use women claiming *more* than men, though probably in the end they'll get more, as they invariably do whenever women agitate for equality with men in any respect.'

This is a strange Bernard Shaw in one way: refusing to help others because he is not injured, urging people to shoot, kill, maim; and yet a perfectly predictable Shaw in another way: giving an unnecessary interview just to help a struggling freelance journalist, making startling and quotable statements, and thinking more about the effect of his words on people's actions than about the eternal truth of the words themselves.

After one act of female militancy in 1906, which consisted largely of walking into the House of Commons uninvited, the government took repressive measures which moved Shaw to use the medium of the ordinary outraged Englishman. He wrote to *The Times*. Opening with a long reminder of the terrible perils England had faced courageously, with special emphasis on the men who have invaded the Houses of Parliament at various times and suffered no greater penalty than removal, Shaw continued:

But the strongest nerves give way last. . . . The peril of to-day wears a darker, deadlier aspect. Two women – two petticoated, long-stockinged, corseted females have hurled themselves on the British Houses of Parliament. Desperate measures are necessary. I have a right to speak in this matter, because it was in my play *Man and Superman* that my sex were first warned of woman's terrible strength and man's miserable weakness.

It is a striking confirmation of the correctness of my views that the measures which have always been deemed sufficient to protect the House of Commons against men are not to be trusted against women. Take, for example, the daughters of Richard Cobden, long known to everybody worth knowing in London as among the most charming and interesting women of our day. One of them – one only – and she the slightest and rosiest of the family – did what the herculean Charles Bradlaugh did. To the immortal glory of our Metropolitan Police they did not blench. They carried the lady out even as they carried Bradlaugh. But they did not dare to leave her at large as they left him. They held on to her like grim death until they had her safe under bolt and bar, until they had stripped her to see that she had no weapons concealed, until a temperate diet of bread and cocoa should have abated her perilous forces. She – and the rest of the terrible ten.

Shaw then suggests that the government quadruple the police staff inside the Houses of Parliament, that Westminster and Vauxhall Bridges be strongly held by the Guards, and special constables be enrolled.

I submit, however, that if these precautions are taken we might, perhaps, venture to let Mrs Cobden-Sanderson and her friends out. As a taxpayer, I object to having to pay for her bread and cocoa when her husband is, not only ready, but apparently even anxious to provide a more generous diet at home. After all, if Mr Cobden-Sanderson is not afraid, surely the rest of us may pluck up a little. . . . If Mrs Cobden-Sanderson must remain a prisoner whilst the Home Secretary is too paralysed with terror to make that stroke of the pen for which every sensible person in the three kingdoms is looking to him, why on earth cannot she be imprisoned in her own house? We should still look ridiculous, but at least the lady would not be a martyr. I suppose nobody in the world really wishes to see one of the nicest women in England suffering from the coarsest indignity and the most injurious form of ill-treatment that the law could inflict on a pickpocket. It gives us an air of having lost our tempers and made fools of ourselves, and of being incapable of acting generously now that we have had time to come to our senses. Surely, there can be no two opinions among sane people as to what we ought to do.

Will not the Home Secretary rescue us from a ridiculous, an intolerable, and incidentally a revoltingly spiteful and unmanly situation?

Thus Shaw speaks, in his irrepressibly gentlemanly fashion, of the horrors which feed his passion for reform as surely as they do Swift's. Shaw knew his Yahoos better than he is supposed to have done, although he shrank from exhibiting their vileness in the unsparing detail to which most satirists feel impelled. An article entitled, 'The Unmentionable Case for Women's Suffrage', which appeared in *The Englishwoman* in 1909, begins:

One of the most blackguardly debates that ever took place in the House of Lords was that in which the women who had sat on the old London Vestries were disqualified from sitting on the new Borough Councils. The argument which prevailed was that the new Borough Councils would include aldermen, and that a woman could not possibly be an alder-*man*. This joke pleased the Peers immensely. It stimulated that vein of facetiousness in which the health of the bridesmaids is proposed at old-fashioned weddings; and women vanished from the London Municipalities for some years.

The logic of the Lords is contemptible, but their laughter is the masculine laughter that accompanied the struggle for women's rights. When militant suffragists on hunger strike were subjected to forcible feeding, Parliament found this subject funny also, even though this procedure is, as Shaw pointed out, a form of torture. 'At first the House of Commons listened to the Home Secretary's accounts of such proceedings with bursts of laughter. . . .' An American journalist reported in 1877 that, on the subject of women's suffrage, 'The majority of the senators found these petitions uproariously funny. . . . The entire Senate presented the appearance of a laughing school practicing side-splitting and ear-extended grins.'

The second incident in 'The Unmentionable Case for Women's Suffrage' also involves masculine laughter:

One day, at a meeting of the Health Committee of the Borough Council of which I was a member, a doctor rose to bring a case before the Committee. It was the case of a woman. The gravity of the case depended on the fact that the woman was pregnant. No sooner had the doctor mentioned this than the whole Committee burst into a roar of laughter, as if the speaker had made a scandalous but irresistible joke. . . . There is only one absolutely certain and final preventive for such indecency, and that is the presence of women. If there were no other argument for giving women the vote, I would support it myself on no other ground than that men will not behave themselves when women are not present.

When Shaw referred to this incident in a talk he made in 1927, he noticed that his audience received it '. . . in a perfectly decorous silence; there does not seem to you anything funny about it. But I assure you that on that Health Committee – and it is not much more than twenty years ago – no sooner had the doctor uttered this revelation than the whole committee burst into a roar of laughter.'

Before coming to the unmentionable subjects with which the article ends, Shaw makes a curious but quite sound reversal of one argument for the presence of women on official bodies. He argues that the kind-heartedness of women is less needed than their tough-mindedness. Women will recognize at once the soundness of Shaw's observation that '. . . the average man is a silly sentimental gossip where women are concerned, and will not keep women up to the mark unless women are present to keep *him* up to the mark'. Shaw's example is that of a young woman stricken with scarlet fever who traveled home by public conveyances, exposing all the other travelers to infection. Out of sympathy for her difficulties and her silliness, the vestrymen refused to prosecute. Shaw maintains that vestrywomen would have been more realistic and that '. . . the influence of women on public bodies is anti-sentimental, and much needed to correct the tendency of men to exceed in the opposite direction.'

On the subject of housing Shaw deals with matters nearly as unmentionable to his fastidious soul as to Edwardian convention. Of the right of husbands and wives to separate beds or bedrooms, he says, 'One just touches this terrible subject, and flies from it.' Here again, as in his view of adultery, Shaw advocates an arrangement that had been taken for granted among the aristocracy, strange as it might seem to the middle classes. Once again, the connection between private lives and public issues is emphasized. 'I strongly suspect that, though we never mention it, the cry for the vote is often really a cry for the key of one's bedroom.'

When Virginia Woolf wrote *A Room of One's Own* twenty years later, she did not stir these depths. She wrote as though she had remained one of the 'glorious old maids of old England'. Shaw, on the other hand, speaks with the voice of the married woman. Since he is not known ever to have gone into a trance, as Mrs George does, one must suppose that some of the married women who made claims on his time and sympathy must have revealed to him those experiences which convert into either bad gossip or good generalizations. There was also, clearly, more to that conference of respectable married men which he attended than he felt bound to report in the preface of *Getting Married*, although the rest is implied.

Then Shaw touches on a subject which, at first thought, seems scarcely relevant to the women's vote. There is a connection, however, in Shaw's belief that any increase in the rights of women would bring about further limitations in the sexual exploitation of the helpless. He never failed to recognize a sharp difference between men and women in their approach to sexual matters, no matter how often he insisted that in other respects woman was merely man in petticoats. His socialism, moreover, is founded on a relentless realism about poverty.

When Lord Shaftesbury and Tennyson tried to startle the conscience of the nation by letting slip the unmentionable fact that the one-room tenement produced incest, we simply pretended not to hear, knowing that nobody dare pursue the subject.

Also, it must be understood that I do not pretend to have exhausted the unmentionable matters. In the borough which I helped to govern for six years there were long sections of main streets in which almost every house was a brothel.

Shaw is reticent about the details of sexual behavior, but in order to remind people of a topic to which they have been wilfully shutting their eyes, just mentioning the unmentionable should be enough. There has always been a tendency, especially among the most noisily masculine of the critics, beginning with Frank Harris, to rate Shaw as somehow deficient because he omits the salacious detail. These writers take it for granted that a man can scarcely have too much of this good thing. Yet Shaw had reason for his omissions, being well aware, as his comments on flogging prove, of what he would have called the psycho-sexual abnormalities that feed on reported horrors.

The connection between private lives and public issues was made even more explicit when Shaw was asked on a questionnaire what he considered the greatest single obstacle to the emancipation of women. He answered in one word: 'Lust.'

It may be unkind, but it can surely not be unfair, to quote here a remark made by Horace Greeley after Mrs Greeley had signed a petition asking that the word 'male' be struck from the Constitution. He said, 'It seems but fair to add that female suffrage seems to me to involve the balance of the family relation as it has hitherto existed.' Precisely.

Shaw pointed out one other hidden element in the opposition to women's suffrage. The subject is women in industry, the play referred to being *La Femme Seule* by Brieux, but the comments apply at least equally well to government.

Brieux shews you the working man as selfish, foul-mouthed, ill-behaved and violent, objecting far more to the woman's capacity, orderliness, and industry, than to her weaknesses; jealous of her attempts to do without him; and afraid of being dominated by her in industry, where he cannot resort to his fists, as he often does in his home. There is nothing new in this resentment of the virtues of your competitor, and nothing unnatural in it; for the virtues of your competitor screw up the standard you are expected to reach. . . . Now women, as it happens, have always had to manage households, however poor, whereas working men have never had to manage anything. Working men feel that women manage them at home; interfere with them; curb their expenditure; lecture them on their conduct; and never relax any advantage they are allowed or can take by moral force. This is bearable at home where the interests of the man and the woman are so far identical that poverty for one means poverty for both. But in industry, where there is the sharpest conflict of interests . . . it opens up a terrifying and humiliating prospect. That is why Brieux, with perfect truth to social facts, represents the men as driving the women out of their industries as ruthlessly as they have driven out the Chinese, yet with a rancor which no Chinaman could excite.

There is no valid way to assess the relative rancor aroused by women and by other disfranchised groups in the political field. In the United States, where abolition and feminism ran nearly parallel courses for a long time, overt bitterness against Negroes far exceeded anything that could possibly, in the nature of things, be exhibited against women. Yet Negro men were, at least theoretically, enfranchised years before white women were. On the other side of the argument, it must be remembered that, once white women were enfranchised, they could actually vote. Ironically, the right to vote has been more important to women than the vote itself, and the vote itself more important to Negroes.

In the United States, feminist political action had been hampered by two factors quite familiar in progressive movements. One factor was that the movement split into two segments, an event always to be feared on the principled side of any political conflict. The other factor was the feminists' involvement with another movement, abolitionism, which came to involve a desperate military crisis. As is common in such cases, the women were asked to defer their hopes until they had helped with the more urgent cause, in exchange, of course, for receiving assistance at a later date. As is also common, once the first task had been accomplished, the feminists found that gratitude could be forgotten. Another complicating factor on the American scene was the Women's Christian Temperance Union, whose funny and touching motto, 'Do Everything', bears out Shaw's diagnosis of the working-man's fear of women.

In England a similar political complication existed in the connection between feminism and socialism. One takes for granted the opposition of the Tories of this world to the disruption of existing patterns. Women looked for and found their natural supporters among those who were dissatisfied with the way of the world in general. But again, although the two groups overlapped considerably, they were by no means identical.

One eminent Fabian, the bitterly antifeminist Ernest Belfort Bax, claimed that the intellectual vacuity of women, especially one's friends' wives, made the society of women highly undesirable, and that the laws of England were unfair to men, especially husbands. Shaw, by the way, had begun to see some justification for the latter claim by the time he was preparing the second edition of *The Quintessence of Ibsenism* in 1912.

The less simple and more dangerous form of opposition was that of H. G. Wells who, as I have mentioned, was at odds with

Shaw from the first over the inclusion of women's suffrage in the Fabian Basis. The danger of men like Wells in any struggle is that, far from making such extreme and often easily discredited statements as those of Belfort Bax, men like Wells give a conditional and partial support which, as it later transpires, omits nothing but the essential points. In *A Modern Utopia*, for example, Wells devotes a whole chapter to 'Women in a Modern Utopia'. The existence of such a chapter is ominous enough. As a matter of fact, the chapter is devoted exclusively to the genetic arrangements in Utopia, with some attention to marriage. All other considerations are dismissed in a single sentence: ' "He" indeed is to be read as "He and She" in all that goes before.' This statement might be either the most enlightened treatment of women's rights, or a mere gesture concealing a complete lack of interest in any issues concerning a woman's life which are not related to her sexual role. Coming from H. G. Wells, the statement seems to be of the latter kind. In another place Wells, writing after the First World War, assesses woman's role in the modern world as follows, '. . . rather than star parts in the future [women will] mother, nurse, assist, protect, comfort, reward and hold mankind together'. If ever a supposedly daring modern novelist sounded like the stuffier of his grandfathers, it is here. Of the suffrage and other rights won by women he says, with some complacency, that they '. . . have widened her choice of what she shall adorn or serve . . .'. By women unsuited to adorning or tired of serving, such offers are ungratefully received. Moreover, the advanced novels of Wells contrive to miss, with uncanny precision, the only new thing about the New Woman, her ability to have a nonsexual goal. The revolt of Ann Veronica, for example, is that of a New Woman who is merely an Old Woman of impaired chastity. 'She wanted to live. She was vehemently impatient – she did not clearly know for what – to do, to be, to experience.' These are the thoughts of a girl ready to be seduced and priggish enough to suppose there is something new about that.

In brief, Shaw's support of women's rights was remarkable even among the 'advanced'. There was one source of opposition more interesting than any other, and that was the women themselves.

One historian says: 'In moments of despair those who were

trying to enlarge the opportunities of women must have felt that they were fighting a hopeless struggle against the general indifference of their own sex and the active hostility of many men.' St John Packe says of John Stuart Mill: '. . . Mill's chief discouragement was the extraordinary reluctance of women to come forward.' The same phenomenon was observed by the opposition and was frequently used as a debating point: Horace Greeley says, 'The best women I know do not want to vote.' The word 'best' now evokes a smile, but Greeley's observation had some validity.

Octavia Hill, for one, did not want to vote. She had no lack of brains, courage or zeal, as her work for the reform of slum housing proves; she did not fear ridicule, censure or violence. The fact that she went from tenement to tenement collecting rents shows that there must have been many other things she was not afraid of. Yet she refused to have anything to do with the suffragists. Her biographer gives a number of possible reasons, but I can only conclude that she was one of those single-minded persons so bent on one task that she cannot bear to think of herself, or for that matter anyone else, wasting a moment in any other pursuit.

Mrs Humphry Ward, another kind of anti-suffragist, went so far as to compose a manifesto against women's suffrage, and this manifesto was signed by Beatrice Webb, then Miss Beatrice Potter. Miss Potter was good-looking, clever and rich. Moreover, her father, fortunately for a man with many daughters, was pro-feminist. Under these circumstances, it is easy to see why she found it no disadvantage to be a woman and asked what all the fuss was about. Much later, in *My Apprenticeship*, Mrs Webb tried to explain what had led her to sign the manifesto in 1889. It is interesting to find this radical thinker citing as one reason her 'conservative temperament'. Another reason she cites, not at all helpful in generalization, is her reaction against her pro-feminist father. The explanation from which one can and must generalize is that, far from finding her femininity a disadvantage, Miss Potter found it a remarkable stroke of luck. Had she been a man, she would have had to take up a profession and prepare to earn a living. As it was, she could mess about to her heart's content in the subjects that interested her, and she found many doors that would otherwise be closed were graciously open to a pretty young lady who looked a bit like a gypsy.

This is the situation which led one writer to say: 'The very success of some outstanding women made them singularly obtuse when it came to considering the position of women in general.'

The sequel to the signing of the manifesto was that, under attack by Millicent Garrett Fawcett, Beatrice Potter withdrew from the controversy but '... delayed my political recantation for nearly twenty years ...'. During those years she had, of course, married Sidney Webb and in his company had become a close associate of Bernard Shaw.

Mrs Humphry Ward, by the way, found herself making an appeal to Shaw years later, in 1910, when the Society of Authors of which she and Shaw were both members, set up some exclusively male committees, which she considered an insult to the women belonging to it. She asked Shaw's support for a rather fussy resolution of protest which she enclosed. Shaw responded fully and helpfully as always, but with a touch of asperity most unlike his usual tone in addressing women, saying among other things:

When, on the announcement of the list, one or two Academicians communicated with me in some bewilderment as to what they ought to do, I at once said that ... a number of fauteuils must be reserved for women. It was immediately objected by an ardent Suffragist (male) that if such a thing were done *you* would be the first person to be elected. I agreed, & said Why not? Of course the reply was that you yourself had proclaimed the unfitness of women for &c &c &c &c &c. Now that is a good debating point, though quite irrelevant as an argument. Saul among the prophets always amuses an audience; and the more unfair the more it tickles. You may, however, turn the difficulty into an advantage if you wish to use the opportunity to show that your opinions about the Suffrage must not be taken to imply any general exclusion of women from representative institutions. I simply point out the situation as an old platform hand; so that you may not be taken by surprise.

The 'old platform hand' in this case is also an old fox. He goes on to warn the lady against promising not to accept an invitation to become a member, saying that it would be like getting a proposal of marriage by promising beforehand not to accept it.

'Besides, everybody hates a self-sacrificing woman; and you will look like a bad case of that.'

But to return to what might be called, by analogy with Marx's phrase, the damned wantlessness of women: Shaw had his explanation of that.

You must have noticed that some of the most imperiously wilful women, unable to bear a moment's contradiction, and tyrannizing over their husbands, daughters, and servants until nobody else in the house can call her soul her own, have been the most resolute opponents of Women's Rights. The reason is that they know that as long as the men govern they can govern the men.

Here feminists and their opponents seem superficially to agree. Horace Greeley voiced the weariest of all anti-suffrage arguments when he said, 'Talk of a true woman needing the ballot as an accessory of power when she rules the world with the glance of an eye.' This point was still, incredible as it seems, being made in 1961 in a sophisticated magazine for women, as though it were a witty invention of the author, Malcolm Muggeridge, who suggests waggishly that discussions between men and women should take place in the bedroom, not in the board-room. Whether this is intended as a plea for more mistresses or fewer board members, it is impossible to say. At any rate, this particular argument, casting woman back eternally on her sexual beguilements, dies hard.

Shaw put this political phenomenon into moral terms. After meeting his sister-in-law, Mary Cholmondeley, who managed her difficult husband in a way that is supposed to have been the inspiration for *Captain Brassbound's Conversion*, we are told that Shaw made the following notes:

A slave state is always ruled by those who can get round the masters. The slavery of women means the tyranny of women. No fascinating woman ever wants to emancipate her sex; her object is to gather power into the hands of Man because she knows she can govern him.

A cunning and attractive woman disguises her strength as womanly timidity, her unscrupulousness as womanly innocence, her impunities as womanly defencelessness: simple men are duped by them.

It is only the proud, straight-forward women who wish not to govern but to be free.

Later Shaw pointed out the exact political application of this idea:

. . . in oligarchies women exercise so much influence privately that the cleverest of them are for giving all power to the men, knowing that they can get round them without being hampered by the female majority whose world is the kitchen, the nursery, and the drawing-room, if such a luxury is within their reach.

A somewhat more thorough and less pleasant explanation had been given by John Stuart Mill: 'In the case of women, each individual of the subject-class is in a chronic state of bribery and intimidation combined.' He concludes therefore that the subjection of women '. . . was certain to outlast all other forms of unjust authority'. There is also some relevance in the observation of Rousseau that 'Men in shackles lose everything – even the desire to shake them off: They cherish their bondage as Ulysses' companions cherished being brutes.'

Because of his awareness that the greatest need of humanity was to create some form of government that could save it from its own cleverness, Shaw very largely ignored the submissive woman and argued about the woman who knew how to dominate. Here Shaw diverges from other supporters of women's rights. One historian of the movement says: 'At every turn such women were faced with the handicap of their utter political impotence, and, with the exception of Miss Dodge, every woman who was to any degree active in the social reform movement [in the U.S.A.] was also an active and articulate suffragist.' The vote was also the right on which John Stuart Mill pinned his hopes.

It seemed to him that once women were properly represented in Parliament, all their grievances would be swept away, as surely as the working-class vote would end in Socialism. 'When that has been gained,' he said, 'Everything else will follow.'

Shaw disagreed thoroughly, although he had the same goals in view. He said:

John Stuart Mill certainly was a little uxorious; and it is well to remind the uxorious that women have all the faults of men, and that Votes for Women will no more achieve the millennium than Votes for Manufacturers did in 1832 or Votes for Working Men in 1867 and 1885. Above all, it may help to effect a reduction to absurdity of Sex Recrimination, that Duel of Sex in which Ibsen and Strindberg were such mighty opposites. It was an inevitable phase; let us hope it will end . . . in frank confession and good-humoured laughter.

There are two separate matters involved here, which Shaw never scruples to combine, as his conclusions on both are almost exactly the same. One is the efficacy of the vote in improving the lot of women, the other its efficacy in improving the lot of humanity. Shaw attributes one author's state of error to his having several brothers and no sisters. 'He is still afraid of women, still unable to conceive that they belong to his own species, still by turns irritated and attracted by these strange monsters.' But Shaw, as he substituted common humanity for the worship of Woman, was bound to see that her common humanity made the average woman a doubtful political asset. Hence his remark that giving women the vote '. . . only doubled the resistance to any change'. There may be a flaw in the mathematics of this statement, but its sociology has proved sound.

In only one instance did Shaw ever speak as though there might be a woman's vote. That was in a message intended for the Women's Suffrage Issue of *Puck* in 1915, which ran as follows:

MESSAGE FOR MRS NORMAN WHITEHOUSE: WHEN ARE THE WOMEN GOING TO TELL US WHAT THEY SURELY MUST HAVE TO SAY ABOUT WAR? AND HOW SOON THEY INTEND TO STOP IT OR HAVE THEY ALL BECOME CHILDISH AND UNREASONABLE OR VILLIANOUS [*sic*] AND COWARDLY OR ROMANTIC AND IMPOSSIBLE LIKE THE OTHER SEX

SHAW

He had answered his own question in a letter to Mrs Patrick Campbell in 1914, written before her son was killed in battle:

And now that they have settled the fact that their stupid fighting can't settle anything, and produces nothing but a perpetual Waterloo that nobody wins, why dont the women rise up and say 'We have the trouble of making these men; and if you dont stop killing them we shall refuse to make any more.' But alas, the women are just as idiotic as the men.

Thirty years later, in the midst of events even more gruesome, Shaw tried to explain the causes of that idiocy:

Now if the race is to survive every woman must have her man and every man his woman: two to the unit. But though the woman has to bear all the labor of childbirth and to nourish and protect the human infant . . . her man is to her more than a mere fertilizer. He must be a fighter who can protect her against rape, and her helpless children against robbery by strange fighters. . . . Consequently before selecting him as her mate she demands proof of his ability to kill strangers.

This is no more than to say that women are caught in the necessities and neuroses of the human lot, that as voters they are bound to be merely 'man in petticoats' and to illustrate again the weakness of democracy. Shaw's most explicit statement of this belief occurs in *The Intelligent Woman's Guide to Socialism and Capitalism*:

Only the other day the admission of women to the electorate, for which women fought and died, was expected to raise politics to a nobler plane and purify public life. But at the election which followed, the women voted for hanging the Kaiser; rallied hysterically round the worst male candidates; threw out all the women candidates of tried ability, integrity, and devotion; and elected just one titled lady of great wealth and singular demagogic fascination, who, though she justified their choice subsequently, was then a beginner. In short, the notion that the female voter is more politically intelligent or gentler than the male voter proved as great a delusion as the earlier delusions that the business man was any wiser politically than the country gentleman or the manual worker than the middle class man.

The one political act which has been most thoroughly entangled with the achievement of votes for women, the Eighteenth Amendment to the Constitution, has become almost as complete a joke as Shaw's sally, 'Give women the vote, and in five years there will be a crushing tax on bachelors.'

Shaw later, in the preface to *Getting Married*, grew more serious in this same vein, without growing much more realistic. With his mind on the appalling state of the laws that govern sexual behavior, he said:

The political emancipation of women is likely to lead to a comparatively stringent enforcement by law of sexual morality (that is why so many of us dread it): and this will soon compel us to consider what our sexual morality shall be. . . . At all points the code will be

screwed up by the operation of Votes for Women, if there be any
virtue in the franchise at all. The result will be that men will find
the more ascetic side of our sexual morality taken seriously by law.
It is easy to foresee the consequences.

The consequence foreseen by Shaw was that men would reconsider their morality and remodel the law along less stringent
lines. This is not the most closely reasoned of Shaw's arguments.
As always, his attention is deeply engaged in the business of
polemics and, in pursuit of what he would have called a good
debating point, misses the logical question of whether women
with enough political power to enforce laws uncongenial to the
male would not, by the same token, have enough political
power to maintain on the statute books the laws already in
effect. This is almost the only occasion on which Shaw considered that there might be 'any virtue in the franchise at all'.

As to the virtue of the franchise in advancing women themselves, the first general election in which women participated
seems to have borne out his belief that women will not vote
for women. The shared delusion of pro-feminists and anti-
feminists was that women *would* vote as a bloc. Belfort Bax,
for example, predicted that women would have half the votes
inevitably and that the few men who would vote for women
out of gallantry would give them always a clear majority.

Shaw's various real and unreal reasons for holding aloof from
the suffrage movement did not satisfy the women who were
active in the movement. His own inconsistencies cannot have
made his position easier to accept. At one moment he told Mrs
Braby that he could not be bothered because he was not a
woman. At another he said that '. . . the vital obstacle to the
vote is its own loathsomeness. . . . When we win equality, no
sane person will cross the street to vote, though everybody will
run down the lane to avoid being elected.' Still later, and obviously with considerable truth, he wrote to Maud Arncliffe
Sennett, a leader of the Votes for Women movement:

Dear Madam

If I could do all these wonderful things with a stroke of my pen,
you would have the vote & Mrs Pankhurst be in parliament. Do you
suppose I should wait to be asked if I had the magical powers which

you attribute to me? Do you suppose that the walls of Jericho, which stand against Mrs Pankhurst's devotion and suffering, will fall at a wave of my pen or a clever platform speech? Such credulity makes me despair of the movement.

Yours sincerely

G. Bernard Shaw

A year later he answered another critic in the same way, but with a touch of pique.

Dear Miss Smyth

In reply to your question as to why I do not interest myself in the Suffrage I can only put a similar question to you. Why is it that you have never thought of devoting yourself to musical composition? It is a light employment though the actual pen and ink work of scoring is tedious. You will find the transposing instruments rather puzzling at first; but if you write down the exact notes you want played, you can easily hire somebody to write the clarinet parts in proper form. You will find the work of devising effective instrumental combinations quite amusing; for instance you might begin with a concerto for a piccolo and six tubas. Just try it.

You now probably feel exactly as I feel when some enthusiastic militant comes along and informs me that I am a blind fool and a dastard because I allow women to be tortured when by a single stroke of my powerful pen I could enfranchise her entire sex.

If you can suggest anything that is worth doing that I can do and that I have not already done five or six times over, by all means let me know what it is. How little effect I am likely to produce is shewn by the fact that even you, who are specially interested in the question, do not even know whether I am in favor of the vote or not.

The letter continues with a reiteration of Shaw's views on the relative unimportance of the vote. Clearly, however, he had begun to find his role uncomfortable. He may even have felt some slight uneasiness about the small superficial comedy which was his only dramatic treatment of the suffrage issue. This trifle, called 'Press Cuttings: A Topical Sketch Compiled From the Editorial and Correspondence Columns of the Daily Papers During the Women's War in 1909', appears as an avowed tomfoolery in the volume, *Translations and Tomfooleries*. Although full of the usual Shavian fun and fascination, the sketch treats its masterful women as only a little less ridiculous than its sticks of men, Balsquith and Mitchener, and the play abounds in remarks like: 'We must adopt Maxim's Silencer for the army rifles if we're going to shoot women. I really couldn't stand hearing it.'

Each time he defended himself against the charge of being a bitter enemy of votes for women, Shaw repeated patiently his own proposal for giving women their proper share of influence in the affairs of the nation. His letter to Ethel Smyth, for example, continues this way:

I may say that I have long been convinced that women are making a mistake in concentrating on the vote. If they would demand that, vote or no vote, every public authority in this country, including the House of Parliament should contain a considerable proportion of women, no matter how selected or elected, the question would take on a new seriousness, and the demand for the mere vote would cease to appear an extreme one, and would fall into something like its proper political perspective. For you have only to consider how little use the vote has been to the men, or indeed to the women in the case of the Municipal Franchise, to foresee how bitterly the results of the Suffrage will disappoint those who are at present expecting so much from it.

This same feminist, by then Dame Ethel Smyth, took part in a meeting in November 1933 at which Shaw was asked to discuss the question, 'Should married women earn?' The small impression Shaw's views on feminism had made on even the active feminists, was demonstrated again on this occasion. Shaw refused to speak but sent, as usual, a long letter about the unimportance of the vote and the great importance of getting, by some means or other, a number of women on every governing body. This plea concludes with a fresh argument for the participation of women in government:

Do not Mussolini, Hitler, and company make you think occasionally that perhaps I was right? What we have now is the spectacle of women's votes keeping women out of the Parliament, and Liberia, the negro republic, reviving the slave trade. What a world!

In answer to this letter, Lady Rhondda, who had actually appeared on a platform with Shaw some years earlier, in a debate on 'The Menace of the Leisured Woman', said that she had no idea that Shaw had ever advocated the co-option of women and was horrified at the suggestion.

For we never fought that fight . . . to put women into positions of authority. That was the last thing we desired. No. We fought in a sense to do the very opposite. We fought to do away with this eternal dividing of the human race into two entirely different and differently treated halves.

Shaw's answer is not based on principle. It was he who had called woman 'man in petticoats' and had said that the slight difference between men and women does not matter 'except on special occasions'. His objection to equal treatment is made on practical grounds:

> I quite understand Lady Rhondda's attitude, and sympathize with it. But I am a man, and know how careful women have to be in dealing with men. If they go no farther than to claim that women belong to humanity equally with men, then the men will claim that a parliament of men, being human, will be representative of women. I know by personal experience that this is not so, and that humanity can be represented only by men and women.

Shaw was later asked in a newspaper interview: 'Talking of home affairs, we now have a new woman Minister. Do you think that female emancipation has reached its goal?' He answered:

> No. Until every public authority contains a representative proportion of women, no matter how elected or co-opted or nominated, the political emancipation of women will be incomplete. Votes for women are useless, as women will not vote for women. They don't want to be emancipated.

One may doubt the prophetic powers of an author whose opinions of July 26, 1939, are issued under the headline: BERNARD SHAW (who is eighty-three today) SAYS WE WILL HAVE PEACE. Shaw's prediction about women had, however, already seen two decades of confirmation, and it has since seen two decades more. I suggest that one could probably show, if the necessary data were collected, that the number of women in important public offices would scarcely be changed at all if the votes of women went uncounted.

Considering the hopelessness of electing women to office by any of the usual political techniques, Shaw comes out firmly for co-option:

> The representative unit must not be a man *or* a woman but a man *and* a woman. Every vote, to be valid, must be for a human pair, with the result that the elected body must consist of men and women

in equal numbers. Until this is achieved it is idle to prate of political democracy as existing, or ever having existed, at any known period of English history.

The staying power of masculine silliness is evident in Arthur Nethercot's comment on this proposal: 'But he somehow neglects to stipulate that, in the interests of the Life Force, the pair should be married, or at least engaged.' This muted echo of the laughter of the nineteenth-century vestrymen shows how hard a purely artificial notion can die. Shaw had wearied of this notion, even as a theatrical convention, by 1895, when he complained of a new play by Pinero:

Off the stage it is not customary for a man and woman to assume that they cannot co-operate in bringing about social reform without living together as man and wife; on the stage, this is considered inevitable.

The more serious objection to the coupled vote as a substitute for women's suffrage is the difficulty of achieving it. We cannot, certainly, envision its enactment tomorrow. On the other hand, Shaw knew that women could be introduced gradually into various public bodies, with results that would encourage further steps in the same direction. Every one of these steps was of importance to Shaw, chiefly because he was so much interested in the actual work women could do in government.

There was, for example, the matter of 'sanitary accommodations for women'. The situation that existed in 1898 while Shaw was a vestryman of the Borough of St Pancras was this:

Women had two grievances in the matter under my Borough Council. The first and worst was, that in most places no sanitary accommodation was provided for them at all. But this, at least, was known and understood. The second . . . was that even where accommodation was provided, it consisted wholly of the separate apartment at a charge of one penny: an absolutely prohibitive charge for a poor woman. . . . The moment it became known that I was one of those ungentlemanly and unromantic men who reject the angelic theory of womanhood, I received piteous anonymous letters from women begging me to get the penny charge at least reduced to a halfpenny. These letters, and the reports and complaints as to the condition of all the little by-ways and nooks in the borough which afforded any sort of momentary privacy, revealed a world of unmentionable suffering and subterfuge.

The one woman on the Vestry of St Pancras, with the help of Shaw and a few others, '. . . succeeded in shaming the Véstry into making the accommodation in the women's convenience partly free'. Six months later this free arrangement was abolished. 'I remonstrated, and was seconded by our lady member. An eminent member of the vestry immediately rose and expressed his horror at my venturing to speak in public on so disgusting a subject. He then accused my seconder of indecency.' One argument against reform was that a woman so unwomanly as to write to a vestryman on the subject could scarcely deserve any consideration. Amid objections of this kind, Shaw's measure was defeated, and nothing more was done during his term of office. Meanwhile, women had been excluded from holding office.

Shaw lost no time in seizing on a quite different subject which put his name in the newspapers, and using that adroitly to publicize his struggles with the Vestry. He told Sidney Webb:

Cunninghame Graham writes a letter to the Chronicle raising the question whether, as a dramatist, I am a pupil of Ibsen or De Maupassant. I reply with a long letter showing that the real force which influences me is the attitude of the St Pancras Vestry on the question of providing free sanitary accommodation for women.

The letter itself ends:

It must not be inferred that vestrymen are an inhuman and merciless class. . . . All their finest instincts are jarred unendurably when their minds are dragged down from the contemplation of photographs of princesses to sanitary conveniences for charwomen.

. . . .

If a dramatist living in a world like this has to go to books for his ideas and his inspiration, he must be both blind and deaf. Most dramatists are.

The dramaturgical question is a pretext, but it serves. The more one puts together Shaw's experience and his plays, the more one sees how his genial comedy was refined out of the bitter comedy of daily life.

The incident of the public toilets of St Pancras, gross as it may seem, shows the fineness of Shaw's mind as well as any. It is easy to speak nobly about general subjects, but the man who will take upon himself distasteful practical matters is one who has a genuine kindness for women. The suffragists would naturally have thought this struggle trivial. In retrospect, however, it argues for the honesty and realism of Shaw's preference for the co-option of women officials over the women's vote.

At the time of this dispute, about the turn of the century, women were permitted to sit on Parish Councils, Urban and Rural District Councils, and Boards of Guardians and School Boards. They were excluded from County Councils and Borough Councils. The nature of the offices that were open indicates that the British muddling approach was based, however unconsciously, on the same kind of insight which inspired Shaw's aware and articulate principle of the need for women on public bodies, for women were allowed to sit on boards which had dealings with the welfare of women and children. Before women were admitted to the vestries, for example, male vestrymen appointed only male inspectors to enforce the provisions of the factory laws. The sanitary accommodations for women workers were out of bounds for these inspectors. A Fabian Tract which bears the unmistakable imprint of Shaw's style points out: 'When the vestries were thrown open to women, this was at last recognized and women inspectors were appointed. It is impossible to describe the state of things which was then discovered.'

Even this minimal participation of women in government was reduced in 1899 by the Dunraven Exclusion Clause. At this time the Vestries were replaced by Metropolitan Borough Councils, and this change was made a pretext for excluding women from the newly constituted body. The Clause was adopted in Parliament by a group of men '. . . who were facetious and rather coarse in the vein usual on such occasions'.

Shaw and the Fabians continued to agitate. Fabian Tract No. 126 proposes that women should be made eligible as county and borough councillors and that every poor law authority should be required to make up by co-option the number of its women members to a minimum of five.

On the formation of an English literary academy, Shaw again put his pen to work on behalf of women. As a substitute for Mrs Humphry Ward's resentful resolution, he suggested that six propositions be put, one of which was:

That the first Academy shall contain a sufficient number of women of letters to make it clear that no sex disqualifications are to be allowed to become traditional in the body.

This un-statistical and un-legalistic attitude is characteristic of Shaw. Disparaging votes for women at the very height of the women's war ('. . . provided every governing body and jury in the country be composed of men and women as the nation is') he carried the rejection of legal and numerical rights even further than he had previously:

But the real vote to go for . . . is the vote in the division lobby. And even that I disparage. If I had to choose between an Act declaring that no Bill shall pass into law, or resolution be carried in either House of Parliament, unless the quorum consists of women as well as men, *even if the women's votes did not count,* and an Act giving the present franchise to women on the same footing as men, I should unhesitatingly choose the former. It is the presence of women, and the contribution of what Mr Asquith disgustedly calls their point of view to the discussion, that will make the vital difference.

. . . .

Who that knows the world has any doubt that the fear of admitting women to parliament is largely the fear that they will screw up the moral standard unbearably? Why not give them the opportunity of shaming it up, leaving the blushing victims to turn the screw on themselves?

This is the voice of a man who has sat through many exclusively male meetings. The 'moral tone' of these gatherings caused him to say, when the possibility of appointing women factory inspectors even in the absence of women council members was offered:

The tone in which questions concerning women are still discussed, by Peers and Vestrymen alike (a tone which is at once silenced by the presence of a woman representative) makes it practically impossible for her to approach male members of the council on the subject of her duties.

Shaw hoped, apparently, for something like the effect which Elizabeth Blackwell, the first woman to take a medical degree in the United States, had on the incorrigibly rowdy medical students who are said to have been subdued into perfect order by her mere presence.

All this, however, is trivial compared to the great question which Shaw, as his life progressed, found more and more compelling: the question of how human society can be governed. The most serious of his arguments for the participation of women goes beyond the rights of women themselves and deals with humanity's most desperate need.

Now political capacity is rare; but it is not rarer in women than in men. Nature's supply of five per cent or so of born political thinkers and administrators are all urgently needed in modern civilization; and if half of that natural supply is cut off by the exclusion of women from Parliament and Cabinets the social machinery will fall short and perhaps break down for lack of sufficient direction.

Competent women, of whom enough are available, have their proper places filled by incompetent men: there is no Cabinet in Europe that would not be vitally improved by having its male tail cut off and female heads substituted.

Shaw was neither the only man nor the first man to hold this view. William Lloyd Garrison had urged that women should sit in Congress and in the state legislatures and that there should be an equal number of men and women on all national councils. John Stuart Mill had given his argument exactly the same theoretical basis:

Is there so great a superfluity of men fit for high duties that society can afford to reject the service of any competent person? Are we so certain of always finding a man . . . for any duty or function of social importance . . . that we lose nothing by putting a ban on one-half of mankind, and refusing beforehand to make their faculties available, however distinguished they may be!

But Shaw – he who called John Stuart Mill uxorious – went on to answer a question he had not been asked:

The only decent government is government by a body of men and women; but if only one sex must govern, then I should say, let it be women – put the men out! Such an enormous amount of work done is of the nature of national housekeeping, that obviously women should have a hand in it. I have sat on committees both with women and without them; and emphatically I say that there ought always to be women on public bodies. Decency demands it – simple common decency. Women at once discover evils and omissions which men never think of, especially in matters of public health, sanitation, and the like. In fact, I've found it impossible to get the most necessary things done when only men are set to do them.

. . . .

However, I am not advocating the exclusion of men from Parliament. I only say that if you ever have the chance to choose between a parliament of men and a parliament of women – which you haven't and never will have – choose the parliament of women. They would prove to be weak precisely where they are supposed to be strong, just as men do; because the ideal man is a woman; and vice versa.

This is only one example of Shaw's recurrent inclination to put the second sex first, an inclination which creeps up on him at times and then is put away by his common sense and his clear-sighted observation. Before he died Shaw took note of a process which he ought to have expected – that in refining men, women were coarsening their own behavior. We see this happening in the personal lives of the characters in *Too True To Be Good*, but the more horrifying example is that of Begonia Brown in *Geneva*. This thoroughgoing *arriviste* and vulgarian is the subject of a Shavian afterthought which one prefers to doubt:'Begonia becomes the first female Prime Minister, too late for inclusion in the play.' Need even the despised techniques of popular politics take us so far from the sound housekeeping M.P.s to whom Shaw was earlier prepared to trust civilization? I think not. Begonia is a bug, not a flower, and her belated election to high office a natural result of her author's being faced with a state of the world which corresponded to nothing except a sane mind's worst nightmares, and far exceeded those. She had better be ignored.

Shaw had provided the antidote earlier, in the two women among the cabinet ministers of *The Apple Cart*. Amanda, who is gay, and Lysistrata, who is earnest, are the only ministers in the cabinet who behave themselves. All the men, whatever their various faults and abilities, behave like schoolboys and seem to feel no connection between principle and action. It is the women who have a regard for reality, and it is the women who recognize the genius of King Magnus and give him what little help and kindness he receives. In spite of the fact that their relationship with him remains entirely one of business, the two women ministers give the king the same kind of protection and solace he has from his sensible queen and his amusing mistress. These female ministers of state – kind, perceptive, conscientious – are not entirely false to the contrast in real life between men and women as officials. How much of this contrast is due to the very different bases of selection for the two sexes, and how much is due to an intrinsic difference of the kind Shaw implies, it is still too early to say. On the other hand, it is by no means too early to say that Shaw was right in treating the vote as a simple and necessary act of justice which, as it continually offers a choice which is no choice, can solve no problems which present real difficulty; and also that Shaw was right in saying that the best contribution women could make would be in running things and bossing men around, a department in which he felt they showed considerable talent.

CHAPTER 9

Second Sex First

THE woman who emerges at last from all Shaw's scolding, wooing, encouraging and instructive words is, like the society he envisions, a little beyond our reach. But even though the superwoman, who is never jealous and always gets her man, who is calm and maternal, and voluptuous without vulgarity, does her national housekeeping with relaxed efficiency, protects a man but never asks for protection, and is in all things a man's dream of perfection, may be impossible, she is made up of elements that already exist in living women and have existed through all the deprivations and deformities that male and female stupidity have combined to impose through the ages. But Shaw never said we could ourselves become supermen – not by being Aryan or by being brainy or by being inspired or by being virtuous. He was unbearable to the ordinary man just because he *would* face facts and allowed scarcely an inch of illusion in a whole painful universe of truth. He said the human race was hopeless and would have to evolve into a new species before it could begin to live decently. But in one way he was kinder to us than the lowly who consider only our failings to be 'human'. He did recognize the existence among us of 'chance attempts at the superman', those rare beings who, we discover with joy, can be admired as well as loved, and who save us from despair. Shaw himself, with his combination of amiability, strictness of intellect and strength of character, might serve as one of those working models for a new species of humanity.

Nothing in his long life's work has more moral elegance than Shaw's consideration of women. He began paradoxically by defending woman against her admirers, those woman-worshippers who demanded a paragon, chaste and selfless. Shaw pointed out that the exaggeration of differences between men and women, like the obsession with chastity, was an obsession with sex. He saw also that preserving the purity of women by keeping them out of business and politics, implied also a desire to preserve the impurity of business and politics and, by separating woman's innocence from man's drive for money and power, to avoid the pangs of confronting Christian and civilized ideals with the realities of *laissez-faire* capitalism. When Shaw speaks of woman as though she might save men's souls (or society, which is not so different a matter as it sounds), he intends quite a different process, one in which women plunge into practical matters and change reality instead of shunning it.

The Shavian woman, instead of being unselfish, is radically selfish. The selfishness Shaw recommends is extreme because only in its extreme form can it resist the insidious temptations of idealism, and also because selfishness, when finally freed from every petty concern, as it is in so many of the women in Shaw's plays, becomes a saintly assurance and strength. Certainly if evil and guilt be as extraneous to human life as they are to Shaw's consciousness, getting to the roots of the self may well be the only way to virtue. At any rate, Shaw's own tastes are so clearly superior to a vulgar, guzzling happiness, that the selfishness he recommends to woman can only mean honesty and self-respect.

The Shavian woman outrages the 'womanly' ideal further by being the aggressor in sex. That phrase has an unpleasant sound, but the Shavian huntress is by no means an unpleasant woman. Shaw considers courtship a game, not a war; therefore he endows his huntress with tact, wit, personal charm, and a strong sense of her own individuality, instead of making her the ferocious woman more timid authors imagine. Her outward pleasantness is matched by nobility of motive. In the woman who interests Shaw, the woman who is a vital genius, even unscrupulous or promiscuous behavior is interpreted as the working of the evolutionary appetite through the promptings of her unconscious self. Those who reject the mystical element in this process must account for Saint Joan's voices, which are no less voices from God for being just common sense or imagination. In the same way, a woman's pursuit of a lover need be no less the pursuit of an impersonal, evolutionary goal (a father for the Superman) simply because it is inspired by sexual attraction. In fact Shaw would claim that a conscious, dutiful choice of a genetically certified mate would be doomed to failure, since we cannot consciously know how to create something better than ourselves; therefore the voice of the unconscious is our only clue.

Shaw separates motherhood from marriage conceptually, taking the view that the best arrangements for one are seldom best for the other. Practically, on the other hand, he views with horror any attempt by a woman in our society to bear children out of wedlock, just as he views with horror all other anarchism in social reform, because of the ghastly troubles it causes the individual without solving anything for society.

The provisions society makes for motherhood are of the utmost importance in Shaw's view, since his despair of political action among Yahoos makes all his hopes for the future of the human race depend upon creative evolution. Here the biological role of women gives them special responsibilities, and Shaw recognizes a primeval difference between woman's immanent work of reproducing and nurturing human life and man's transcendent work as an artist and philosopher. This distinction does not blind him, as it does so many abstract and dogmatic thinkers, to the obvious fact that civilized women have artistic and intellectual impulses just as men have, and that women's ability to act upon these impulses is hampered far more by social than by biological handicaps.

To permit the evolutionary appetite full play, Shaw proposes in various ways four different reforms of our present arrangements. The first of these is equality, which for Shaw means equality of income. That this pure socialist doctrine should be useful to Shaw's evolutionary theories is only one example of the beautiful coherence of his views, a coherence particularly pleasing because it is in no way contrived, but results directly from the clarity and passion of his thought. Equality is essential to selective breeding because it removes the class barriers which may prevent marriage between two people instinctively attracted to each other.

A second reform that goes back to socialist principles is state support of mother and child, which has evolutionary advantages quite aside from its inescapable logic. These advantages are: first, to change the pattern of adverse selection by which at present the least civilized mothers breed most freely, while those who have more intelligence and a greater sense of responsibility limit themselves more nearly to the number of children they can care for; second, to free women from economic dependence on their husbands so that even the most provident could marry the man they find sexually attractive. These two reforms illustrate the way Shaw's proposals for long-range improvements are also considerate of each individual woman during the little space of one life.

A third reform which would permit the evolutionary appetite to work unhindered is the substitution of polygamy for monogamy. Here Shaw is assuming that marriage will continue to go with motherhood. Polygamy would 'sterilize' the inferior men by letting a woman choose, as Shaw says the maternal woman always will, to share a superior man with other women, rather than to have an inferior man all to herself. The financial drawbacks are already solved (in theory) by the state support of mother and child. The emotional drawbacks, as Shaw points out, have never deterred any society in which polygamy had practical advantages.

It is never quite clear how literally Shaw intends us to take his references to polygamy. At times he uses the term to describe the network of liaisons which represents our society's *de facto* revision of the marriage laws. If, however, Shaw does intend, as he seems to, a legal form of multiple marriage, then another name is needed for the instances in which the mother is not married to the father. This pattern I have called adultery, since Shaw implies clearly that at least one of the parents will be married to someone who is sexually less fascinating but far more congenial as a domestic partner When Shaw claims that the sexual relation is not a personal relation, his brutality is only the brutality of truth He is referring to the unmistakable fact that physical attraction is never a rational response to all the attributes of a human being.

To recognize adultery as a way of begetting children 'without loss of honour' would be of value to two kinds of women. The first of these are the natural old maids, women whose superiority shows itself in a taste for an orderly, quiet, independent life. Shaw sees the possibility that these women would dedicate themselves to the rearing of a few children with the same lavishness and wisdom that our present arrangements cause them to divert to the care of animals, plants and committees. The other women who would benefit are those fatally attracted to men with whom they cannot live tolerably for even a few days, let alone a lifetime. Such incompatible pairs may give us, as Shaw points out, much the same advantages that 'crossing' gives in the breeding of animals.

Shaw's opinions on the subject of marriage differ somewhat, depending on whether he is writing as a social critic, a husband, an evolutionist, or a playwright. As a playwright, he is in rebellion against the sentimental notion that marriage is a happy ending, and the convention that love interest is the one kind of interest essential to a play or novel. When Shaw does treat marriage as a happy ending, that is not with a view to personal happiness, but as a reminder of the supra-personal meaning with which he endows even the most fragile flirtation. Shaw's criticism of our marriage laws and customs is so radical and so well known, that it obscures the meaning of the many delightful marriages glimpsed in his plays. It would be difficult, in fact, to name any other writer (except the obvious sentimentalists) who has given so consistently pleasant a picture of married couples dwelling together in harmony, affection and infidelity. The genuine kindness and companionability of these marriages is the result of personal qualities in the partners, particularly the wives, which outweigh the cruelty of the customs and laws governing marriage.

In *Getting Married* Shaw's indictment of marriage is consolidated, and the various ways in which marriage can become a slavery are both dramatized and described. Under capitalism, marriage means economic slavery for the dependent woman. The parallel between marriage and prostitution has a historical foundation in the venerable custom of buying wives and shows itself in our own times in the demand for virginity in brides and absolute fidelity in wives. Furthermore, as long as marriage remains an economic arrangement it cannot cease to be a spiritual slavery as well, for men and women alike. The more civilized and conscientious the man, the more he will feel compelled to sacrifice his inclinations and even his principles when they are in conflict with his obligations to his wife and children.

In spite of all its disadvantages, Shaw continues to feel that marriage is inevitable. The application of two simple principles could make it tolerable as well. First, custom must sanction many kinds of relationship under the name of marriage. Second, marriage must remain as it begins, a voluntary association. Marriage, in other words, is defined by divorce, and Shaw's belief is that divorce should be granted at the request of either party without asking for any reasons. To the women who consider so much freedom a backward step, Shaw would answer that their objections are valid only for the woman who is economically dependent, especially if she is also debarred from all the satisfactions men have outside that mythical happy home in which middle-class women have for so long been immured.

On the subject of that late-flowering luxury called love, for all his assurance, Shaw maintains his respect for the mysteries, subtleties and inconsistencies which remain even after the last reasonable word has been said, and therefore his attitude cannot be dismissed with the simple formulations that are customary. There is not a trace of bawdy in his writings; on the other hand, there is not a single character rendered unsympathetic by any breach of the sexual rules, not a single condemnation of any sexual act in itself. Shaw does employ a kind of euphemism which those born in the twentieth century find unnecessary; on the other hand, the euphemism of his language does not hide the realism of his thought, and he defends without reservation the writers who speak in the plainest terms about sexual experience, to the point of suggesting that budding girls be absolutely required to read *Lady Chatterley's Lover*. His marriage was sexless by agreement, as far as we know, and he did his best to remain faithful to it, even though his best was not always quite good enough to please a wife; on the other hand, he had remained single until forty, and before his marriage had been involved in an inconvenient number of intense love affairs, sometimes several at once, and at no time, even forty years after his marriage, did he find it possible to resist entirely the attraction of sexually interesting women, whatever their failings in other respects. He is scornful of people who allow sexual infatuation to rule their lives; on the other hand, he believes that the right to complete sexual experience is one which every political constitution should guarantee. Above all, he grants sexual freedom to women on absolutely equal terms, his feminine 'varietists' being, if anything, more at ease with themselves and more delightful to others than the philandering men.

Shaw's theories about women's right to work for a living are clearly set forth in his prose tracts. They are founded, like all his theories, on a desire for a sensibly arranged society: women's energy and abilities are needed if the work of the world is to be done; women's wages must be equal or the women's wage will drive the man's wage down below subsistence level; governing ability is so rare that when we rule out the competent women we can only fill their places with incompetent men; and so on. When the case for the working woman is put on this basis, it need not evoke the punitive response which most men make to women's demand for work on equal terms. Even in this coldly practical approach, Shaw goes beyond the claims of the feminists themselves by emending the plea for equal opportunity so that it becomes a plea for equal consideration. If democracy were to mean equal consideration, then working mothers would have to be granted maternity leaves, maternity pensions and specially arranged working hours. As matters stand at present, every working mother is engaged in denying the undeniable fact that a conscientious mother is, in a special sense, a handicapped worker. Shaw's method puts the burden of overcoming that handicap on the whole society instead of on the individual woman.

Shaw does something even more valuable for the career woman than asserting her right to equal treatment: he asserts her right to be feminine as well. The woman who engages Shaw's interest is always the woman whose work is a career, usually in the fine arts. The most interesting and vivid of these women, especially in Shaw's early work, are on the stage, several as actresses, one as an acrobat, one as a concert pianist. It is significant that these are the careers that divorce a woman most completely from the home, simultaneously robbing her of shelter and freeing her from convention. As a consequence, these women are tough and self-reliant egotists. I cannot help feeling that one of Shaw's reasons for so insistently dramatizing their 'unwomanly' traits, including physical strength, is to emphasize as strongly as possible their charm, their femininity, and the final, unanswerable evidence of their imperial success in love.

The complete woman, then, is as absolute a concept as the complete man. Her entry into such masculine strongholds as the professions is not made contingent upon her giving up the privileges of the home-bound woman. In Shavian logic there is no more reason for a successful woman to give up her femininity than for a successful man to give up his masculinity. Again Shaw's argument is based rather on society's needs than on those of the individual woman. What our world lacks, he says, is precisely the feminine point of view.

It is never quite clear whether Shaw merely believes that the feminine view is needed to counterbalance the masculine, or whether he believes the feminine view is actually to be preferred. He does say flatly that if one had to choose between a parliament of women and a parliament of men, one should choose the women. After making the usual allowance for Shaw's playfulness and also his penchant for hitting a debating point as hard as possible, there are still two factors to consider. First, women have never had a chance to govern the world. A detached observer of the cruelty, waste and folly of our man-made society might well conclude that women could hardly have done worse, that almost anything done differently, in fact, must have been done better. This line of argument stands on emotion, not logic, but that does not prove it wrong. Shaw's remark about the parliament of women is also one step beyond logic, even though he tried to justify it rationally.

The second factor is even less rational. There may have been, deep in Shaw's consciousness, a sense that it is the women who take care of us, in whom the final refuge and final comfort is to be found, and that whatever instinct it is that guides women in dealing with their sons and lovers, might guide them also in ruling the world. Psychologists (predominantly male) would no doubt claim that such feelings go back to the infant's dependence on his mother. A woman cannot be quite so certain about that, since it does not take into account a feeling fairly common among women that the male represents safety, rescue, a relief from responsibility. Either these two feelings have to be traced to two different sources – the male infant's to the mother, the adult woman's to the man's physical strength – or there may be one common source: traces in some stratum of consciousness of the perfect sexual relationship, with its momentary but total sense of refuge and revelation, its apparent resolution of all the discords of existence. If this idea have any validity, it may explain why no woman makes such extravagant claims for women as Shaw does.

None of his proposals, however, depends on this final reduction of the difference between the sexes to a mystical perception. Every one is made on solid, rational grounds. The flavor, however, the spirit in which the proposals are offered, not as grudging concessions, but as the gifts of a delighted giver, seems to result from the overflowing gratitude of love. Of course Shaw gives more reasoned arguments for his belief in the saving woman – chiefly the practical and life-conserving qualities of the mother-woman. Whatever his reasons, it is clear that all arguments are secondary to the presence of the saving woman in Shaw's plays. Candida, Major Barbara, Saint Joan – even the wild millionairess – and also the soothing wives and mistresses in the late plays, all indicate a sense that women have some resource that men have not. But whereas the traditional saving woman of literature saved by her innocence, these Shavian women do so by their unflinching realism. Male egomania falls in flimsy shreds when it encounters their clarity and decisiveness, the strength of which Shaw says (as others have said) comes of transcending the self. Yet again these women, so sensible, downright and unilluded, remain bewitchingly feminine.

Shaw's views on women's suffrage cannot possibly be misunderstood by anyone who understands both how much he admired and trusted women and how little value he saw in the suffrage under a democracy run by party politics. Suffragists of his own time can be forgiven for not grasping, in the rush of battle, Shaw's longer and more complicated train of thought. Having declared himself fully on behalf of equal political rights for women, he later tried to explain to various suffragists why he felt that the vote as such was, though necessary, an inadequate and misguided final goal, since, as he accurately predicted, there would never be a 'women's vote', women would not vote for women, and the vote at the polls is, for men and women alike, an illusory means of political power.

Even while he was reminding women that the vote would be no panacea, Shaw was also giving the women's war a certain profundity of meaning that few women have found in it. Shaw points out the personal implications of civil rights for women, seeing the obscure but essential connection between the right to vote and the right not to have one's body violated, a right far less common than middle-class optimists have supposed.

One matter in which Shaw recognizes a marked difference between men and women is in their attitudes toward sexual conduct. He feels that women, because of their role in reproduction, have far more serious and sensible views about sexual behavior than the ordinary man. Therefore he allows himself to hope that the women's vote, even though ineffective for the rights of women themselves, might have at least a preventive or a modifying influence on questions of sexual consequence, such as factory wages, slum houses, laws affecting prostitution and the rights of parent over child.

On the other hand, Shaw feels that this purpose and every other purpose for which women sought the vote would be better served by making mandatory the coupled vote. As a means of seeing that women have the vote that counts, which is the vote for measures rather than the vote for candidates, Shaw proposes that every vote be cast for a man *and* a woman, so that the representative body shall consist of equal numbers of men and women.

In all this, however, getting the woman's point of view into government seems less important to Shaw than getting the woman's share of brains and governing ability. Granting that intelligence is about equally distributed between the two sexes, and granting also the Shavian premise that intelligence, especially political intelligence, is at once the rarest and the most necessary of human qualities, one can hardly disagree with Shaw's conclusion that debarring half the citizens from participating in government is one of the most dangerous of human follies.

Shaw's belief in the slight superiority of women would be highly suspect had he not first made another kind of statement, more basic, more valid and far more needed. Shaw said early and often, in various ways, that woman is merely man in petticoats; in other words, that the apparent difference between men and women has been greatly exaggerated by costume, education, occupation and habit. The soul, he points out, is very largely androgynous. In this sense, Shaw also minimizes the role of sex in human life, though not in evolution, pointing out that we spend the larger part of our lives in activities in which the difference between the sexes is irrelevant. There is no contradiction between this view and Shaw's belief that the best contribution women can make is that of the distinctively feminine viewpoint: none, that is, unless one considers masculinity as a human standard and femininity as a deviation. The androgynous nature to which Shaw refers is by no means a masculine nature.

It is fair to say, then, that Shaw advocates all the equality between the sexes that nature will allow. He even goes so far as to favor a greater similarity between the sexes than has ever existed before. In the face of the irreducible differences which remain, however, he places the second sex first, but with a most important qualification. Woman may well be first in the sense that she has a closer connection with the evolutionary work of the Life Force; first in the sense that equal consideration will always dictate certain special privileges for her; first in the sense that her inspired practicality may be the salvation of a society that is heading for the rocks under masculine leadership. On the other hand, woman is never first for her own sake. Her evolutionary instinct, her reproductive labors and her place in the councils of state, all benefit her whole society. Shaw's inclusive spirit easily reconciles the good of society with the good of the individual woman, just as it reconciles a new appreciation of our common humanity with an unspoiled delight in sexual love. These are the fruits of an imagination which puts human qualities above all abstractions, and a spirit in which criticism and the joy of life are inseparable.

Notes

Page numbers in the following notes refer to the editions listed in the Bibliography. In the case of unpublished letters, I have obtained the texts from the manuscript of volumes two and three of the *Collected Letters of Bernard Shaw*, which the editor, Mr Dan H. Laurence, has kindly allowed me to examine and quote from. These letters may not be further quoted or in any way used without the permission of Mr Laurence and that of the Shaw Estate, which holds copyright.

Chapter 1. *Shavianism and Feminism*

Page 11   'Actual freedom has . . .': Camus, *The Rebel*. New York, p. 20; London, p. 26.

Page 12   '. . . no change that . . .: *Our Theatres in the Nineties*, I, p. 108.

'A writer who . . .: Samuel Johnson, *Lives of the English Poets* (ed. G. B. Hill). New York: Oxford University Press; and Oxford: Clarendon Press, 1905, I, p. 411.

Page 13   'But the whirligig . . .': *Three Plays for Puritans*, pp. xxxv–xxxvi.

On Mrs Clandon see: *Plays Pleasant and Unpleasant*, II, pp. 197-8.

'Now that Ibsen . . .': 'The Quintessence of Ibsenism', *Major Critical Essays*, p. 5.

Page 14   '. . . treated the male . . .': G. K. Chesterton, *The Victorian Age in Literature*, p. 69.

'The reply may . . .': *Ibid.*

'. . . perpetually making the . . .': *Ibid.*

'I am certain . . .': Keats' *Letters*. New York, p. 156; London, p. 153.

Page 15   '. . . evil thoughts, malice . . .': *Ibid.* New York, p. 157; London, p. 154.

'equally smokeable': *Ibid.* New York, p. 197; London, p. 207.

On Dickens's Women see Shaw's preface to C. Dickens, *Great Expectations*, p. xviii.

On prototypes of Strindberg see F. Harris, *Bernard Shaw*. New York, p. 114; London, p. 124.

'. . . all these books . . .': *The Intelligent Woman's Guide to Socialism and Capitalism*, p. 465.

Page 16   'At heart, he . . .': C. Brontë, *Shirley*, I, p. 166.

'The Women are . . .': 'Getting Married', *The Doctor's Dilemma, etc.*, p. 328.

Page 17   'Men are waking . . .': 'The Quintessence of Ibsenism', *Major Critical Essays*, p. 8.

'I am a . . .': *Bernard Shaw and Mrs Patrick Campbell: Their Correspondence*. New York, p. 15; London, p. 21.

'In feminine details . . .': Henderson, *Shaw*, p. 678.

Page 18 '. . . unlovable, unpleasing . . .': Constance A. Barnicoate, 'Mr Bernard Shaw's Counterfeit Presentation of Women'. *Fortnightly Review*, 85 (March 1906), pp. 516-17.

'. . . no one else . . .': *Ibid.*, p. 518.

'. . . we are not . . .': *Ibid.*

'The term "lady" . . .': *Ibid.*, p. 517.

'Stir your stumps': *Plays and Players*, p. 215.

'sexless dolls': F. Harris, *Bernard Shaw*. New York, p. 189; London, p. 191.

'. . . distinctly unpleasant, practically . . .': *Ibid.* New York, p. 189; London, p. 189.

'. . . vital defect in . . .': *Ibid.* New York, p. 190; London, p. 191.

Page 19 'Mr Valentine: You . . .': *Plays Pleasant and Unpleasant*, II, p. 291.

Page 20 'Nothing will persuade . . .': *Ellen Terry and Bernard Shaw: A Correspondence*, Letter VII (November 1, 1895). New York, p. 16; London, p. 17.

On Mrs Tanqueray and Mrs Warren see: Martin L. Kornbluth, 'Two Fallen Women: Paula Tanqueray and Kitty Warren', *The Shavian*, No. 14 (February 1959), pp. 14-15.

On Strindberg *vs.* Shaw see: A. Hamon, *Le Molière du XXe Siècle: Bernard Shaw*, p. 224.

Page 21 'La triomphatrice': *Ibid.*

'La théâtre de . . .': *Ibid.*

'I declare that . . .': *Plays Pleasant and Unpleasant*, p. xviii.

'. . . Woman, projecting herself . . .': *Man and Superman*, p. xviii.

'I am a . . .': 'As Bernard Shaw Sees Woman', *The New York Times Magazine*, June 19, 1927, p. 2.

Page 22 '. . . many women, including . . .': Priestley, *Thoughts in the Wilderness*, p. 35.

'Press Clippings', *Translations and Tomfooleries*, pp. 131-71.

'. . . dressed them up . . .': 'Woman Since 1860', *Time and Tide*, I (October 8, 1920), p. 443.

'. . . like the parlor . . .': 'As Bernard Shaw sees Woman', *loc. cit.*, p. 1.

'Masculine affectations were . . .': 'Woman Since 1860', *loc. cit.*, p. 443.

Page 23 'I remember when . . .': H. Pearson, *G. B. S. A Postscript*. New York, p. 72; London, p. 104.

'She has never . . .': *Plays Pleasant and Unpleasant*, II, p. 201.

'I do not . . .': 'Woman Since 1860', *loc. cit.*, p. 445.

'It was clear . . .': *Ibid.*, p. 444.

Page 24 'For life, as . . .': H. James, *Washington Square*. New York, p. 291; London, p. 188.

Page 25 'Rich, complex portraits . . .': E. Fuller, *The Image of Man in Modern Fiction*, p. 94.

'They are vessels . . .': *Ibid.*, p. 121.

'Thus humanity is . . .': Simone de Beauvoir, *The Second Sex*. New York, p. xvi; London, p. xv.

' . . . it is not . . .': 'The Quintessence of Ibsenism', *Major Critical Essays*, pp. 36-7.

'Is the cultured, . . .': *Ibid.*, pp. 110-11.

Page 26 'To see the . . .': J. S. Mill, *Subjection of Women*, p. 260.

Page 27 On Shaw's debt to his predecessors see: Julian B. Kaye, *Bernard Shaw and the Nineteenth-Century Tradition*.

Page 28 '. . . entirely and completely . . .': *The Case for Equality*, 1913, p. 4.

'a gallant evening': Winsten, *Jesting Apostle*, p. 66.

On self-control see: *Back to Methuselah*, pp. li-lii; *Man and Superman*, pp. 182-3.

' . . . the masculine silliness . . .': *Three Plays for Puritans*, p. xiii.

Page 29 On Shaw's love affairs see: *Collected Letters of Bernard Shaw*, and St J. Ervine, *Bernard Shaw*, pp. 145-7, 160-1, 444-51.

On Mollytompkins see: *To a Young Actress: The Letters of Bernard Shaw to Molly Tompkins*.

Page 30 'a chaos of . . .': G. K. Chesterton, *George Bernard Shaw*, p. 233.

Page 33 'Don't argue': E.g. in 'The Menace of the Leisured Woman', *Time and Tide*, VIII (February 4, 1927), p. 106.

'Still, a thing . . .': *Plays Pleasant and Unpleasant*, I, p. ix.

'If you call . . .': 'The Quintessence of Ibsenism', *Major Critical Essays*, p. 7.

Page 34 'They prove too . . .': *Immaturity*, p. xxxix.

Chapter 2. *Pedestals and Petticots, Paragons and Parrots*

Page 37 On the proletariat see: R. Hoggart, *The Uses of Literacy*, p. 74.

On the Bank of England see: P. Green, *Kenneth Grahame*. Cleveland, pp. 77-8; London, pp. 76-7.

Page 39 'Victorian propriety is . . .': Monroe Engel, *The Maturity of Dickens*, p. 149.

'combined coercion and . . .': J. S. Mill, *On the Subjection of Women*, p. 228. See p. 190.

'I often feel . . .': E. Hall (ed.), *Miss Weeton: Journal of a Governess, 1807-1811*, p. xvii.

Page 41 ' . . . had two possible . . .': M. Dalziel, *Popular Fiction 100 Years Ago*, p. 87. See also pp. 107, 116-17.

' . . . she makes you . . .': *Man and Superman*, p. 22.

Page 42 'For nearly seventy . . .': G. Raverat, *Period Piece*, p. 104.

'Be as selfish . . .': *My Dear Dorothea*, p. 25.

'Let your rule . . .': *Ibid.*

'Always strive to . . .': *Ibid.*, p. 15.

' . . . be careful not . . .': *Ibid.*

Page 43 ' . . . because politeness is . . .': *Ibid.*, p. 47.

'I am sure . . .': *Ibid.*, p. 43.

'When you make up your mind . . .': *Ibid.*, pp. 25-6.

Page 44 'My dear friend . . .': *Ibid.*, p. 30.

Page 45 On *Emma* see: L. Trilling, introd. to *Emma* (Boston: Houghton Mifflin, 1957), pp. ix-xi.

'I think I . . .': E. Hall (ed.), *Miss Weeton: Journal of a Governess, 1807-1811*, p. xvii.

Page 46 '. . . an example of . . .': 'The Quintessence of Ibsenism', *Major Critical Essays*, p. 31.

'. . . had toyed with . . .': Winsten, *Jesting Apostle*, pp. 75-6.

On William Stead see: 'The Quintessence of Ibsenism', *loc. cit.*, p. 32.

Page 47 'No *man* pretends . . .': *Ibid.*, pp. 33-4.

'digression': 'The Quintessence of Ibsenism', *loc. cit.*, p. 40.

'. . . traversed my loop . . .': *Ibid.*, pp. 40-1.

*'Do not do . . .': *Man and Superman*, p. 211.

Page 48 'If we have . . .': *Ibid.*, p. 39.

'All the same, . . .': *Ibid.*, p. 40.

'Home is the . . .': *Man and Superman*, p. 222.

'Woman has thus . . .': 'The Quintessence of Ibsenism', *loc. cit.*, pp. 77-8.

'. . . on no account . . .': 'Getting Married', *The Doctor's Dilemma, etc.*, p. 181.

'Both/And.': E. Bentley, *Bernard Shaw*. New York, pp. 32, 58, *et passim*; London, pp. 56, 82, *et passim*.

'. . . not women at . . .': 'The Quintessence of Ibsenism', *loc. cit.*, p. 38.

Page 49 On rumors about Sojourner Truth see: A. H. Fauset, *Sojourner Truth*, p. 139.

' . . . there is no . . .': 'The Quintessence of Ibsenism', *loc. cit.*, p. 130.

*'What she considered . . .': M. Dalziel, *Popular Fiction 100 Years Ago*, p. 87.

Page 50 'All I can . . .': *Ellen Terry and Bernard Shaw: A Correspondence*, Letter XXI (September 6, 1896). New York, p. 26; London, p. 42.

'. . . Esther is not . . .': Preface to C. Dickens, *Great Expectations*, p. v.

'In our novels . . .': 'The Quintessence of Ibsenism', *loc. cit.*, p. 25.

Page 51 'Tannhäuser may die . . .': *Ibid.*, p. 36.

'Therefore Woman has . . .': *Ibid.*, p. 40.

Page 52 'for lover or . . .': *ibid.*, p. 32.

'. . . certainly made her . . .': 'Getting Married', *The Doctor's Dilemma, etc.*, p. 263.

'You see, she's . . .: *Ibid.*, p. 264.

'. . . that fond of . . .': *Ibid.*, pp. 263-4.

'. . . like a bird . . .': *Ibid.*, p. 262.

Page 53 'the sort of . . .': from a letter dated April 23, 1895, quoted in Henderson, *Shaw*, p. 442.

'Now Archer was . . .': Foreword to William Archer, *Three Plays*. New York, p. xxvii; London, p. xxix.

Page 54   'But they are . . .': 'The Perfect Wagnerite', *Major Critical Essays*, p. 172.

'Strindberg, the only . . .': *Three Plays for Puritans*, p. xxviii.

'The women, who . . .': *Plays Pleasant and Unpleasant*, I, p. xv.

'In the middle . . .': *Ibid.*, I, p. xvi.

Chapter 3. *The Comedy of Courtship*

Page 59   '. . . was an advanced . . .': *Man and Superman*, p. 15.

Page 60   On Ann as Everywoman see: *Ibid.*, p. xxviii.

'Unashamed': 'Major Barbara', *John Bull's Other Island, etc.*, p. 326.

'Though it is . . .': *Plays Pleasant and Unpleasant*, I, p. 166.

For Tanner's speech on shame see: *Man and Superman*, p. 14.

'You scandalous woman . . .': *Ibid.*, p. 38.

Page 61   'A cunning and . . .': Winsten, *Jesting Apostle*, p. 119.

'Forgive my brutalities . . .': *Man and Superman*, p. 40.

Page 62   'Whether Ann is . . .': *Ibid.*, pp. 15-16.

'Not at all . . .': *Ibid.*, p. 16.

Page 63   'A father! a . . .': *Ibid.*, p. 131.

'Do you know . . .': *Ibid.*, p. 6.

'He must, one . . .': *Ibid.*, p. 4.

Page 64   'With them, to . . .': C. Brontë, *Shirley*, I, p. 280.

'A drama of . . .': *Man and Superman*, p. 3.

'A slave state . . .': Winsten, *Jesting Apostle*, p. 119.

Page 65   On Shaw's view of Candida's immorality see: J. Huneker, *Iconoclasts*, p. 254.

'. . . chiefly noteworthy for . . .': G. J. Nathan, 'Shaw as a Lover', *American Mercury*, XIII (February 1928), pp. 246-8.

'We go once . . .': 'Candida', *Plays Pleasant and Unpleasant*, II, pp. 139-40.

Page 66   'I give myself . . .': *Ibid.*, II, pp. 137-8.

Page 67   '. . . as unscrupulous as . . .': J. Huneker, *Iconoclasts*, p. 254.

'She seduces Eugene . . .': *Ibid.*

Page 68   '. . . I gather that . . .': letter of July 1, 1919; prospectively in *Collected Letters of Bernard Shaw* (ed. Dan H. Laurence).

Page 69   'I try to . . .': *Ellen Terry and Bernard Shaw: A Correspondence*, Letter CCXXV (August 8, 1899). New York, p. 248; London, p. 312.

'. . . between 30 and 40 . . .': 'Captain Brassbound's Conversion', *Three Plays for Puritans*, p. 215.

'. . . to be in hell . . .': *Man and Superman*, p. 128.

Page 70   'LADY CICELY Thoughtful man . . .': 'Captain Brassbound's Conversion', *loc. cit.*, p. 216.

Page 71   'What a pleasant . . .': *Ibid.*, p. 217.

'You must not . . .': *Ibid.*, pp. 217-18.

'Why? Has any . . .': *Ibid.*, p. 220.

'Well, why not? . . .': *Ibid.*, p. 221.

'You know, really . . .': *Ibid.*, p. 223.

Page 72   'LADY CICELY The important thing. . .': *Ibid.*, p. 228.

'. . . no man ever . . .': *Ellen Terry and Bernard Shaw: A Correspondence*, Letter XII (April 6, 1896). New York, p. 22; London, p. 25.

'Of the two . . .': *Ibid.*, Letter XIX (August 28, 1896). New York, p. 34; London, p. 39.

'like a bloomin . . .': 'Captain Brassbound's Conversion', *loc. cit.*, p. 232.

'And oh, while . . .': 'Captain Brassbound's Conversion', *loc. cit.*, p. 238.

Page 73   'And then you . . .': William Morris, *News from Nowhere*. Boston, p. 84; London, p. 85.

'Bless me! your . . .': 'Captain Brassbound's Conversion', *loc. cit.*, p. 248.

'Have you any . . .': *Ibid.*

Page 74   'Now before I . . .': *Ibid.*, p. 250.

'I can see . . .': *Ibid.*, p. 282.

'It's quite simple . . .': *Ibid.*, p. 283.

'Mr Bernard Shaw . . .': Susan L. Mitchell, *George Moore* (Dublin: Maunsell, 1916), as quoted in *Daily News*, October 23, 1916, p. 7: 4.

Page 75   'They make us . . .': *Man and Superman*, p. 22.

'I dunno about . . .': *Ibid.*, p. 67.

'Without an instant's . . .': *Ellen Terry and Bernard Shaw: A Correspondence*. New York, p. xxvii; London, pp. xxiv-xxv.

Page 76   '. . . a woman seeking . . .': *Man and Superman*, p. 115.

'Yes, as a . . .': *Ibid.*, p. 23.

'. . . all the unscrupulousness . . .: ' *Ibid.*, p. xx.

'. . . a sublime altruist . . .': *Ibid.*

Page 77   'Be as selfish . . .': *My Dear Dorothea*, p. 25.

'This is the . . .': *Man and Superman*, p. xxxi.

'. . . for the great . . .': 'The Shewing-up of Blanco Posnet', *The Doctor's Dilemma, etc.*, p. 457.

Page 79   'Poor wretch! Oh . . .': *Heartbreak House*, p. 122.

On pregnancy as a cure see: *Ibid.*, p. 137.

'danger and unutterable . . .': *Man and Superman*, p. xix.

'Yes, but, damn it . . .': *Heartbreak House*, p. 137.

Page 80   'There is no . . .': *Ibid.*, p. 120.

Page 81   'In the Romantic . . .': *Our Theatres in the Nineties*, III, p. 174.

'You cannot think . . .': *Florence Farr, Bernard Shaw, W. B. Yeats Letters*. New York, p. 76; London, p. 54.

Notes

Chapter 4. *Mothers Married and Unmarried*

Page 83 On the sources of Shaw's evolutionary theory see: *Back to Methuselah*, pp. xviii-xx, xliv-xlv.

On will *vs.* chance selection see: *Ibid.*, pp. xxi-xxvii.

Page 84 On the inheritance of acquired characteristics see: *Ibid.*, pp. lxxx-lxxxvi.

'I leave it . . .': ' "In Good King Charles's Golden Days",' *Geneva, etc.*, p. 159.

'We must eliminate . . .': *Man and Superman*, p. 203.

'The mere transfigurations . . .': *Ibid.*, p. 171.

'There is a . . .': *Ibid.*, p. xxii.

'. . . chance attempts at . . .': *Ibid.*, p. 179.

'. . . what is proposed . . .': *Ibid.*, pp. 182-3.

Page 85 'The matter must . . .': *Ibid.*, p. 206.

'a general secret . . .': *Ibid.*, p. 204.

'Even a joint . . .': *Man and Superman*, p. 205.

'. . . Miss Murby . . .': *Florence Farr, Bernard Shaw, W. B. Yeats Letters*. New York, p. 28; London, pp. 19-20.

Page 86 '. . . we should not . . .': *The Case for Equality*, p. 15.

'. . . we shall still . . .': *Man and Superman*, p. 174.

'What is really . . .': *Ibid.*

'indispensable to the . . .': *Ibid.*

'a great number . . .': *Ibid.*, p. 175.

'Though more costly . . .': *Ibid.*

'. . . the survival of . . .': *Ibid.*, p. 183.

Page 87 '. . . it took the form . . .': *Ibid.*, pp. 114-15.

'The modern devices . . .': *Ibid.*, p. 182.

'. . . human equality . . .': *The Case for Equality*, 1913, p. 4.

'. . . until you widen . . .': *Ibid.*, p. 16.

'The question, . . .': 'Getting Married', *The Doctor's Dilemma, etc.*, p. 208.

Page 88 For the 'Revolutionist's Handbook' version see: *Man and Superman*, pp. 214-15.

'. . . the revolt of . . .': *Ibid.*, p. 214.

On the sterilization of the schoolmistress see: the preface to: 'Getting Married', *loc. cit.*, pp. 210-11.

'. . . the one point . . .': *Ibid.*, pp. 206-7.

Page 89 'There is no . . .': 'Getting Married', *Ibid.*, p. 210.

'There are certain . . .': *Ibid.*, p. 316.

Page 90 'I ought to . . .': *Ibid.*, p. 267.

On The Old Maids of England see: *Ibid.*, pp. 210-11 and *Three Plays for Puritans*, p. xvii.

'The best mothers . . .': 'Getting Married', *The Doctor's Dilemma*, etc., p. 211.

'Everything that can . . .': *Man and Superman*, p. 186.

Page 91 For medical memoirs see: S. Maugham, *The Summing Up*, and E. Jones, *Free Associations*.

On Esther Waters' mother see: G. Moore, *Esther Waters*, pp. 133-4.

On birth as an economic disaster see: B. L. Hutchins, *The Working Life of Women*, 1911; Mrs Pember Reeves, *Family Life on a Pound a Week*, 1912.

On the price of housing and the death of children see: Mrs Pember Reeves, *op, cit.*, pp. 9-12.

'. . . . preserved very carefully . . .': 'Misalliance', *Misalliance, etc.*, p. 73.

'endowment of motherhood': Sidney Webb, *The Decline of the Birth-Rate*, pp. 18-19.

On maternity pensions see: Henry Harben, *The Endowment of Motherhood*, 1910, pp. 12-15.

Page 92 'Place the work . . .': 'Getting Married', *loc. cit.*, p. 254; cf. Ellen Key *et al.*, *The Woman Question*, p. 43.

'You call yourself . . .': As quoted by Meta Maynard, 'George Bernard Shaw', *The Actor's Society Monthly Bulletin*, February 1904, p. 6.

Page 93 On the replacement of marriage by agreement see: 'Getting Married', *loc. cit.*, pp. 212-13.

On adultery see Chapter 6, pp. 133-136.

'are not married . . .': 'Getting Married', *loc. cit.*, p. 210.

'There is no . . .': *Man and Superman*, p. 175.

'Marriage remains practically . . .': 'Getting Married', p. 182.

'In short, for . . .': Note on Francis Galton's paper on 'Eugenics', in *Sociological Papers* (London: Macmillan, 1905), I, 74-5.

Page 94 '. . . he is absolutely . . .': F. Harris, *Bernard Shaw*. New York, p. 167; London, p. 168.

Page 95 'Parents and Children': 'Misalliance', *Misalliance, etc.*, pp. 3-106.

'I think if . . .': *To a Young Actress: The Letters of Bernard Shaw to Molly Tompkins*, p. 161.

Page 96 On Mrs Collins see: 'Getting Married', *loc. cit.*, p. 315.

'. . . is indeed, perhaps . . .': H. C. Duffin, *The Quintessence of Bernard Shaw*, p. 74.

On Shaw's advice to O'Casey see: S. O'Casey, *Sunset and Evening Star*, pp. 255, 257. Considerations of this kind might have modified somewhat the findings of Louis Simon's *Shaw on Education*.

Page 97 Hamon's statement is:'. . . Mme Clandon, l'héroïne de la pièce, raisonnable, pondérée, franche, sincère, separée de son mari, M. Crampton. . . .' Augustin Hamon, *Le Molière du XXᵉ Siècle: Bernard Shaw*, p. 135.

Hamon's statement on the children's attitude is: 'Mme Clandon est, dans le théâtre de Shaw, la seule mère que les enfants aiment, estiment et respectent.' *Ibid.*, p. 135.

'. . . was an advanced . . .': *Man and Superman*, p. 15.

On children and emotion see the preface to 'Misalliance', *loc. cit.*, p. 18.

'I have a . . .': *Ellen Terry and Bernard Shaw: A Correspondence*, Letter LX (November 4, 1896). New York, p. 86; London, p. 106.

On the dangerous use of love see: 'Misalliance', *loc. cit.*, pp. 16-18; 'Getting Married', *loc. cit.*, p. 194.

On Mrs Clandon see: 'You Never Can Tell', *Plays Pleasant and Unpleasant*, II, p. 207, *et passim*.

'Why did't you . . .': *Ibid.*, p. 253.

Page 98 For another view of the Victorian family see: G. M. Young, *Victorian England*, pp. 224, 226-8.

On Shaw's authorship of Tract No. 2 see: Edward R. Pease, *The History of the Fabian Society*, p. 43.

'. . . The state should . . .': As quoted. *Ibid.*, p. 42.

'All one can . . .': 'Misalliance', *loc. cit.*, p. 85.

For Shaw's defense of Ellen Terry see: *Ellen Terry and Bernard Shaw: A Correspondence*. New York, pp. xii-xiii; London, pp. xii-xiv.

Page 99 '. . . to be an . . .': *To a Young Actress: The Letters of Bernard Shaw to Molly Tompkins*, p. 162.

Chapter 5. *Marriage: The Mystery of the Unhappy Ending*

Page 100 'And what an . . .': *Three Plays for Puritans*, p. 286.

Page 102 'Eliza's instinct tells . . .': 'Pygmalion', *Androcles and the Lion, etc.*, pp. 295-307.

On the law of his own nature see: *Three Plays for Puritans*, p. xxxvi.

On romantic love and romantic marriage see especially *Three Plays for Puritans* and ' Getting Married'.

'Go on talking': *Man and Superman*, p. 166.

Page 103 '. . . the slave of . . .': *The Intelligent Woman's Guide to Socialism and Capitalism*, p. 197.

Page 104 On Harriet Taylor see: M. St J. Packe, *Life of Mill*, p. 125. See also Mill's *Autobiography*, Chapter VII.

'I am far . . .': Mill, *Subjection of Women*, p. 248.

'There are certain . . .': 'Getting Married', *The Doctor's Dilemma, etc.*, p. 316.

'. . . he can claim . . .': Mill, *op. cit.*, p. 248.

'. . . in the most . . .': *Ibid.*, p. 262.

'Marriage is the only . . .': As quoted in Packe, *op. cit.*, p. 125.

'Any sentiment of . . .': Mill, *Subjection of Women*, pp. 260-1.

Page 105 On family life and the public welfare see: 'Misalliance', *loc. cit.*,
pp. 59-60, 105-6.

On the danger to the souls of men see: 'The Quintessence of
Ibsenism', *Major Critical Essays*, p. 8

'The only way . . .': *Plays Pleasant and Unpleasant*, pp. 212-13.

'The one is . . .': E. Belfort Bax, *Outlooks from the New Standpoint*,
1891, p. 160.

On injustices to men see: E. Belfort Bax, 'The Everlasting Female',
Outspoken Essays on Special Subjects, pp. 23-45.

Page 106 On marriage and prostitution see: 'Getting Married', *loc. cit.*,p.241.

'What is any . . .': *Plays Pleasant and Unpleasant*, p. 211.

'. . . just like a . . .': *Ibid*', pp. 209, 212-13, 211-12.

'How could you . . .': *Ibid.*, p. 212.

'In short, Capitalism . . .': *The Intelligent Woman's Guide to Socialism
and Capitalism*, p. 201.

Page 107 'In certain occupations . . .': *Ibid.*

'. . . an early attempt . . .': *The Irrational Knot*. New York, p. xxv;
London, p. 19.

'Matrimony is all . . .': *Ibid*, both editions, p. 67.

'I confess I . . .': *The Irrational Knot*. New York, p. 220; London,
p. 183.

On marriage as slavery see: 'Getting Married', *loc. cit.*, p. 235.

'an inhuman standard . . .': 'Cymbeline Refinished', *Geneva, etc.*,
p. 135.

Page 108 'At the point . . .': 'Getting Married', *loc. cit.*, p. 246.

'I do not . . .': 'Mrs Warren's Profession', *Plays Pleasant and
Unpleasant*, p. 172.

On canonical law see, for example, A. P. Herbert, *Made for Man*.

'. . . that the effect . . .': 'Androcles and the Lion,' *Androcles and the
Lion, etc.*, p. 69.

Page 109 'The greatest sacrifice . . .': *Ibid.*, p. 72.

'an absolute right . . .': 'Getting Married', *loc. cit.*, p. 206.

'Thus, though it . . .': 'Androcles and the Lion', *loc. cit.*, p. 71.

'. . . make the individual . . .': *Ibid.*, p. 72.

'And that is why . . .': *Ibid.*, p. 70.

On Cherry-Garrard see: 'Too True to be Good', *Too True To Be
Good, etc.*, p. 9.

On Alfred Gattie see: 'The Apple Cart', *St Joan, etc.*, pp. 186-
191.

Page 111 Dalziel, *Popular Fiction 100 Years Ago*, p. 109.

On Cashel Byron's attractions see: *Cashel Byron's Profession*,
pp. 43, 51.

'You are perfectly . . .': *Ibid.*, p. 253.

'Family Life in England', *Berliner Tageblatt*. March 23, 1913,
Beiblatt, 1 : 3.

Notes

Page 112 On attitude of other radicals to marriage see: J. B. Kaye, *Shaw and the Nineteenth-Century Tradition.*

'Do not forget . . .': F. Harris, *Bernard Shaw.* New York, p. 245; London, p. 238.

Page 113 On Shaw's marriage see: *Sixteen Self Sketches,* p. 115; and Janet Dunbar, *Mrs G. B. S.,* p. 153.

'. . . its inevitable preliminary . . .': Henderson, p. 419.

'. . . would never have . . .': H. Pearson, *G. B. S. A Postscript.* New York, p. 72; London, p. 101.

'. . . but sometimes I . . .: *ibid.* New York, p. 70; London, p. 101.

'The second, whose . . .': 'The Quintessence of Ibsenism', *Major Critical Essays,* p. 13.

**'I also am . . .: *Florence Farr, Bernard Shaw, W. B. Yeats Letters,* p. 1.

Page 114 '. . . a guilty society . . .': *Ibid.,* pp. 13-14.

'In the very . . .': *Ellen Terry and Bernard Shaw: A Correspondence.* New York, p. xii; London, p. xiii.

'Marriage is popular . . .': *Man and Superman,* p. 214.

'a little Alsatia': 'Getting Married', *The Doctor's Dilemma, etc.,* p. 342.

Page 115 'Peter the Great . . .': *Ibid.,* p. 188.

'Compared with statesmen . . .': *Ibid.,* p. 189.

'As a husband . . .': ' "In Good King Charles's Golden Days",' *Geneva, etc.,* pp. 156-7.

On passion and marriage as irreconcilable see: D. de Rougement, *Love in the Western World,* p. 288.

Page 116 '. . . healthy marriages are . . .': 'Getting Married', *loc. cit.,* p. 244.

'When one has . . .': Pearson, *G. B. S. A Postscript.* New York, p. 72; London, p. 101.

'. . . when a tie . . .': *Short Stories, Scraps and Shavings.* New York, p. 134; London, p. 153.

'. . . may mask all . . .': Preface to *Three Plays by Brieux.* New York, p. xxxix; London, p. 31.

Page 117 'a carnal disgust': Packe, *Life of Mill,* p. 319.

'Man is the . . .': as quoted in Ervine, *Shaw,* p. 381.

'. . . whenever it is . . .': 'Getting Married', *loc. cit.,* p. 234.

'. . . to make marriage . . .': 'Androcles and the Lion', *Androcles and the Lion, etc.,* p. 72.

'1. Make divorce . . .': 'Getting Married', *loc. cit.,* p. 253.

Page 118 'Should not divorce . . .': Letter to *The Times* [London], headed 'Divorce Law Reform', July 14, 1950, p. 7: 5.

'. . . attained by *any* . . .': as quoted in Packe, *Life of Mill,* p. 125.

Page 119 On divorce see: 'Getting Married', *loc. cit.,* pp. 234-5, 253-4.

'If he were . . .': 'Too True To be Good', *Too True To Be Good, etc.,* p. 23.

Page 120 'The familiar libertine's . . .': letter to 'Proteus' in *Westminster Gazette*, headed 'Letters to the Well-Known', November 22, 1911, p. 3: 1-2.

'This is the . . .': *Man and Superman*, p. xxxi.

'Any tolerable western . . .': 'Getting Married', *loc. cit.*, p. 233.

Page 121 'the only women . . .': 'G. B. S. and a Suffragist', interview, in the [London] *Tribune*, March 1, 1906, p. 3: 3-4.

'a regular old hen . . .': 'Getting Married', *loc. cit.*, p. 261.

'glorious strong-minded . . .': *Ibid.*, p. 344. See also *Three Plays for Puritans*, p. xviii.

'He married a . . .': 'Getting Married', *loc. cit.*, p. 262.

Page 122 'Oh, I dont . . .': *Ibid.*, p. 325.

'Love costs a . . .': letter to Maud Churton Braby (Mrs Percy Braby), May 18, 1908; Charles E. Feinberg Collection.

Page 123 'We are all . . .': *Ellen Terry and Bernard Shaw: A Correspondence*, Letter XII (April 6, 1896). New York, p. 22; London, p. 25.

'The attack on . . .': 'Getting Married', *loc. cit.*, p. 186.

Chapter 6. *The Real Thing*

Page 124 '. . . when the question . . .': as quoted in Henderson, *Shaw*, p. 501; and in Ervine, *Shaw*, p. 375.

'When I began . . .': letter to St John Ervine, as quoted in Ervine, *op. cit.*, p. 384.

Page 125 On Bellamy and Wells see: *Three Plays for Puritans*, p. xviii.

'. . . must proceed upon . . .': *Ibid*, p. xvi.

On the romantic play see: *Ibid.*, p. xvii.

'Since most people . . .': *Our Theatres in the Nineties*, I, p. 7.

Page 126 'When we want . . .': *Three Plays for Puritans*, p. xxvi.

'. . . the law of . . .': *Ibid.*

On Dick Dudgeon's motives see: *Ibid.*, pp. xxvi-xxvii.

'Besides, I have . . .': *Ibid.*, p. xxix.

Page 127 '. . . people who sacrifice . . .': *Plays Pleasant and Unpleasant*, I, p. 154.

'. . . modern English plays . . .': *Man and Superman*, pp. viii-ix.

'Let it kill . . .': *Ibid.*, p. 163.

'You propound a . . .': *Ibid.*, p. xv.

The French critic is Augustin Hamon, author of *Le Molière du XXᵉ Siècle*.

Page 128 'Better than Shakespear . . .': *Three Plays for Puritans*, p. xxvii.

'. . . only a mere . . .': *Man and Superman*, p. 187.

Page 129 'wounding our self- . . .': *Ibid.*

'The prudery of . . .': *Ibid.*, p. 186.

On Mrs Tarleton's prudery see: 'Misalliance', *Misalliance, etc.*, pp. 119-21; see also 'Overruled', *Androcles and the Lion, etc.*, p. 156.

'I do not . . .': 'The Need for Expert Opinion in Sexual Reform', *Platform and Pulpit* (London: Hart-Davis, 1962), pp. 201, 203.

Page 130 'Taboo in the Schools.': 'Misalliance', *loc. cit.*, pp. 28-30.

'. . . its dignity, its . . .': 'Getting Married', *The Doctor's Dilemma, etc.*, p. 249.

'If I had . . .': as quoted in F. Harris, *Bernard Shaw*. New York, pp. 238-9; London, pp. 232-3.

'. . . the obsolete Elizabethan . . .': *Our Theatres in the Nineties*, I, p. 28.

'whore' . . . 'mistress' . . .: F. Harris, *Bernard Shaw*. New York, p. 240; London, p. 233.

'I liked sexual . . .': letter to Frank Harris, as quoted in F. Harris, *Bernard Shaw*. New York, p. 244; London, p. 237.

Page 131 'Lawrence had delicacy . . .': *Ibid.* New York, p. 239; London, p. 233.

'naughty ladies': Preface to *Three Plays by Brieux*. New York, p. xiii; London, p. 6.

'Sexual irregularities began . . .': *Ibid.* New York, p. ix; London, p. 3.

'. . . assumed that unmentionability . . .': *Ibid.* New York, pp. xiii-xiv; London, p. 7.

'Thank goodness, they . . .': Henderson, *Shaw*, pp. 531-2.

'. . . with coarse frankness . . .': *Three Plays for Puritans*, p. xiii.

Page 132 'I found that . . .': *Ibid.*

'. . . the English novelist . . .': *Ibid.*, pp. xvii-xviii.

'Where the sexes . . .': George Meredith, *Essay on Comedy*. New York, p. 30; London, p. 56.

'I have said . . .': Winsten, *Jesting Apostle*, p. 139.

'Tannhäuser may die . . .': 'The Quintessence of Ibsenism', *Major Critical Essays*, p. 36.

'. . . because it is . . .': 'Getting Married', *The Doctor's Dilemma, etc.*, p. 245.

Page 133 On Freud's views see: E. Jones, *Life of Freud*. New York, II, pp. 291-4; London, II, pp. 328-30.

'. . . probably because of . . .': *Ibid.* New York, II, p. 314; London, II, p. 351.

'. . . all sorts of . . .': as quoted in Henderson, *Shaw*, p. 501; and in Ervine, *Shaw*, p. 375.

'Ce qui distingue . . .': Hamon, *Le Molière du XXᵉ Siècle*, p. 228.

On the French theater see: M. Moore, *Shaw et la France*, p. 172.

On polygamy see: 'Overruled', *Androcles and the Lion, etc.*, p. 151.

Page 134 '. . . a sentimental old . . .': *Man and Superman*, p. 151.

On Shaw's opinion of *The Philanderer* see: Ervine, *Shaw*, p. 251.

On the background of *The Philanderer* see: F. Harris, *Bernard Shaw*. New York, p. 238; London, pp. 233-4.

'Of course the . . .': *Our Theatres in the Nineties*, II, p. 259.

Page 135 'the best of . . .': ' "In Good King Charles's Golden Days",'
    Geneva, etc., p. 155.

Hamon says: '. . . nous avons vu que l'amour qu'il met en l'âme de
ses personnages féminins est toujours teinté de maternité.' (*Le
Molière du XXe Siècle*, p. 228.)

On eternal babies and mothers see: *Ellen Terry and Bernard Shaw:
A Correspondence*, Letter XIX (August 28, 1896). New York,
p. 34; London, p. 39.

'Being my wife . . .': 'The Apple Cart', *Saint Joan, etc.*, pp. 241-5.

'We were frightfully . . .': *Heartbreak House*, p. 36.

Page 136 'Now I am . . .': *Ibid.*

'Beauty's Duty': *Short Stories, Scraps and Shavings*, pp. 121-3.

'Every good wife . . .': 'A Glimpse of the Domesticity of Franklyn
Barnabas', *Short Stories, etc.*, p. 187.

'You make too . . .': *Ibid.*

'I have all . . .': 'Memories of Oscar Wilde', in New York edition
of F. Harris, *Oscar Wilde*, II, p. 393.

'abominably superstitious . . .': letter to Henry Seymour, editor
of *The Adult*, II (September 1898), pp. 230-1.

'Sex is an . . .': 'Androcles and the Lion', *Androcles and the Lion, etc.*,
p. 68.

Page 137 'Would you believe . . .': 'Too True To Be Good', *Too True To Be
Good, etc.*, p. 63.

'If we are to judge . . .': *The Case for Equality*, 1913, p. 16.

Page 138 'AUBREY You had . . .': 'Too True To Be Good', *loc. cit.*, p. 63.

'. . . in all the . . .': *Our Theatres in the Nineties*, I, p. 6.

Page 139 'Who are the . . .': 'Too True To Be Good', *loc. cit.*, p. 66.

'. . . a woman of . . .': *Our Theatres in the Nineties*, I, p. 47.

'Wells was a . . .': H. Belloc, as quoted in J. B. Priestley, *Thoughts
in the Wilderness*, p. 182.

On pretending to be shocked see: G. Raverat, *Period Piece*, p. 129.

Page 140 'Take this tip . . .': 'Too True To Be Good', *loc. cit.*, p. 65.

'No doubt its . . .': *Ibid.*

'When you loved . . .': 'Getting Married', *The Doctor's Dilemma,
etc.*, p. 338.

Page 141 '. . . their prey; and . . .': *Ibid.*, p. 339.

'I am a woman: a human creature . . .': *Ibid.*

'I am a woman; and you are a man . . .': 'Village Wooing', *Too
True To Be Good*, p. 114.

'You will find . . .': *Ellen Terry and Bernard Shaw: A Correspondence*,
Letter XXX (September 21, 1896). New York, p. 54; London,
p. 65.

'. . . the bodily contacts . . .': 'Village Wooing', *loc. cit.*, pp. 136-7.

'Your secondhand gabble . . .': *Ibid.*

Notes

Page 142 'I liked sexual . . .': F. Harris, *Bernard Shaw*. New York, p. 244; London, p. 237.

Page 144 On Shaw's advice to young ladies see: 'Getting Married', *The Doctor's Dilemma, etc.*, p. 181.

Page 145 '. . . a sort of . . .': V. Woolf, *A Room of One's Own*, pp. 19-23.

'Yes: you are . . .': 'The Millionairess', *The Simpleton, etc.*, p. 193.

Page 146 On Shaw's apology for his gallantry see: *Ellen Terry and Bernard Shaw: A Correspondence*. New York, pp. x-xi; London, p. xi.

Chapter 7. *Bread and Circuses: The Career Woman*

Page 150 On Shaw's view of *Mrs Warren's Profession* see: Henderson, *Shaw*, pp. 531-2.

On the woman's wage see: 'Women in the Labor Market', *The Intelligent Woman's Guide to Socialism and Capitalism*, pp. 196-204.

Page 151 ' "Well," said he . . .': W. Morris, *News from Nowhere*, p. 83.

'When it is complicated . . .': *Man and Superman*, p. xx.

Page 152 On happiness see: *Man and Superman*, p. xxxi; 'Too True To Be Good', *Too True To Be Good, etc.*, pp. 10-11; *The Intelligent Woman's Guide to Socialism and Capitalism*, pp. 45-6.

On selfishness see: 'The Quintessence of Ibsenism', *Major Critical Essays*, pp. 30-45.

Page 153 On bullying as flirtation see: W. Morris, *News from Nowhere*. Boston, p. 84; London, p. 85.

'If the Examiner . . .': *Plays Pleasant and Unpleasant*, II, p. 154.

'Women arists are . . .: Mill, *The Subjection of Women*, p. 288.

'Indeed, he remarks . . .': Harris, *Bernard Shaw*. New York, pp. 219-20; London, p. 217.

Page 154 On Miss Lockett see: Ervine, *Shaw*, pp. 114-15; also the *Collected Letters of Bernard Shaw*.

On Lucy's resemblance to Ellen Terry see: Ervine, *Shaw*, p. 59.

On actresses in Shaw's life see: *Ibid.*, pp. 160, 162, 260-1, 443.

Page 155 'I hate my . . .': *Cashel Byron's Profession*, p. 9.

'I say, Archer, . . .': as quoted in Henderson, *Shaw*, p. 103.

On Shaw's mother see: Ervine, *Shaw*, p. 17.

On Mrs Byron see: *Cashel Byron's Profession*, p. 2.

Page 156 On living in sin see: *The Irrational Knot*. New York, pp. 163, 221, *et passim*; London, pp. 94-5, 111, 183, *et passim*.

On being thin-skinned see: *Ibid.* New York, pp. 406-7; London, p. 223.

*'. . . in all the . . .': 'Two Plays', *Plays and Players*, p. 2.

Page 157 '. . . can sing A . . .': *The Irrational Knot*. New York, p. 16; London, p. 28.

'Conolly sat down . . .': *Ibid.*

'You must not . . .': *Saint Joan*, p. 67.

Page 158 On the home-bound woman see: 'Misalliance', *Misalliance, etc.*, p. 84.

On the daughter's revolt see: *Plays Pleasant and Unpleasant*, I, p. xvi.

'. . . all the unscrupulousness . . .': *Man and Superman*, p. xx.

On instinct *vs.* women see: L. Fiedler, *Love and Death in the American Novel*, *passim*.

Page 159 On artist man and mother woman see: *Man and Superman*, pp. xx-xxi.

'. . . Woman meets a . . .': *Ibid.*, p. xx.

On Florence Nightingale see: 'Too True To Be Good', *Too True To Be Good, etc.*, p. 9.

Page 160 'You cant cover . . .': 'Misalliance', *Misalliance, etc.*, p. 168.

On Lina's frankness see: *Ibid.*, pp. 195-6.

'He don't exclaim . . .': Gilbert and Sullivan, *The Complete Plays*, New York, p. 373; *Savoy Operas*, London, p. 345.

Page 161 'Art and nature, . . .': *Ibid.* New York, p. 372; London, p. 344.

Page 162 'And now let . . .': *Misalliance, etc.*, p. 260.

'[Pinero] has fallen . . .': 'Mr Pinero's New Play', *Plays and Players*, p. 28.

Page 163 'These critics must . . .': *Plays Pleasant and Unpleasant*, I, p. 168.

On Lydia Carew, see p. 155.

Page 164 Shaw's image: '. . . Bunsby dropping like a fascinated bird into the jaws of Mrs MacStinger . . .': *Man and Superman*, p. xviii.

On loving eminence see: 'The Quintessence of Ibsenism', *Major Critical Essays*, pp. 32-35.

'the female Yahoo': Shaw's words to portray Strindberg's attitude, not his own. *Three Plays for Puritans*, p. xxviii.

'cut the paragon . . .': *Ellen Terry and Bernard Shaw: A Correspondence*, Letter XXI (September 6, 1896). New York, p. 36; London, p. 42.

Page 165 'The author, though . . .': *Too True To Be Good, etc.*, p. 108.

On Candida Shaw says: 'Don't ask me conundrums about that very immoral female, Candida.' Letter to James Huneker, as quoted in Huneker, *Iconoclasts*, p. 254; see above, p. 65.

Page 166 'Besides, it is . . .': *The Simpleton, The Six, and The Millionairess*, p. 155.

On Ellen Terry's performance see: Ervine, *Shaw*, pp. 337-8.

'trading on the . . .': *Ellen Terry and Bernard Shaw: A Correspondence*, Letter CCXXV (August 8, 1899). New York, p. 248; London, p. 312.

On the higher moral number see: *Man and Superman*, p. 63.

Page 167 On the moral resemblance of opposites see: 'Captain Brassbound's Conversion', *Three Plays for Puritans*, pp. 247-50.

On the managing genius, Stephen Winsten says Lady Cholmondeley charmed Shaw '. . . especially as she manœuvred her fire brand of a husband with tact and success' (*Jesting Apostle*, p. 119).

Page 168 '... there is nothing ...': *Heartbreak House*, p. 129.

'On the flying ...': *Misalliance, etc.*, p. 157.

'Come, You need ...': *Ibid.*, p. 158.

'man-woman or ...': *Ibid.*, p. 159.

'... all ambassadors make ...': *Ibid.*, pp. 149-50, 155, 195-6.

Page 170 'You have killed ...': *The Simpleton, The Six, and The Millionairess*, p. 163.

'But the decider ...': *Ibid.*, p. 124.

'You do not ...': *Ibid.*, p. 155.

'... a pulse in ...': *Ibid.*, p. 199.

Page 171 'He stripped well ...': *Ibid.*, p. 139.

On Cashel in tights see: *Cashel Byron's Profession*, pp. 45, 51; see above, p. 111.

Page 173 'The reasonable man ...': *Man and Superman*, p. 221.

Page 174 On Shaw's disgust at nineteenth-century London see: *Ibid.*, pp. 102-4, 107, 223.

Page 175 '... the spectacle of ...': as quoted in Ervine, *Shaw*, p. 51.

'Incidentally, I would ...': E. Jones, *Free Associations*, p. 76.

'You may add ...': C. S. Lewis, *Surprised by Joy*, p. 9.

Page 176 'Curious, how little ...': *Ellen Terry and Bernard Shaw: A Correspondence*, Letter XL (October 2, 1896). New York, p. 66; London, p. 81.

Chapter 8. *Emancipation and its Discontents* ·

Page 177 'My father shall ...': 'Major Barbara', *John Bull's Other Island with How He Lied to Her Husband and Major Barbara*, p. 339.

'Why mayn't we ...': G. Raverat, *Period Piece*, p. 267.

Page 178 'That Men no ...': as quoted in Pease, *History of the Fabian Society*, p. 43.

On the Basis see: Ervine, *Shaw*, p. 417.

Page 179 'The suffrage is ...': 'G. B. S. and a Suffragist', Interview in the [London] *Tribune*, March 12, 1906, p. 3: 3-4.

Page 180 'But the strongest ...': letter to the editor of *The Times*, headed 'Woman Suffrage', October 31, 1906, p. 8: 4.

'I submit, however, ...': *Ibid.*

Page 181 'One of the most blackguardly ...': 'The Unmentionable Case for Women's Suffrage', p. 112.

On a form of torture see: 'Forcible Feeding', unsigned article by Shaw in *The New Statesmen*, April 12, 1913, pp. 8-9.

'At first the ...': *Ibid.*, p. 8.

'The majority of ...' as quoted in Lutz, *Susan B. Anthony*, p. 54; see also Octavia Hill's *Letters* (ed. C. E. Maurice), p. 73.

'One day, at . . .': 'The Unmentionable Case for Women's Suffrage', *The Englishwoman*, I, No. 2 (March 1909), 112-21.

Page 182 '. . . in a perfectly . . .': 'As Bernard Shaw Sees Women', p. 2.

'. . . the average man . . .': 'The Unmentionable Case', *loc. cit.*, pp. 113-14.

'One just touches . . .': *Ibid.*, pp. 117-18.

'I strongly suspect . . .': *Ibid.*, p. 119.

Page 183 'glorious old maids . . .': *Three Plays for Puritans*, p. xvii; 'Getting Married', *The Doctor's Dilemma, Getting Married, etc.*, p. 344.

On the conference of married men see: 'Getting Married', pp. 188-9.

'When Lord Shaftesbury . . .': 'The Unmentionable Case', *loc. cit.*, p. 120.

Page 184 On flogging see: 'Crude Criminology', *Doctor's Delusions*, pp. 261-88.

'Lust': F. Harris, *Bernard Shaw*. New York, p. 227; London, p. 223.

'It seems but fair . . .': Horace Greeley, letter to Moncure D. Conway, August 25, 1867, as quoted by Alma Lutz, *Susan B. Anthony*, p. 127.

'Brieux shows you . . .': 'The Play and Its Author', souvenir program, 1913, pp. 10-12.

Page 185 'Do Everything': Alma Lutz, *op. cit.*, pp. 108-20.

On unfairness to men see: Ernest Belfort Bax, 'Marriage', *Outlooks from the New Standpoint*, pp. 151-60.

For Shaw's 1912 addendum see: 'The Quintessence of Ibsenism', *Major Critical Essays*, pp. 37-8, n.

Page 186 ' "He" indeed is . . .': H. G. Wells, *A Modern Utopia*, p. 186.

'. . . rather than star . . .': H. G. Wells, *Work, Wealth and Happiness of Mankind*. New York, p. 576; London, p. 585.

'. . . have widened her . . .': *Ibid.*, New York, p. 579; London, p. 586.

'She wanted to . . .': H. G. Wells, *Ann Veronica*, pp. 4-5.

'In moments of . . .': Doris Stenton, *The English Woman in History*, p. 312.

Page 187 '. . . Mill's chief discouragement . . .': Packe, *Life of Mill*, p. 497.

'The best women . . .': as quoted in A. Lutz, *Susan B. Anthony*, p. 126.

On Octavia Hill see her *Letters*, pp. 263-4.

On the manifesto see: Margaret Cole, *Beatrice Webb*. New York, p. 34; London, p. 35. See also Ervine, *Shaw*, p. 220.

On Miss Potter's reasons see: M. Cole, *op. cit.*, New York, pp. 34-5; London, pp. 35-6; Beatrice Webb, *My Apprenticeship*, New York, pp. 342-3; London, pp. 302-4.

Page 188 'The very success . . .': Doris Stenton, *op. cit.*, p. 312.

On Beatrice Webb's withdrawal see: M. Cole, *op. cit.* New York, p. 35; London, p. 36.

'. . . delayed my political . . .': B. Webb, *op. cit.* New York, pp. 341-2; London, p. 302.

'When, on the . . .': unpublished letter to Mrs H. Ward, September 10, 1910; prospectively in the *Collected Letters of Bernard Shaw* (ed. Dan H. Laurence).

Page 189 'You must have . . .': *The Intelligent Woman's Guide to Socialism and Capitalism*, pp. 451-2.

'Talk of a . . .': as quoted in A. Lutz, *Susan B. Anthony*, p. 123.

On bed and board see: Muggeridge, *Harper's Bazaar*, January 1961, pp. 106-7.

'A slave state . . .': as quoted in Winsten, *Jesting Apostle*, pp. 118-19.

Page 190 '. . . in oligarchies women . . .': ' "In Good King Charles's Golden Days", ' *Geneva, etc.*, pp. 158-9.

'In the case . . .': Mill, *Subjection of Women*, p. 228.

'Men in shackles . . .': Rousseau, *The Social Contract*, p. 5.

'At every turn . . .': Eleanor Flexner, *Century of Struggle*, pp. 204-5.

'It seemed to . . .': Packe, *Life of Mill*, p. 500.

'John Stuart Mill . . .': 'Sir Almroth Wright's Polemics', *The New Statesman*, II (October 18, 1913), p. 47.

Page 191 'He is still . . .': *Ibid.*

'. . . only doubled the . . .': ' "In Good King Charles's Golden Days", ' *Geneva, loc. cit.*, p. 159.

'MESSAGE FOR MRS . . .': telegram to Gertrude Kingston, January 25, 1915, *Puck* [New York]. LXXVII (February 20, 1915), p. 6.

'And now that . . .': *Bernard Shaw and Mrs Patrick Campbell: Their Correspondence*, p. 189.

Page 192 'Now if the . . .': *Everybody's Political What's What?*, p. 132.

'Only the other . . .': *The Intelligent Woman's Guide*, pp. 452-3.

On the woman's vote and the Eighteenth Amendment see. Eleanor Flexner, *Century of Struggle*, pp. 184-6, 224-5, 296-8.

'Give women the . . .': *Man and Superman*, p. xix.

'The political emancipation . . .': 'Getting Married', *The Doctor's Dilemma, etc.*, p. 227.

Page 193 On the women's majority see: Ernest Belfort Bax, 'The Everlasting Female', *Outspoken Essays on Social Subjects*, pp. 37-8.

For the interview with Mrs Braby, see p. 179.

'. . . the vital obstacle . . .': 'What Is Mr Asquith up to Now?' *The Independent Suffragette*, No. 3 (October 1916), pp. 10-11.

'Dear Madam, If . . .': to Maud Arncliffe Sennett, June 2, 1913; British Museum.

Page 194 'Dear Miss Smyth': to Ethel Smyth, June 25, 1914; British Museum.

'We must adopt . . .': *Translations and Tomfooleries*, p. 139.

Page 195 'I may say . . .': to Ethel Smyth, *loc. cit.*

'Do not Mussolini . . .': 'Mr G. B. Shaw on Women's Rights',
Manchester Guardian, November 4, 1933, p. 16: 6-7.

'For we never . . .': *Ibid.*, p. 16: 7.

Page 196 'I quite understand . . .': *Ibid.*, p. 16: 6-7.

'Talking of home . . .': *Daily Express*, July 26, 1939, p. 8: 3-6.

'The representative unit . . .': ' "In Good King Charles's Golden
Days",' *Geneva, etc.*, p. 157.

Page 197 'But he somehow . . .': Nethercot, *Men and Supermen*, p. 253.

'Off the stage . . .': *Our Theatres in the Nineties*, I, p. 62.

'Women had two . . .': 'The Unmentionable Case for Women's
Suffrage', *The Englishwoman*, I, No. 2 (March 1909), pp. 113-14.

Page 198 '. . . succeeded in shaming . . .': letter to the editor of the [London]
Daily Chronicle, headed 'Mr Shaw's Method and Secret', April
30, 1898, p. 3: 6.

'I remonstrated, and . . .': *Ibid.*

On the struggle in the Vestry of St Pancras see: 'The Unmentionable Case', *loc. cit.*, pp. 115-16.

'Cunninghame Graham writes . . .': as quoted in Henderson,
Shaw, p. 367.

'It must not . . .': letter to the editor of the [London] *Daily
Chronicle*, headed 'Mr Shaw's Method and Secret', April 30,
1898, p. 3: 6.

Page 199 On offices open to women see: *Women as Councillors*, 1906, p. 1.

'When the vestries . . .': *Ibid.*

'. . . who were facetious . . .': *Ibid.*

On co-option see: *The Abolition of Poor Law Guardians* (London:
The Fabian Society, 1906), pp. 14-15.

'That the first . . .': unpublished letter to Mrs H. Ward, September 10, 1910; prospectively in the *Collected Letters of Bernard
Shaw* (ed. Dan H. Laurence).

Page 200 '. . . provided every governing . . .': 'What is Mr Asquith up to
Now?', *The Independent Suffragette*, No. 3 (October 1916), p. 10.

'But the real . . .': *Ibid.*

'The tone in . . .': *Women as Councillors*, *loc. cit.*, p. 1.

On Elizabeth Blackwell see: Inez Irwin, *Angels and Amazons*, p. 46.

Page 201 'Now political capacity . . .': ' "In Good King Charles's Golden
Days",' *Geneva, etc.*, p. 159.

On Garrison's views see: A. Lutz, *Susan B. Anthony*, p. 71.

'Is there so . . .': Mill, *Subjection of Women*, pp. 267-8.

'The only decent . . .': 'G. B. S. and a Suffragist', Interview in the
[London] *Tribune*, March 12, 1906, p. 3: 3-4.

Page 202 'Begonia becomes the . . .': *Everybody's Political What's What?*, p. 44.

Bibliography

A. THE WORKS OF BERNARD SHAW

1. *Collected Works*

Androcles and the Lion, Overruled, Pygmalion. London: Constable, 1932.

Back to Methuselah: A Metabiological Pentateuch. London: Constable, 1931.

Buoyant Billions, Farfetched Fables & Shakes Versus Shav. New York: Dodd, Mead and Co., 1951. London: Constable, 1950.

Cashel Byron's Profession. London: Constable, 1921.

Doctors' Delusions, Crude Criminology and Sham Education. London: Constable, 1932.

The Doctor's Dilemma, Getting Married, & The Shewing-up of Blanco Posnet. London: Constable, 1932.

Essays in Fabian Socialism. London: Constable, 1932.

Everybody's Political What's What? New York: Dodd, Mead and Co., 1944. London: Constable, 1944.

Geneva, Cymbeline Refinished, & Good King Charles. London: Constable, 1946.

Heartbreak House. London: Constable, 1931.

Immaturity. London: Constable, 1931.

The Intelligent Woman's Guide to Socialism and Capitalism. New York: Brentano, 1928. London: Constable, 1928.

The Irrational Knot. New York: Brentano, 1911. London: Constable, 1914.

John Bull's Other Island with How He Lied to Her Husband and Major Barbara. London, Constable, 1931.

Love Among the Artists. London: Constable, 1932.

Major Critical Essays: The Quintessence of Ibsenism. The Perfect Wagnerite. The Sanity of Art. London: Constable, 1932.

Man and Superman. A Comedy and a Philosophy. London: Constable, 1931.

Misalliance, The Dark Lady of the Sonnets, & Fanny's First Play. London: Constable, 1932.

My Dear Dorothea. London: Phoenix House, 1956.

Our Theatres in the Nineties. 3 vols. London: Constable, 1932.

Platform and Pulpit (Ed., with intro., Dan H. Laurence). New York: Hill and Wang, 1962. London: Hart-Davis, 1962.

Plays and Players (Selected by A. C. Ward). World's Classics. London: Oxford University Press, 1952.

Plays Pleasant and Unpleasant. 2 vols. London: Constable, 1931.

Saint Joan, A Chronicle, and The Apple Cart, A Political Extravaganza. London: Constable, 1932.

Shaw on Theater (Ed. E. J. West). New York: Hill and Wang, 1958. London: MacGibbon and Kee, 1960.

Shaw's Dramatic Criticism. A selection by John F. Matthews. New York: Hill and Wang, 1959.

Short Stories, Scraps and Shavings. New York: Dodd, Mead and Co., 1934. London: Constable, 1934.

The Simpleton, The Six, and The Millionairess. London: Constable, 1936.

Sixteen Self Sketches. London: Constable, 1949.

Three Plays for Puritans. The Devil's Disciple, Caesar and Cleopatra, and Captain Brassbound's Conversion. London: Constable, 1931.

Too True To Be Good, Village Wooing, & On the Rocks. London: Constable, 1934.

Translations and Tomfooleries. London: Constable, 1926.

An Unfinished Novel (Ed. Stanley Weintraub). London: Constable, 1958.

An Unsocial Socialist. London: Constable, 1932.

2. *Correspondence*

Advice to a Young Critic and Other Letters (Ed. E. J. West). New York: Crown Publishers, 1955. London: Peter Owen, 1956.

Bernard Shaw and Mrs Patrick Campbell: Their Correspondence (Ed. Alan Dent). New York: A. Knopf, 1952. London: Gollancz, 1952.

Collected Letters of Bernard Shaw (Ed. Dan H. Laurence). Reinhardt, 1964.

Ellen Terry and Bernard Shaw: A Correspondence (Ed. Christopher St John). New York: G. Putnam, 1931. London: Reinhardt, 1949.

Florence Farr, Bernard Shaw, W. B. Yeats Letters (Ed. Clifford Bax). New York: Dodd, Mead and Co., 1942. London: Home and Van Thal, 1946.

To a Young Actress: The Letters of Bernard Shaw to Molly Tompkins (Ed. Peter Tompkins). New York: Clarkson N. Potter, 1960.

3. *Miscellaneous Works*

'As Bernard Shaw Sees Woman', *The New York Times Magazine*, June 19, 1927, pp. 1: 1-4, 2: 1-5.

'Bernard Shaw (who is eighty-three today) Says We Will Have Peace', Interview in the [London] *Daily Express*, July 26, 1939, p. 8: 3-6.

Bibliography

The Case for Equality. London: National Liberal Club, Political and Economic Circle Transactions, Part 85, 1913.

Do We Agree? (A debate between G. K. Chesteron and Bernard Shaw.) London: Cecil Palmer, 1928.

'Family Life in England', Contribution to a symposium, 'Das häusliche Leben: Beiträge zur Charakteristik der Familien in Europa', *Berliner Tageblatt*, 4 (March 23, 1913), Beiblatt, 1: 3. English translation published in the [Cincinnati, Ohio] *Commercial Tribune*, April 5, 1913, p. 1: 4-5.

'Forcible Feeding', unsigned article in *The New Statesman*, April 12, 1913, pp. 8-9.

Foreword: William Archer. *Three Plays.* New York: Henry Holt, 1927. London: Constable, 1927.

'G. B. S. and a Suffragist', Interview by Maud Churton Braby in the [London] *Tribune*, March 12, 1906, p. 3: 3-4.

The Impossibilities of Anarchism. Fabian Tract No. 45. London: Fabian Society, 1893.

'Memories of Oscar Wilde', Appendix to Frank Harris, *Oscar Wilde.* New York: Brentano, 1916.

'The Menace of the Leisured Woman', *Time and Tide*, VIII (February 4, 1927), pp. 106-7.

'Mr G. B. Shaw on Women's Rights', *Manchester Guardian*, November 4, 1933, p. 16: 6-7.

'The Play and Its Author', Souvenir program for Brieux, *La Femme Seule.* Women's Theatre Inaugural Week, Coronet Theatre, London, December 8, 1913.

Preface to Charles Dickens, *Great Expectations.* Edinburgh: Printed for the Members of the Limited Editions Club by R. and R. Clark, 1937.

Preface to *Three Plays by Brieux.* New York: Brentano, 1911. London: Fifield, 1910.

'The Root of the White Slave Traffic', *The Awakener*, I, No. 1 (November 16, 1912), pp. 7-8.

'Sir Almroth Wright's Polemics', *The New Statesman*, October 18, 1913, pp. 45-7.

'The Unmentionable Case for Women's Suffrage', *The Englishwoman*, I, No. 2 (March 1909), pp. 112-21.

'What is Mr Asquith up to Now?', *The Independent Suffragette*, No. 3 (October 1916), pp. 10-11.

'Woman Since 1860', *Time and Tide*, I (October 8, 1920), pp. 442-4.

Women as Councillors. Fabian Tract No. 93. London: Fabian Society, 1906.

B. CONCERNING BERNARD SHAW

Bab, Julius. *Bernard Shaw*. Berlin: S. Fischer, 1926.

Barnard, Eunice Fuller. 'G. B. S. The Father of the Flapper', *New Republic*, July 1926, pp. 272-3.

Barnicoate, Constance A. 'Mr Bernard Shaw's Counterfeit Presentation of Women', *Fortnightly Review*, 85 (March 1906), pp. 516-19.

Bentley, Eric. *Bernard Shaw*. New York: New Directions, 1947. London: Hale, 1950.

Duffin, Henry C. *The Quintessence of Bernard Shaw*. London: Allen and Unwin, 1939.

Ervine, St John. *Bernard Shaw: His Life, Work and Friends*. New York: W. Morrow, 1956. London: Constable, 1956.

Hamon, Augustin. *Le Molière du XXe Siècle: Bernard Shaw*. Paris: E. Figuière, 1913.

Harris, Frank. *Bernard Shaw: An Unauthorized Biography Based on First Hand Information with a Postscript by Mr Shaw*. New York: Simon and Schuster, 1931. London: Gollancz, 1931.

Henderson, Archibald. *George Bernard Shaw: Man of the Century*. New York: Appleton-Century-Crofts, 1956.

Joad, C. E. M. (ed.). *Shaw and Society*. London: Odhams, 1953.

Kaye, Julian B. *Bernard Shaw and the Nineteenth-Century Tradition*. Norman, Oklahoma: University of Oklahoma Press, 1958.

Kornbluth, Martin L. 'Two Fallen Women: Paula Tanqueray and Kitty Warren', *The Shavian*, No. 14 (February 1959), pp. 14-15.

Molnar, Joseph. 'Shaw's Living Women', *Shaw Society Bulletin*, 49: 7-11, June 1953.

Moore, Mina. *Bernard Shaw et la France*. Paris: Librairie Ancienne Honoré Champion, 1933.

Nathan, George Jean. 'Shaw as a Lover', *American Mercury*, XIII (February 1928), pp. 246-8.

Nethercot, Arthur. *Men and Supermen: The Shavian Portrait Gallery*. Cambridge, Mass.: Harvard University Press, 1954.

—— 'The Schizophrenia of Bernard Shaw', *The American Scholar*, 21: 455, October 1952.

Ohmann, Richard M. *Shaw: The Style and the Man*. Middletown, Conn.: Wesleyan University Press, 1962.

Pearson, Hesketh. *G. B. S. A Postscript*. New York: Harper and Brothers, 1950. London: Collins, 1951.

Rattray, R. F. *Bernard Shaw: A Chronicle*. Luton, England: The Leagrave Press, 1951.

Bibliography

Rhondda, Lady. 'Shaw's Women', *Time and Tide*, XI (March 7-April 11, 1930), pp. 300-1, 331-4, 364-6, 395-6, 436-8, 468-70.

Robertson, J. M. *Mr Shaw and 'The Maid'*. London: Cobden-Sanderson [1925].

Scott, Dixon. 'The Innocence of Bernard Shaw', *Men of Letters*. London: Hodder and Stoughton, 1923.

Simon, Louis. *Shaw on Education*. New York: Columbia University Press and London: Oxford University Press, 1958.

Strauss, E. *Bernard Shaw: Art and Socialism*. London: Gollancz, 1942.

Ward, A. C. *G. Bernard Shaw*. New York and London: Longmans, Green and Co., 1951.

Wilson, Edmund. 'Bernard Shaw at 80', *The Triple Thinkers*. New York and London: Oxford University Press, 1938.

Winsten, Stephen. *Jesting Apostle: The Private Life of Bernard Shaw*. New York: E. P. Dutton, 1957. London: Hutchinson, 1956.

C. OTHER REFERENCES

Annan, Noel Gilroy. *Leslie Stephen*. Cambridge, Mass.: Harvard University Press, 1952. London: MacGibbon, 1951.

Arnold, Armin. *D. H. Lawrence and America*. London: Linden Press, 1958.

Beauvoir, Simone de. *The Second Sex*. New York: Bantam Books, 1961. London: Jonathan Cape, 1953.

Belfort Bax, Ernest. *Outlooks from the New Standpoint*. London: Swan Sonnenschein, 1891.

—— *Outspoken Essays on Social Subjects*. London: W. Reeves, 1897.

Bessborough, The Earl of (ed.). *Georgiana: Extracts from the Correspondence of Georgiana, Duchess of Devonshire*. London: J. Murray, 1955.

Briffault, Robert. *The Mothers*. New York: Macmillan Company, 1959. London: Allen and Unwin, 1960.

Brittain, Vera. *Lady into Woman: A History of Women from Victoria to Elizabeth II*. New York: Macmillan Company, 1953. London: Andrew Dakers, 1942.

Brontë, Charlotte. *Shirley*. 2 vols. The Thornton Edition of the Novels of the Sisters Brontë. London: Downey, 1899.

Burnett, Constance Buel. *Five for Freedom*. New York: Abelard Press, 1953.

Camus, Albert. *The Rebel*. New York: Vintage Books, 1956. London: Hamish Hamilton, 1953.

Chesterton, G. K. *The Victorian Age in Literature*. Home University Library. London: Oxford University Press, 1946.

Cole, Margaret. *Beatrice Webb*. New York: Harcourt Brace, 1946. London: Longmans, Green and Co., 1945.

Craig, Edward Gordon. *Ellen Terry and Her Secret Self: Together with A Plea for G. B. S.* New York: E. P. Dutton, 1932. London: Sampson Low, Marston & Co., 1931.

Dalziel, Margaret. *Popular Fiction 100 Years Ago*. London: Cohen and West, 1957.

De Mille, Agnes. 'Artist or Wife', *The Atlantic*, 202: 52-8, September 1958.

Dickens, Charles. *Sketches by Boz*. The Fireside Dickens. London: Chapman and Hall, n.d.

Dobrée, Bonamy. *The Lamp and the Lute*. Oxford: Clarendon Press, 1929.

Dunbar, Janet. *Mrs G. B. S. A Portrait*. New York and Evanston: Harper & Row, Publishers, 1963. London: Harrap, 1963.

'Enfranchisement of Women', *The Westminster and Foreign Quarterly Review*, LV (October 29, 1850), pp. 289-311.

Engel, Monroe. *The Maturity of Dickens*. Cambridge, Mass.: Harvard University Press and London: Oxford University Press, 1959.

Epton, Nina. *Love and the French*. Cleveland: The World Publishing Company 1959. London: Cassell, 1959.

Fauset, Arthur Huff. *Sojourner Truth*. Chapel Hill: University of North Carolina Press, 1938.

Fiedler, Leslie. *Love and Death in the American Novel*. New York: Criterion Books, 1959.

Finley, Ruth E. *The Lady of Godey's: Sarah Josepha Hale*. Philadelphia: J. B. Lippincott Company, 1931.

Flexner, Eleanor. *Century of Struggle*. Cambridge, Mass.: Harvard University Press and London: Oxford University Press, 1959.

Friedan, Betty. *The Feminine Mystique*. New York: W. W. Norton & Co., 1963. London: Gollancz, 1963.

Fuller, Edmund. *The Image of Man in Modern Fiction*. New York: Random House, 1958.

Gilbert, W. S. *The Complete Plays of Gilbert and Sullivan*. New York: The Modern Library, n.d. As *Savoy Operas*, London: Macmillan, 1926.

Green, Peter. *Kenneth Grahame, a Biography*. Cleveland: World Publishing Company, 1959. London: John Murray, 1959.

Hall, Edward (ed.). *Miss Weeton: Journal of a Governess, 1807-1811*. London: Oxford University Press, 1936.

Harben, Henry D. *The Endowment of Motherhood.* Fabian Tract No. 149. London: Fabian Society, 1910.

Hill, Octavia. *The Life of Octavia Hill as Told in Her Letters.* Edited by C. Edmund Maurice. London: Macmillan, 1913.

Hoggart, Richard. *The Uses of Literacy: Changing Patterns in English Mass Culture.* Fair Lawn, New Jersey: Essential Books, 1957. London: Chatto and Windus, 1957.

Hsu, Francis L. K. *Americans and Chinese: Two Ways of Life.* New York: H. Schuman, 1953. London: Cresset Press, 1955.

Huneker, James. *Iconoclasts.* New York: Scribner, 1907. London: T. Werner Laurie, 1906.

Hutchins, B. L. *The Working Life of Women.* Fabian Tract No. 157. London: Fabian Society, 1911.

Irwin, Inez Haynes. *Angels and Amazons.* Garden City, New York: Doubleday, Doran and Co., 1934.

James, Henry. *Washington Square.* New York: Modern Library, 1950. Chiltern Library, London: Lehmann, 1949.

—— *The Wings of the Dove.* New York: Modern Library, n.d. London: Eyre and Spottiswoode, 1948.

Jones, Ernest. *Free Associations: Memories of a Psychoanalyst.* New York: Basic Books, 1959. London: Hogarth Press, 1959.

—— *The Life and Work of Sigmund Freud.* 3 vols. New York: Basic Books, 1953-57. London: Hogarth Press, 1953-57.

Jones, L. E. *A Victorian Boyhood.* London: Macmillan, 1955.

Keats, John. *The Selected Letters of John Keats.* (Ed. Lionel Trilling) Garden City, New York: Doubleday Anchor Books, 1956. (Ed. F. Page) London: Oxford University Press, 1954.

Key, Ellen, *et al. The Woman Question* (Ed. T. R. Smith). New York: Boni and Liveright, 1918.

Laver, James. *Edwardian Promenade.* Boston: Houghton Mifflin, 1958. London: Vista Books, 1960.

—— *Victorian Vista.* London: Hulton Press, 1954.

Lewis, C. S. *Surprised by Joy.* New York: Harcourt, Brace and Co., 1956. London: Geoffrey Bles, 1955.

Lutz, Alma. *Susan B. Anthony: Rebel, Crusader, Humanitarian.* Boston: Beacon Press, 1959.

Lynd, Helen Merrell. *England in the Eighteen-Eighties.* New York and London: Oxford University Press, 1945.

Maugham, W. Somerset. *The Summing-Up.* London: Heinemann, 1938.

Meredith, George. *An Essay on Comedy.* New York: Doubleday Anchor Books, 1956. London: Archibald Constable, 1897.

Mill, John Stuart. *On the Subjection of Women.* Everyman's Library, London: Dent, 1929.

Moore, Doris Langley. *E. Nesbit: A Biography.* London: Benn, 1933.

Moore, George. *Esther Waters.* New York: Brentano, 1922. London: Heinemann, 1894.

Morris, William. *News from Nowhere or, An Epoch of Rest.* Boston: Roberts Brothers, 1890. And in *Selected Writings.* London: Nonesuch Library, 1934.

O'Casey, Sean. *Sunset and Evening Star.* New York and London: Macmillan, 1954.

Olivier, Sydney. *Letters and Selected Writings* (Ed. Margaret Olivier). London: George Allen and Unwin, 1948.

Packe, Michael St John. *The Life of John Stuart Mill.* New York: Macmillan Company, 1954. London: Secker and Warburg, 1954.

Pease, Edward R. *The History of the Fabian Society.* New York: International Publishers, 1926. London: Fifield, 1916.

Pope-Hennessy, James. *Monckton Milnes: The Flight of Youth 1851-1885.* London: Constable, 1951.

Priestley, J. B. *Thoughts in the Wilderness.* New York: Harper and Brothers, 1957. London: Heinemann, 1957.

Raverat, Gwen. *Period Piece: A Cambridge Childhood.* New York: W. W. Norton, 1953. London: Faber, 1952.

Reeves, Mrs Pember. *Family Life on a Pound a Week.* Fabian Tract No. 162. London: Fabian Society, 1912.

Rougement, Denis de. *Love in the Western World.* Garden City, New York: Doubleday Anchor Books, 1957.

Rousseau, Jean Jacques. *The Social Contract.* Chicago: Henry Regnery Company, 1954. Everyman's Library, London: Dent, 1955.

Scott-Maxwell, Florida. *Women and Sometimes Men.* New York: A. Knopf, 1957. London: Routledge, 1957.

Stenton, Doris May. *The English Woman in History.* London: George Allen and Unwin, 1957.

Sudermann, Hermann. *Magda.* New York: Samuel French, 1923.

Terry, Ellen. *The Story of My Life: Recollections and Reflections.* New York: McClure Company, 1908. London: Hutchinson, 1908.

Trilling, Lionel. Introduction to Jane Austen, *Emma.* Boston: Houghton Mifflin (Riverside Editions), 1957.

Tynan, Kenneth. *Curtains.* New York: Atheneum, 1961.

Webb, Beatrice. *My Apprenticeship.* New York: Longmans, Green and Co., 1926. London: Longmans, Green and Co., 1950.

Webb, Sidney. *The Decline of the Birth-Rate.* Fabian Tract No. 131. London: Fabian Society, 1907.

Wells, H. G. *Ann Veronica: A Modern Love Story.* New York: Harper and Brothers, 1909. Everyman's Library, London: Dent, 1943.

—— *Experiment in Autobiography.* New York: Macmillan Company, 1934. London: Gollancz; Cresset Press, 1934.

—— *A Modern Utopia.* New York: Scribner, 1905. London: Chapman and Hall, 1905.

—— *The Work, Wealth and Happiness of Mankind.* 2 vols. Garden City, New York: Doubleday, Doran, 1931. London: Heinemann, 1934.

White, William Hale. *The Autobiography of Mark Rutherford.* New York: Dodd, Mead and Co., n.d. London: Oxford University Press, 1936.

Wollstonecraft, Mary. *The Rights of Woman.* Everyman's Library, London: Dent, 1929.

Woolf, Virginia. *A Room of One's Own.* New York: Harcourt, Brace and Co., 1929. London: Hogarth Press, 1929.

—— *Three Guineas.* New York: Harcourt, Brace and Co., 1938. London: Hogarth Press, 1952.

Young, G. M. *Early Victorian England.* London: Oxford University Press, 1934.

—— *Victorian England: Portrait of an Age.* Garden City, New York: Doubleday Anchor Books, 1954. London: Oxford University Press, 1960.

Index

A

Achurch, Janet, 53
Acton, Sir John, 104
adultery, 93-4, 115-16, 119, 120,
    133-6, 207-8
Amanda, 202
Anderson, Judith, 102
Androcles, 17, 71
Androcles and the Lion, 69, 131
Anouilh, Jean, 53
Apple Cart, The, 68, 72, 99, 115,
    122, 133, 134, 135, 162, 163 n.,
    168, 172, 202
Archer, William, 49, 53, 124
Ariadne (Lady Utterword),
    78-80, 134
Arms and the Man, 160
Aubrey, 137
Austen, Jane, *Emma*, 16, 45

B

Back to Methuselah, 51, 84, 116
Bagehot, Walter, 110
Bagnold, Enid, *The Door of Life*,
    95
Barbara, 68, 72, 77, 79, 95, 105,
    126, 157, 159, 166-7, 168, 170,
    177, 212
Barnicoate, Constance, 18
Barrie, J. M., *What Every Woman
    Knows*, 65
Bashkirtseff, Marie, 46-7, 49,
    159, 160

'Beauty's Duty', 136
Beauvoir, Simone de, 25; *The
    Second Sex*, 178
Begonia Brown, 124, 202
Belfort Bax, Ernest, 105-6, 185-6,
    193
Bellamy, Edward, 125
Bennett, Arnold, 139
Bentley, Eric, 48
Blackwell, Elizabeth, 200
Blanco Posnet, 77, 86, 105, 126
Braby, Maud Churton, 179,
    193
Brailsford, Madge, 155, 158
Brassbound, Captain, 63-74,
    100, 101, 105, 166
Bridgenorth, Mrs, 121
Brieux, Eugène, 18, 116, 121,
    131; *La Femme Seule*, 184
Britomart, Lady, 95
Brontë, Charlotte, 64; *Shirley*,
    16, 45
Brontë sisters, 14, 16
Buoyant Billions, 77
Butler, Samuel, 83
Byron, Cashel, 111
Byron, Mrs, 111, 155, 156

C

Caesar, 17
Caesar and Cleopatra, 163 n.
Campbell, Mrs Patrick, 17, 29,
    119, 175, 191

245

Camus, Albert, *The Rebel*, 11
Candida, 17, 64-8, 69, 95, 122,
    133, 134, 161, 165, 171
Candida, 55, 64-8, 69, 72, 73, 79,
    123, 134, 161, 162, 165-6, 170,
    212
capitalism, 32, 106-7, 117, 205
Captain Brassbound's Conversion,
    17, 68-74, 100, 161, 189
Carew, Lydia, 45, 155, 163, 171
Carlyle, Thomas, *Past and
    Present*, 27
'Case for Equality, The', 85
Cashel Byron's Profession, 45, 111,
    155, 171
Catherine, Queen, 72
Charles, King, 17, 115, 135, 172
Cherry-Garrard, Apsley, 109
Chesterton, G. K., 14, 30
Cholmondeley, Lady Mary, 166,
    189
Christianity, 52, 69, 73, 77,
    107-9, 132, 205
Cicely, Lady, 68-74, 77, 95, 101,
    124, 138, 157, 161, 162, 165,
    166, 173-4
Clandon, Mrs, 13, 19, 23, 96-7
Cobden-Sanderson, Mrs, 180
Collins, Mr, 52, 121
Collins, Mrs, 52, 96, 121, 155
Congreve, William, *The Way of
    the World*, 20, 38
Conolly, Ned, 154, 156, 157
Conolly, Susanna, 107, 154,
    155-7
Craven, Julia, 53
Creative Evolution, 32, 83-8, 93,
    103, 205-7, 214
Cruickshank, George, 110
Cusins, 126, 167

D

Dalziel, Margaret, *Popular
    Fiction 100 Years Ago*, 41, 111
Dartington Hall, 96
Darwin, Erasmus, 83
Daumier, Honoré, 110
'Decline of the Birth-Rate, The',
    91
democracy, 84, 190-5, 212-13
Desdemona, 20
Devil's Disciple, The, 52, 53, 102
Dickens, 15, 39, 74, 91, 97;
    Bleak House, 38, 50, 164, 165
divorce, 46, 117-20, 208-9
Doctor's Dilemma, The, 67, 135,
    158
Don Juan, 87
'Don Juan in Hell', 59
Dona Ana, 87
Drinkwater, 71
Dubedat, Jennifer, 67, 135
Dubedat, Louis, 158
Dudgeon, Dick, 17, 86, 102, 126
Dudgeon, Mrs, 52, 53
Duffin, H. C., 96
Dunn, Mazzini, 78

E

Edith, 121
Eliot, George, 16; *Middlemarch*,
    103
Eliot, T. S., *The Cocktail Party*, 77
Eliza (Doolittle), 17, 62, 99,
    101-2, 173
Ellie (Dunn), 79, 168
Ellis, Havelock, 130; *The
    Psychology of Sex*, 136
Ervine, St John, 166

F

Fabian Society, 45, 90, 178, 186
Fabian Tracts, 90-1, 98, 178, 199
Faguet, Emile, 30
'Family Life on a Pound a
  Week', 91
Fanny, 162
Fanny's First Play, 162
Farr, Florence (Mrs Emery), 29,
  81, 85, 113 n.
Fawcett, Henry, 22
Fawcett, Millicent Garrett, 188
Fiedler, Leslie, *Love and Death in
  the American Novel*, 25, 158
Freddie, 101
Freud, Sigmund, 132-3
Fuller, Edmund, *The Image of
  Man in Modern Fiction*, 25

G

Garrison, William Lloyd, 201
Gattie, Alfred, 109
Geneva, 202
George, Mrs, 16, 52, 115, 121-2,
  129, 138, 140-1, 144, 183
Getting Married, 16, 17, 31, 52,
  88, 95, 96, 115, 117, 121-2,
  129, 155, 183, 192, 208
Gilbert, W. S., 111, 160-1
Gloria, 19, 97
Goethe, 34
Goldsmith, Oliver, 127
Graham, Cunningham, 198
Great Catherine, 163 n.
Greeley, Horace, 184, 187, 189
Gwyn, Nell, 156, 171-2

H

Hamon, Augustin, 20-1, 96, 97,
  133, 135

Harris, Frank, 18, 94, 112, 130,
  142, 183
Heartbreak House, 59, 72, 78-82,
  115, 122, 126, 133, 134, 135, 168
Henderson, Archibald, 17
Herbert, Adrian, 158
Herbert, H. W., 49
Hesione (Mrs Hushabye), 72,
  78, 80, 135-6, 168
Higgins, Henry, 101-2
Hill, Octavia, 157, 187
Hogarth, William, 110
Howard, Sir, 70-1
Hsu, Francis L. K., *Americans and
  Chinese*, 81
Hushabye, Hector, 78, 79, 115,
  135

I

Ibsen, Henrik, 13, 14, 17, 26, 41,
  42, 44, 45-7, 116, 121, 131,
  141, 191, 198; *A Doll's House*,
  107; *Little Eyolf*, 134
Immaturity, 34
Imogen, 164, 165
'Impossibilities of Anarchism,
  The', 48
Inge, Dean, 28
'*In Good King Charles's Golden
  Days*', 72, 115, 122, 125, 133,
  134-5, 156, 171-2
*Intelligent Woman's Guide to
  Socialism and Capitalism, The*',
  15, 33, 150, 166, 192
Irrational Knot, The, 45, 107, 154,
  155

J

Jack Owen, 158-9
James, Henry, 16; *Washington
  Square*, 24

Jemima, Queen, 72, 79, 95, 135

Jesus, 108, 109

Joan (Jeanne d'Arc), 20, 68, 77, 78, 79, 108, 138, 145, 157, 161, 166, 168-9, 170, 174, 175, 205, 212

Johnson, Samuel, 12, 44

Jones, Ernest, 91, 133, 175

K

Karenina, Anna, 67

Keats, John, 14-15

L

Lamarck, 83

Lawrence, D. H., 26, 27, 144; *Lady Chatterley's Lover*, 130, 131, 209

Leo, 121

Lesbia (Grantham), 88, 89, 95, 104, 121

Lessing, Doris, 19

Lewis, C. S., 175

Life Force, the, 54, 77-8, 103, 107, 108, 205, 214

Linnaeus, 83

Lockett, Alice, 154

Louisa, 59

Love Among the Artists, 45, 155, 158

Lysistrata, 68, 79, 99, 162, 202

M

Macbeth, Lady, 20

McCarthy, Mary, 19

McNulty, Edward, 174

Magnus, King, 17, 115, 135, 172, 202

Mailer, Norman, 53

Major Barbara, 17, 44, 60, 61, 64, 68, 150, 163 n.

Malone, Hector, 59, 166

Man and Superman, 17, 18, 28, 31, 41, 51, 53, 59-64, 74, 75, 84, 85, 96, 98, 102, 126, 127, 134, 170, 180

Mangan, Boss, 78

Marchbanks, Eugene, 66, 67

marriage, 31, 32, 46, 48, 83, 89-90, 100-3, 144-5, 207-8

Martineau, Harriet, 39

Maugham, Somerset, 91

Maupassant, Guy de, 198

'Menace of the Leisured Woman, The', 195

Mendoza, 59

Meredith, George, *Diana of the Crossways*, 16; *An Essay on Comedy*, 38, 132

Mill, John Stuart, 22, 26, 39, 104, 116, 117, 153, 187, 190, 201

Millamant, 20, 38

Millionairess, The, 17, 64, 79, 162, 163, 165-6, 169-71, 174, 212

Mirabell, 38

Misalliance, 18, 95, 97, 98, 129, 159, 168, 172

'Modest Proposal, A', 150

Molière, 127-8, 133

Moore, George, 74, 91

Moore, Mina, 133

Morell, James, 65-7, 76

Morris, William, *News from Nowhere*, 73, 151

motherhood, 79, 83-99, 206-7, 210

Mozart, 59

Mrs Warren's Profession, 17, 18, 20, 60, 91, 131, 150

Muggeridge, Malcolm, 189

Murby, Miss, 85

Murdoch, Iris, 19
Mussolini, 33
My Dear Dorothea, 40-4, 52

N
Napoleon, 79
Nathan, George Jean, 65
Negroes, 19, 49, 184-5
Nethercot, Arthur, 197
Newcombe, Bertha, 29
Nietzsche, 79
Nightingale, Florence, 108, 157, 159

O
O'Casey, Sean, 96
Octavius, 59, 62, 63, 76, 126, 134
On the Rocks, 168
Orinthia, 79, 172
Overruled, 133
Owen, Robert, 33

P
Packe, Michael St John, 116, 118, 187
Pankhurst, Emmeline and Christabel, 157, 193-4
'Parents and Children', 95
Patterson, Jenny, 29
Payne-Townshend, Charlotte, *see* Shaw, Charlotte
Pearson, Hesketh, 113
Philanderer, The, 53, 94, 134
Pinero, Arthur Wing, 40, 162, 197; *The Second Mrs Tanqueray*, 20, 139
polygamy, 87-9, 133-4, 207
Potter, Beatrice, *see* Webb, Beatrice
'Preface on Bosses', 170

Press Cuttings, 22, 194-5
Priestley, J. B., 22
Prola, 124
prostitution, 32, 60, 105-7, 108, 133-4, 183, 207, 213
'Proteus', 119-20
Pygmalion, 17, 62, 99, 100, 101

Q
Quintessence of Ibsenism, The, 13, 17, 45-55, 113, 132, 185

R
Ramsden, Roebuck, 59, 63, 97
Randall (Utterword), 78-80, 126, 134
Rankin, 70-1
Raverat, Gwen, *Period Piece*, 42, 139, 177-8
Restoration comedy, 28, 125, 127
'Revolutionist's Handbook, The', 47, 60, 88, 128, 173
Rhondda, Lady, 195-6
Richardson, Samuel, *Pamela*, 38, 164
Romanticism, 100-3
Rougemont, Denis de, 115
Rousseau, 190

S
Saint Joan, 17, 27, 64, 78, 163 n., 168-9
Saint Vincent, 119
Sartorius, Blanche, 53
Sennett, Maud Arncliffe, 193
Shakespeare, 20, 28, 49, 50, 115, 127-8, 130, 165
Shaw, Bernard: amorous encounters, 28-9, 113, 119, 130, 142, 143, 145, 209; as

Shaw, Bernard—*cont.*
  Vestryman of St Pancras,
    81-2, 183, 197-8; his marriage,
    112-13, 209; his reputation,
    12-13
Shaw, Charlotte (Mrs G. B. S.),
    23, 112-13
Shaw, George Carr, 175
Shaw, Lucinda, 155, 175
Shaw, Lucy, 154, 156
She, 124
Shelley, 114
Shewing Up of Blanco Posnet, The,
    69
Shotover, Captain, 78,79
Smyth, Dame Ethel, 194-5
socialism, 83, 89, 110, 185, 190, 206
Society of Authors, 188
Stead, William, 46, 47
Stephen, Leslie, 49
Stevenson, R. L., 155, 163
Straker, Henry, 59, 75
Strindberg, August, 15, 20, 54,
    164, 191
suffrage, women's, 31, 177-203,
    211, 212-13
Summerson, Esther, 38, 50, 164,
    165
superman, the, 62, 84-5, 86, 87,
    204, 206
Sweetie, 124, 137-9, 140, 142, 165
Swift, Jonathan, 172-6, 181
Szczepanowska, Lina, 159-60,
    163, 168
Szczymplica, Aurélie, 155, 158-9

T
'Taboo in the Schools', 130
Tanner, Jack, 41, 59, 60, 61, 63,
    75, 76, 80, 98, 126, 127, 143

Tarleton, John, 168
Tarleton, Johnny, 172
Tarleton, Mrs, 18, 129
Taylor, Harriet, 104, 116, 118
Tennyson, 117
Terry, Ellen, 50, 68, 72, 75, 97,
    98, 123, 154, 156, 164, 166,
    175, 176
Three Plays by Brieux, 131
Three Plays for Puritans, 31
Tolstoy, 121
Tompkins, Molly, 29, 95, 98, 99
Too True To Be Good, 137, 157,
    165, 202
Translations and Tomfooleries,
    194-5
Trilling, Lionel, 45
Trotter, 162
Truth, Sojourner, 49
Tynan, Kenneth, 20

U
Undershaft, Andrew, 32, 44, 60,
    61, 107, 167, 169, 170
United States, the, 49, 109, 110
    184-5
'Unmentionable Case for
    Women's Suffrage, The',
    181-2

V
Valentine, 31
Veblen, Thorstein, 81
Village Wooing, 102, 124, 141-2
Violet, 59, 98
Voltaire, 30, 126

W
Wagner, Richard, 54
Ward, Mrs Humphry, 187-8,
    199

Warren, Mrs, 20, 32, 79, 95, 105,
106, 107, 138, 139, 163
Warren, Vivie, 18, 20, 32, 79,
95, 105-6, 107, 108, 149, 161,
163
Webb, Beatrice, 157, 187-8
Webb, Sidney, 91, 188, 198
Weeton, Miss, 39, 45
Wells, H. G., 125, 139, 178,
185-6; *Ann Veronica*, 143-4,
186; *A Modern Utopia*, 186
Whitefield, Ann, 53, 59-64, 65,
67, 68, 69, 74, 76, 79, 102, 124,
127, 134, 137, 138, 170
Whitefield, Mrs, 18, 63, 96
Widowers' Houses, 53, 91
Wilde, Oscar, 136, 161
Williams, Tennessee, 40, 53, 164
Winsten, Stephen, 46
Wollstonecraft, Mary, *A
Vindication of the Rights of
Women*, 37

'Woman Since 1860', 22, 23
Women's Christian Temperance
Union, 185
Woolf, Virginia, 145-6; *A Room
of One's Own*, 45, 178, 183;
Three Guineas, 66, 178
'Working Life of Women, The',
91
Wright, Frank Lloyd, 150
Wylie, Philip, 53, 96, 164

Y

Yeats, W. B., 81
You Never Can Tell, 13, 19, 23, 31,
96-7
Yum-Yum, 160-1

Z

Z., 124, 141
Zola, Emile, 39